To Ton[...]

Best Wishes

Hope you Enjoy

Terry Crowley

YOU DON'T
REMEMBER ME
DO YOU?

YOU DON'T REMEMBER ME DO YOU?

THE AUTOBIOGRAPHY OF TERRY CONROY

TERRY CONROY
FOREWORD BY TONY PULIS

First published by Pitch Publishing, 2015

Pitch Publishing
A2 Yeoman Gate
Yeoman Way
Durrington
BN13 3QZ
www.pitchpublishing.co.uk

A CIP catalogue record is available for this book
from the British Library.

ISBN 978-178531-019-5

Typesetting and origination by Pitch Publishing

Printed in Malta by Melita Press

Contents

Acknowledgements

THERE are many people without whom this book would not have happened. From my publishers Pitch Publishing – Paul and Jane Camillin, Gareth Davis, Graham Hales and Derek Hammond; thank you everyone. Simon Lowe has helped me collate my experiences into what I hope are entertaining chapters and none of this would have happened without Michael Colley; his persistence in persuading me to finally write this book has lasted over a decade. I am very proud to have eventually got round to it... pester power worked!

I would also like to thank two great photographers, Eddie Fuller and Phil Greig for not only taking superb photos of me over the years, but also allowing me to use them in this book.

There would not be a tale to tell without Laszlo Papp, Maureen Cooper, Angela Peake, Regina Gibbons, Arun Pherwani, Josep Sule-Suso and all the superb staff at the University Hospital of North Staffordshire. And I must give a mention to my old mate Jimmy Greenhoff for helping me back to fitness on our regular walks together, along with many of my former Stoke team-mates. Thanks lads.

My family deserve a very special mention; my dad Jack, mum Esther, and siblings Ollie (R.I.P.), Lar, Donnie, Rita, Peter (R.I.P.), Michael, Vincent, Paul and Marie.

Of course my wonderful daughters Tara, Niamh and Sinead should receive special mention, along with Tara's husband Mike and my three wonderful grandchildren Estela, Lola and Rafa.

Last, but never ever forgotten, my long-suffering wife Sue, for her love, care, dedication and support through many difficult times. This is for you.

Terry Conroy

Preface

WHEN you bought this book, you probably thought 'That's an odd title?' Of course, if you didn't know who I am then the title made complete sense, but let's face it most people buy autobiographies of people that they know something about, that they do remember and that they want to both learn and remember more about. That's the point.

So why choose the title? It's a perfectly reasonable question.

Just in case you are wondering, it isn't some oblique reference to the lyrics of 'It Started With A Kiss' by 1970s supergroup Hot Chocolate – one of my favourite bands. It stems from the fact that over nearly 50 years, since I arrived in Stoke-on-Trent from Dublin in March 1967, I've had people coming up to me and starting their welcome with a smile, a hand offered in friendship, and asking me that very question by way of introducing themselves to me. Or should I say re-introducing; because apparently I've met them before and I should remember them. Of course, almost all of the time they are right. I don't remember them. But what happens is that they then launch into a detailed explanation of why I might. And that's where the fun begins.

I first recall it happening to me back in 1971. April 1971 to be exact. It was a couple of weeks after we'd lost to Arsenal in the FA Cup semi-final in a humdinger of a tie, which went to a replay, although we should have won the first game as we led going into injury time.

But more of that controversy later. I was leaving the Victoria Ground after training one day when a chap came up to me and smiled, offered his hand out, which I shook, and said the immortal words for the first time, 'You don't remember me, do you?'

'No,' I had to admit. 'I don't.'

'Well,' he continued, 'you played in the semi-final at Hillsborough, didn't you?'

'Yes.'

'And there were over 50,000 in the crowd, weren't there?'

'Yes.'

'And thousands were cheering for Stoke, weren't they?'

'Yes.'

'Well,' he said proudly, 'I was the one booing Arsenal. Could you hear me?'

I couldn't believe that he thought that not only might I have heard him above the din which had been created by our wonderful supporters that day in Sheffield, but that I might have realised it was him!

That was but the first instance of hundreds, though. It must happen about once a month still and I always say that if I had £1 for every time I've heard it I'd be a millionaire.

I remember another occasion it happened, when I was hosting over 300 guests on a matchday in the Waddington Suite, Stoke City's hospitality suite, before a Premier League game just after City had been promoted back into the big time in 2008. This feller came up to me, held out his hand and with a big smile said, 'You don't remember me, do you?'

Well, by now I was well practised in dealing with this circumstance, so I'd say something like, 'Of course I do. Your face looks very familiar.'

He laughed and said, 'Oh, so you do remember awarding me a prize for cribbage at the Abbey Hulton Working Men's Club 40 years ago, then. I wondered if you might.'

I'd made this feller's day. I'm sure he probably dines out even now on my incredible powers of recollection.

The thing is, I have met so many wonderful, warm people and given out so many prizes and conversed with so many people at dinners, opened countless fetes and the like over the years that I rarely can actually recall the exact details. As a matchday host nowadays at the Britannia Stadium I welcome guests into the hospitality areas of the club at least 20 times each season. I can guarantee that on about half of those occasions someone comes up to me with a smile on their face, hand extended for a warm handshake and says, 'Terry... you don't remember me, do you? But...' And then we'll be off. It will be a fond recollection from ten or 15 years ago or even longer. Something which has stayed with this person for all those years. That is quite a special thing really. The point is that it makes the fans feel great and it allows me the opportunity to bring a smile to both their faces and, for very different reasons, my own.

A sense of humour is very important to me. I played the game of football with a smile on my face and loved to socialise with supporters as well as with my team-mates. I really hope you find that as you read through the book and learn more about me, this shines through. This book is about my life as much as my football career; and I have packed it full of stories not just about what went on during games, but also about the thousands of supporters I have had the pleasure of meeting and the great times and challenges I have faced both on and off the pitch. Throughout them all this question – 'You don't remember me, do you?' – has been a constant theme, so when it came to choosing a title I couldn't really choose anything else, could I?

Foreword by Tony Pulis

HARD though it is to believe, I know, but Terry Conroy and I once played against each other in a professional football match. It was April 1978 and I was a mere whippersnapper trying to keep this old stager quiet. Obviously I was magnificent and he was average and that was the only reason why my team Bristol Rovers beat his Stoke side 4-1. If Terry has a different recollection then I'm right and he's wrong! I had a really easy afternoon and he was a piece of cake to mark.

I'd known all about Terry, with his flame red hair and white legs, for many years before this. He was one of the major stand-out stars of the Stoke City team which won the 1972 League Cup. Stoke were never a glamorous club like your Manchester Uniteds, Liverpools or Arsenals, but that team was fantastic. Terrific. Gordon Banks, Denis Smith, Jimmy Greenhoff and the incomparable George Eastham, among many others. Apart from the team I put together it most probably is the best Stoke City team ever!

Somehow Terry stood out because of his looks and his skill. He was a naturally gifted player who could beat a man with a trick and a burst of pace and he was a terrific crosser of the ball, a dying art these days. That was on those dreadful pitches they had to play on and with those balls which collected water like sponges and then after about ten minutes would turn into cannonballs. Mind you, I'd never have picked Terry in any of my sides. Far too ill-disciplined!

When I became manager of Stoke I came across Terry again as he was by now the matchday host in the main hospitality suite and working in the commercial department of the club. I warmed to him immediately as he is such a fun, bubbly and impish character. He has this (in)famous sense of humour, with one-liners being cracked every second sentence and, if you like, he's a typical Irishman in that sense; very quick-witted, with the gift of the gab. I'm fairly sure he got away with murder as a player and reading about how he managed to pick up the most literary booking in British football history in this book has put the biggest smile on my face I've had for many a year.

They say football has changed and that certainly is a great example. You get the sense from talking to his team-mates that the 1970s squad were great lads, with a terrific affinity with the football club. That rarely happens these days. The game is very different in so many ways, including the money they earned and the difference in exposure the media gives to modern players too. Players had a lot more fun back then and I think that's one of the things which shines through both in this book and when you meet Terry. He had a whale of a time.

Often Terry would bring former players from his era down to the training ground and we'd sit and have lunch together, chewing the fat over the old days and how times have changed. Some of the stories he told me in those sessions may have made it into this book, although I'm fairly sure there will be a few that haven't! What is certain is that whenever Terry is around there is fun and laughter to be had. I always enjoyed his company.

It was lovely being involved in helping the Stoke City Old Boys' Association with various events to raise money for some of the former players that they have helped. Terry has always been at the hub of all of that, among many other good causes which he has championed. I'd never been at a club which had such an active network of old pros before and it was a truly wonderful thing. Terry worked so hard on keeping those lads together and involving them and it is to his eternal credit and great testament to him as an individual. He really is Stoke City through and through.

I'll never forget learning about Terry's terrible illness. I couldn't believe it. I think he used two of his lives up in that one day. He tells me he's still got seven left, though. Myself and David Kemp decided we'd go round to his house to help him recuperate (I know that there will be many people who think the last thing a man who has survived a near-death experience needs is us pair turning up, but on this occasion it seemed to work). We insisted that if we won the semi-final against Bolton then he had to be fit enough to come to the final. It was only right that he was there for that special Wembley day in the club's history. We made it and so did TC.

If there's one thing I hope you take from this book it's that Terry Conroy is one of the warmest and greatest people you could possibly come across. Someone you would definitely want on your side, both on the pitch and in life; great character and tremendous human being.

1

A Heart-Stopping Moment

THERE'S nothing funny about almost dying. Not even remotely. I should know as I'm the very fortunate survivor of what's known as an Abdonimal Aortic Aneurysm (AAA). It's a very serious condition, which is actually a swelling (the aneurysm) of the aorta – the main blood vessel that leads oxygenated blood away from the heart, down through the abdomen to the rest of the body. This is the largest blood vessel humans possess and is usually around 2cm wide – roughly the width of a garden hose. However, when weakened it can swell to over 5.5cm – at which point it can burst, causing huge internal bleeding. This is usually fatal. Usually.

The events of Sunday 20 March 2011 are ingrained in my memory. It was the St Patrick's Day celebration in the Parish Hall of Holy Trinity, my local church in central Newcastle-under-Lyme in north Staffordshire. Consequently the church hall was packed, which was to prove something of a salvation for me. The music was playing, fiddles flying, both Irish stew and drink were in abundance. Typical church do, you might say. Well, for us Irish folk, anyway.

The previous day I had been at the Britannia Stadium fulfilling my duties as matchday host as Stoke had thrashed Newcastle United 4-0 in the Premier League. This had followed quickly on from the previous home game in which Stoke had defeated West Ham United to clinch a first FA Cup semi-final place since I had appeared for the club in monumental tussles with Arsenal in 1971 and 1972. Not only that, but Ireland had hammered England 24-8 to deny them the Grand Slam in the Six Nations Championship in Dublin that night. It was an incredibly exciting month and I was loving every minute of being involved in my club as it achieved success, just as we had in my days wearing the red and white stripes.

So, here I was having a whale of a time with my friends at the church when suddenly I felt a pain inside my back, as if someone had stuck a knife in me. I often have back pains, although not as severe as this, and I thought it would just go away. It didn't.

I excused myself and tottered outside on my own to catch a breath of air. It was a lovely, sunny spring day. I leant against the wall, trying to ease the pain and looked up at the sky, which seemed to be twisting and turning round, and I thought, 'This can't be right.' I'd suffered several horrendous knee injuries through playing football but had never experienced pain such as this. It was excruciating.

The next thing I knew was being surrounded by paramedics. I'd collapsed. But fortunately for me a lady called Maureen Cooper, who had been involved in putting the event on, had brought something out to her car and found me slumping to the ground. The very fact of there being so many people there had caused her to have to tidy things away into her car boot. It saved my life.

Maureen had raced into the hall and raised the alarm. Luckily for me the nearest hospital, University Hospital of North Staffordshire, was only just around the corner from my church and within five minutes I was being attended to by paramedics and within 20 minutes I would be admitted to hospital and was being seen by a specialist. There is no doubt that this was a major factor in saving my life. In fact, had I been at home and not bothered going to church that Sunday I probably wouldn't have survived, as I would have been too far away from medical assistance. Not only that, but there was a doctor in attendance at the church service that day, a cancer specialist (and mad keen Barcelona fan), Josep Sule-Suso, who had raced out to see what he could do to help.

Josep was worried I would vomit and choke on it, so he rolled me into the recovery position, allowing me to breathe again; he was helped in this by two ladies, Angela Peake and Regina Gibbons. So actually my life was saved twice that day – once from choking to death and once from the aneurysm. I will be forever indebted to the care and quick attention of Josep, Maureen, Angela and Regina that day.

I can't remember much about what happened after that at all and most of what I am able to tell you is pieced together from other people's recollections as they are far more lucid than mine, but I do remember lying there and being for some reason conscious that I was wearing a purple polo shirt and swearing to myself that to my dying day I would never wear purple again... Josep seemed to share this opinion as at this moment he got some scissors and cut the shirt off me, shearing it right down the middle of the front so he could check me out.

I had no idea what was wrong with me. I knew it couldn't be my heart as I'd had that checked regularly and had been told only recently that it was a strong as an ox's. I drifted in and out of consciousness, although I can vaguely remember a portion of the very short journey to Accident and Emergency in the ambulance with its siren going. I was wheeled in on a stretcher and in the busy reception area several people recognised me and enquired, 'How are you, Terry?' Now, I know they meant well, but when you've an oxygen mask on, are pumped full of morphine and are being hurriedly rushed into a hospital you're unlikely to be tip top, are you?

The drugs were barely disguising the pain, but at least caused me to dip in and out of consciousness some more. When I awoke again it was to find the specialist shaking me to tell me that he needed me to sign a consent form. Well, I could barely lift the pen, so had no chance of writing my full signature. I settled for my initials, TC, which is how many people know me anyway.

Then came the news. Document signed, the specialist said, 'Thank you for that. It's my duty to inform you that the chances of you surviving this operation are one in ten.'

'You'd better get on with it, then,' was all I could muster before I succumbed to the morphine.

The enormity of that statement didn't really hit me until I came round after the operation and was trying to piece everything that had happened together.

By that time I had actually been given the Last Rites twice! Once by the hospital priest and once by the Parish Priest of St Gabriel's in Alsager, Father Tony Grace. I never realised I had so much influence with the great man above!

Now, where was my family when all this happened, you may well ask? Sue, my beautiful wife, was over in Australia for a month visiting Niamh, the middle one of my three wonderful daughters, who was living in Sydney at the time. Meanwhile my eldest daughter Tara was in London along with her husband, Mike, celebrating his birthday. Back at the church my friends were looking through my mobile phone to try and find some contact numbers to let my family know what was happening. The first one they happened upon was for my youngest daughter Sinead, so they called her, but as she was out having Sunday lunch somewhere in deepest rural Shropshire they couldn't get hold of her. Eventually they managed to get through and Sinead started to relay messages to the others as she headed back to Newcastle to come to the hospital to await the end of my surgery, fretting and very upset.

As soon as she heard the news, Tara rushed to catch a train from Euston to Stoke. They were all thinking the worst, and were trying to get hold of their mum, Sue. The problem there was that Sue and Niamh had gone on a tour to see the sun rise at Ayers Rock, just about the most isolated place on earth, slap bang in the middle of Australia. There was no mobile signal until they got back to the hotel, at which point their phones went off like Christmas trees. They knew something was wrong as that never happens unless something is up. As soon as they learned I was gravely ill they organised flights home and set off, but of course that's a day and a half's journey at least, so it would be some time before they made it back to the Potteries. The worst thing for them was that they knew that my condition was so serious that I might not be alive once they returned. They were fretting so much during the journey that they decided not to turn their phones on at all, even between flights, just in case bad news came through and they would have to suffer the rest of the journey home in the full knowledge that I was gone.

Thankfully I wasn't. I'd made it into that ten per cent window of opportunity and came through the operation. One by one my family arrived to find out that I had survived despite all the odds and was now feeling as right as rain. When Sue rushed in, on the Tuesday lunchtime after a long and tortuous journey, the first thing she said was, 'I am never leaving you again.' That was lovely. But it was followed quickly by, 'Because I can't trust you to do anything without causing a fuss!' It was just great to see her and it gave me a huge boost.

My survival was entirely due to the skill of the vascular surgeon who operated on me, a Hungarian called Laszlo Papp. I was very lucky that he was working at the hospital and that dealing with an AAA was one of his specialities. We have become friends through the course of my recovery and Laszlo confided in me about a year after this all happened that he thought he had lost me at one stage. So he almost literally did perform miracles by bringing me back to life that day.

It was only once I was out of the high dependency unit and off the critical list that I began to learn about what had happened to me, what an AAA is and how it had nearly done for me. Apparently it hadn't initially fully burst. It had, though, begun to leak, which is what had caused the initial back pain. Had it burst then I would have been a goner and no level of skill on Laszlo's behalf could have saved me. The immediate action of those people at the church had almost certainly saved my life as it burst just after they laid me on the operating table, but by then the staff had been able to stabilise me and were able to cope. Just. Apparently it took ten litres of blood to keep me going – twice the normal amount that humans have in their entire body.

During the procedure, they replaced the part of my aorta which had burst with something called a graft, which is a piece of plastic the size and shape of a small tube of toothpaste. Once this is grafted on, the body just starts functioning properly again. Good as new. The recovery time is actually quite short really, considering the seriousness of the condition, and you don't need any medication to recover, it's just getting yourself active again.

Interestingly news of my untimely demise had reached the outside world pretty quickly. The local paper, the *Sentinel*, had received a call telling them that I'd got no chance of survival and began preparing an obituary, so it's comforting to know that they're well prepared! I know a lad who had seen me rushed in on the stretcher who rang BBC Radio Stoke and went one step further and told them I'd died. Thankfully they checked with the hospital before putting that news out on air. I even had my own strapline on Sky Sports News – 'Stoke legend Terry Conroy in serious condition in hospital'. Now there's something I never thought would happen!

Because of all this publicity and the speed of modern communications as the news spread like wildfire, there was so much interest pouring in to the hospital that we had to devise a system of communication so that the hospital would know who should and shouldn't be allowed to learn about my progress. Apparently the switchboard was chaotic, but anyone who didn't know the special code word didn't get put through. Well-wishers would turn up asking if they could come in and see me. It was wonderfully warming to hear, but having visitors outside the immediate family was barred in order to aid my full recovery.

I am flabbergasted to this day at the level of interest that was shown in my well-being. I'd been out of the game of football for years and it was hard to take in the places that Get Well Soon cards arrived from; not just England and Ireland, but France, Norway and America. It was surprising and phenomenal. It just wasn't possible to even begin to respond to the thousands of cards, so let me take this opportunity to say thank you to everyone from the bottom of my heart.

Everything lined up to save my life when my aneurysm came – from the people who had raised the alarm and stopped me choking to where I was when I collapsed in relation to the hospital to the genius of the surgeon who operated on me and the incredible staff at University Hospital of North Staffordshire who nursed me back to health. I was very lucky. I had never heard of AAA before so I began to research it more. I was given a leaflet about Abdominal Aortic Aneurysm screening which was incredibly informative. I became fascinated by this unheard of condition and, having become something of an expert, I am now a very keen campaigner to raise awareness of it. It has become a cause which is – literally – close to my heart.

Because of my position at Stoke City Football Club it seemed the most obvious thing was to get the club involved, as it turns out that men are far more prone to his problem than women, especially males over the age of 65. In fact the stats say that around one in 50 of all deaths in men in this age group – a total of 6,000 deaths in England and Wales each year – are down to AAA.

I approached the club, who were delighted to get involved, and we've so far arranged two screening days at the Britannia Stadium, which were well attended, following great publicity offered by the *Sentinel*, and the two local radio stations, BBC Radio Stoke and Signal Radio. The campaign centred on my near-death experience and the fact that, because AAAs usually cause no symptoms until they reach a critical stage and start leaking or worse, burst, they tend to only be diagnosed as a result of proactive screening.

Each screening day saw staff from the North Staffs Hospital testing people down at the Britannia Stadium. The club provided four beds – the type on which players receive treatment – and people came in for a simple ultrasound scan, which takes around ten minutes and is completely free. It's a very simple process and we always arrange for some former players to come down to meet the fans while they are waiting, and they will be screened themselves as well. So it's a social occasion and a chance for fans to meet some Stoke City greats, as well as a very worthwhile cause.

In my research I'd discovered that if a large AAA is detected before it ruptures, most people will be advised to have planned surgery to replace the weakened section of the blood vessel with a piece of synthetic tubing, just like the one I had inserted. For one man who attended our sessions this was exactly what happened. The scan revealed an aneurysm which was reaching a critical stage and he was able to have a planned procedure and emerge on the other side fully fit and raring to go. It was the perfect outcome for me as I'd averted a disaster for someone as he might not have been as fortunate as I was with how things worked out for me. Indeed this gentleman, Owen Bennion, agreed. He sent Stoke chairman Peter Coates a letter thanking him for setting up the screening day he had attended which had highlighted the problem and signed off by saying Stoke City had saved his life. It was such a worthwhile thing for the club to have done for its fans and the wider community and I'm so passionate about spreading the word far and wide. In fact when Bolton Wanderers ran a similar testing day in the Spring of 2015 they identified four men who needed immediate help to stop their Aneurysms bursting. In my view football clubs could all run these supporter testing days, and attract fans in by getting a few former players to come down, chat with fans and be tested themselves. We could save many hundreds of lives by juts being that bit more proactive.

The experts on AAA don't yet know everything they would like to know about the condition, for example exactly what causes it. It may be hereditary, so for that reason I have made sure all of my family, including my three daughters, have been screened. They are all fine, thankfully, but you can't be too careful and the screening procedure is quick and simple. Go and get it done and tell all your friends about it too – especially if they are male and over 65. Age, lack of exercise, a high fat diet, having high blood pressure and cholesterol levels are all thought to increase the risk of an aneurysm by weakening the aorta, but these are risk factors you can do something about – as is getting screened. So, go on, do it.

The close shave that I had gave me huge pause for thought. I'd considered writing a book for years, at least a decade. But I had never had the impetus to actually sit down and go through all of my memorabilia, photo albums and dredge my memory to put something comprehensive together about my life. So now I had a reason. Having been though this experience, I wanted to leave a legacy behind for my family. I hope that's a very unselfish reason for producing this tome. Certainly, it isn't either for the money or the glory, you can be assured of that!

With being one of ten siblings myself and then all of us having had children, grandchildren and even great grandchildren, who are spread all over the world, this book is my way of telling my story to help them to understand where they came from, how their parents grew up and how their Uncle Terry or Great Uncle

Terry made his way in the world. I hope that it may serve to inspire them a little as they find their path through life. Many of these kids haven't even met me as they live in far-flung places. In fact just before I started writing this book I met up with my three nieces, my sister Rita's children, who I hadn't seen for some time. They told me that people in our family talk about me all the time, but that they didn't really know the full story. It was one of the clinching moments that made me think it was time to put down on the page how I'd come from a Dublin estate to surviving a major health scare via Wembley. It will be something tangible to be left behind for them. And I hope that you find it interesting, amusing and informative too.

2
Home Farm

I GREW up in a suburb of Dublin called Cabra, about two miles north of the city centre. We lived on a big estate of 1930s-built terraced houses; our road was called Annaly Road and we lived at number 50. Ironically enough, Cabra is the modern version of a word which in old Gaelic means 'the poor land'. This was entirely accurate as neither my family, the Conroys, nor anyone else we knew had any money. This hasn't stopped the area being a source of a huge amount of talent over the years; a hotbed, in fact. For example actor Michael Gambon, world champion boxer Steve Collins, Martin Faye of the band The Chieftains (who lived around the corner from us), and folk singer Dickie Rock, just about the most famous singer in Ireland in the 1950s and 60s, all hailed from Cabra, as did author and journalist Gene Kerrigan and even WWE superstar Sheamus (real name Stephen Farrelly). Many of these talented and determined people would follow me, although admittedly probably unwittingly in many cases, in both dreaming of and pursuing a life and career outside Cabra, showcasing their particular talents to the world along the way.

There was also a plaque on a nearby bridge, the Broombridge, to famous mathematician William Hamilton which we all saw, but had no idea what he did. So in the course of writing this book I've looked it up... and I still don't understand it! He must have been brilliant, though, as the city council put the plaque up in 1958 in honour of his discovery in 'a flash of inspiration' of quaternions. No, I've no idea what those are either, but the thought of a flash of inspiration to a 12-year-old desperate to impress at football was enough to inspire me further.

Because all I cared about was football and for me, my hero was Manchester United inside-forward Liam 'Billy' Whelan. He was a neighbour back then, his family lived in nearby St Attracta's Road, with our respective mothers going down town shopping together and even today his family remain friends with the Conroys. The Whelans were very religious and when Liam used to come home in the summers after finishing the season with Manchester United I remember that he used to pass our house on the way to the church of Christ the King, down our road, to celebrate Mass. Even then he was an impressive man, whose exploits with United were becoming the stuff of legend, particularly in terms of being a goalscoring winger or inside-left. But the best thing for us was that after Mass Liam would love nothing more than to join in our street football games with us young lads. I aspired to be like Liam. To play with him in one of those pitch-battle street football games was the stuff of dreams as far as I was concerned.

Liam was born in 1935 and progressed through our local youth football club, Home Farm, to be signed by Manchester United and develop under the wing of Matt Busby into a key member of that great side known as the Busby Babes. He was actually Manchester United's top scorer in the 1956/57 season, netting 26 goals in the First Division and 33 in total as United won their second successive league title and reached the semi-finals of both the FA Cup and the fledgling European Cup.

In keeping with the theme, Liam now has a bridge named in his honour in Cabra, near Dalymount Park, the home of Irish football, with the unveiling having been performed by Sir Bobby Charlton, Liam's team-mate, in December 2006. The naming of the bridge was to honour the fact that Liam was one of the 23 people killed when a plane carrying Manchester United's team and accompanying staff and journalists home from a European Cup away leg in Belgrade crashed while attempting to take off on a snowy runway at Munich airport on 6 February 1958. He was only 22.

I remember exactly where I was when I heard the news. I was coming out of school on to Annaly Road on a dank afternoon when the gossip started flying around that there had been a crash and many of the Manchester United team were dead, including Liam. I was devastated and numbed by this turn of events. It was a huge thing for Dublin, brought all the more into focus when the city came to a standstill on the day of Liam's funeral. His family lived about half a mile from the church of Christ the King, which stood next door to our school about 100 yards along our road from our house and the cortege arrived after slowly making its way through the streets with stunned onlookers bidding a fond farewell to one of their own who had made such a name for himself in just 22 short years. Liam had known my older brothers well as he was a similar age, so I identified hugely with him and I was proud to be an altar boy at his funeral. The church was packed and, although I don't recall anything about the service itself, I do remember distinctly that not only was there such a huge air of sadness about the place, but for at least a year afterwards a cloud of disbelief lay over the entire area. We all had sympathy for Liam's family and the community closed around the Whelans and supported them amid the sadness of having lost someone so special.

Cabra was quite a football hotbed. John Giles, who was about five or six years older than me, also grew up in Cabra, having moved to the area as a young boy, as did Roddy Collins, brother of boxer Steve, who would follow me in playing for Home Farm and Glentoran. Roddy has gone on to manage in both England, with Carlisle United, and Malta (Floriana), as well as at a clutch of Irish clubs including Bohemians and Shamrock Rovers, winning some famous European victories along the way. Another Cabra-born player who I ended up playing against a lot was Mick Martin, who starred for Manchester United, Newcastle United and West Bromwich Albion.

Giles made his international debut for the Republic of Ireland at the age of 18 in November 1959 at Dalymount Park in Dublin – a stone's throw from Cabra. Opponents Sweden had finished as the runners-up in the previous year's World Cup finals, only losing to Pele's Brazil in the final. John scored in the 16th minute as Ireland won a superb game 3-2, coming back from two goals down in the process, with Dermot Curtis, who had started at Shelbourne but by 1959 had moved on to Ipswich Town where he won the league title under Alf Ramsey in 1961/62, scoring the other two goals. Giles grew to be another Cabra icon while Joe Carolan was another lad who first joined Manchester United and then went on to play for Brighton and win caps for the Republic of Ireland, and Gerry Daly and Ashley Grimes would both go on to play for Manchester United in the 1970s and 80s.

So this was the background of football in which I grew up, but I also had pretty good genes, it's fair to say. I was born into a wonderful, loving, Catholic family; one which had football running through its veins and never lacked a witty word or some banter or other flying around. You had to be quick-witted and switched on in our house as the jokes and one-liners would fly constantly. My mother's name was Esther and my father was called John, although everyone called him Jack. My mother was undoubtedly the boss and my dad, bless his soul, was utterly useless at disciplining us. He was very, very laid back. Unbelievably so. He had a soft spot for everybody. Many's the time that my mother would come down in the morning to find some stranger sleeping in the front room. He'd taken pity on a tramp on the street and offered him a bed for the night. Dad thought the best of everybody, was a sucker for a hard luck story and my mother had to put up with this, although she was a lot more perceptive and a lot less happy to extend hospitality to our 'visitors' for any longer than she had to. As the door closed behind them, she'd turn to dad and say, 'Oh Jack, you're a gobshite. They see you coming a mile off.' Gobshite was her favourite word. As I say we were a true Catholic family…

My parents produced eight boys and two girls. In order of age the eldest was christened Alphonsus (although everyone called him Ollie), then Laurence (affectionately known as Lar), John (always called Donny, nobody ever called him John), Rita, Peter (the only one of the boys in the family who didn't have the Conroy distinctive shock of red hair, which caused some consternation and comment at the time!), Michael (who was born exactly five years before me on 2 October 1941), Vincent, Gerard, Paul and then the youngest of the family, Marie.

So, as you can see, my sizeable family had something of a tradition of christening children with one name then pretty much straight away confusing everyone by calling them something else in practice. This is why you may have spotted that my name that you know me by – Terry – is not on that list. So, was I adopted into this huge and seemingly every-growing family? Did dad take in yet another waif and stray? Was I sent to them in disgrace from some distant cousin in a branch of the family down in County Kerry? No, none of these. Simply the family tradition was continued and my given name of Gerard was quickly amended to Terry. There was a reason behind this particular re-christening which was that apparently when I was learning to speak I just couldn't say my name. The whole family would find my efforts hilarious. I would hold my hand out and say 'that' when I wanted something, but then I got really ambitious and added my name, along the lines of 'Gerard wants that'. The problem was the name Gerard was a little trickier for a youngster to say than anyone expected and it quickly morphed into Terry, so I would actually say 'Terry that' when holding my hand out for something I wanted. So my name got changed to Terry because I just couldn't say Gerard and it stuck.

This still causes the odd problem for me today. For example, when I go into the bank I'm often asked to somehow prove that the person they know as Terry Conroy is the same as the one whose name is actually Gerard on my passport. There was a very famous occasion in my family when this caused even more confusion. Only about five or six years ago I was on a Mediterranean cruise with my wife, Sue. My knee, as it often does following years of knee-high tackles and playing on sub-standard pitches, had swollen up. So I went below decks to see the doctor, an Asian chap, who took one look at my documents and said, 'Gerard!' in a very excited fashion. 'Yes,' I said, slightly taken aback that he'd used my given name, rather than the one everyone knows me by. 'The footballer!' he continued, almost beside himself now. Obviously my reputation and that dodgy spell in Hong Kong, which I'll relate to you later in the book, had had a far deeper impact in the Far East than I thought. Buoyed by this, although also thinking 'how on earth does he know', I replied, 'Yes, that's right.' I was totally unprepared for what came next. 'Steven, Steven Gerrard,' he cried, almost hugging me. Dear reader, I can honestly say that even I never thought I'd be mistaken for the Liverpool and England captain. Not ever.

We Conroys were a traditional Catholic family, which means we lived in fear of my mother. If you did anything wrong like wear out your shoes playing football you'd get a clip round the ear. It wasn't unusual to get punished for misbehaving, but for us it was our mother rather than father who'd dish out the discipline and that was unusual. It wasn't brutal at all. It was just the way of the world then. It was more humbling than painful and it kept us in line. It certainly made sure we knew that mother was in control. She was also in control of the finances. When eldest brothers Ollie or Lar came home with their wages at the end of each week they would have to hand over the majority of it to our mother, who then used it to manage the purchase of food for the coming week. They didn't get to keep much for themselves.

Mother was an incredible worker and had this amazing ability to juggle countless things simultaneously, which she had to given the imbalance of money coming into the house versus ever-growing number of mouths to feed. One of the funniest things that happened was when I was about 12 and mother was holding down two jobs at the time. During the day she worked on the production line canning peas at the Batchelor's factory up the road. She would come home and make the tea at the end of her shift, then go out again and clean at the Electricity Supply Board offices in central Dublin. I don't know how she managed two jobs and a family of ten kids, but that was our mother.

Part of the regime was that in order to get by each week some of us schoolboys would have to take my father's best suit to the pawnshop each Monday in order to realise some cash to get us through to the following payday on Friday, when we'd also be able to liberate the suit in time for dad to wear it to church on the Sunday. Vincent, Paul and myself were responsible for doing this while mum and dad were at work. We would come home from school at lunchtime, get the suit and head to Weaver's pawnbrokers on Dorset Street on the number 12 bus to drop the suit in and collect the 30 shillings which would see us through the week. Weaver's was run by Jews, as pawnshops mostly were in those days, but the Jewish community was well integrated into Dublin and I can't say enough about how unbelievably supportive they were to Dubliners during that period. The interest they charged was actually very low and there was never any hint of 'heaviness' if you were struggling to repay.

I always felt that having to do this was a bit embarrassing as our name was very well known due to the older brothers' decent amount of success on the football field and so when the pawnbroker shouted out 'Conroy' to the waiting queue everyone knew it was us who were pawning dad's suit. I knew people gossiped and that it was a bit of a stigma to have to do this each week and I wasn't comfortable with it. Over the years of course the suit became more and more worn and had less and less value and mum would warn us that she still wanted the 30 bob for it and not to let the pawnbroker be stingy and give us less, as even losing a few shillings would make a massive difference to the weekly budget. So, when the pawnbroker started to try to fob us off with 27 shillings we'd have to come up with some sob story to win him over. We'd always tell him that our mother would tan our hides and then come down and sort him out unless he gave us the full 30 bob. We'd make a big palaver about it and eventually he would cave in as our mother's reputation preceded her. So it was useful in some ways! It became a kind of game with him offering us a low amount to start off with and eventually giving us what we needed to have.

The 12 and 22 buses stopped right outside the pawnshop and, in order to avoid embarrassment, we tried to make sure that the coast was clear before we exited the shop. One day, however, we got our timing wrong and came out just as the 22 was at the stop opposite. On the top of the bus looking straight across at us was a lad who knew us well at school. We were devastated, thinking he would tell everyone we knew where we had been, but great credit to him he never mentioned it. Phew! Major embarrassment averted. Looking back now pawning that suit was a vital way of getting through the week and not going without. We were never hungry, and I suppose you could say that we were better off than many other families at that time.

In the grand tradition of Cabra families our house was cramped to say the least. We had to eat in two sittings just so we could get around the table. The eldest went first and then us younger ones. Washing was interesting as we didn't have a bathroom as such, or hot running water at first. We had a bath once a week in an old metal tub in front of the fire. Our sleeping arrangements saw us crammed in like sardines to the three bedrooms upstairs, especially as mother and father had the one room, then the girls shared with the four youngest boys, although with a sheet pulled across a piece of rope to divide the room up, while the eldest four boys shared the other room. In our half of the partitioned room I slept top-to-toe with the youngest, Paul, in a single bed, while Vincent and Michael shared in another single next to us. It wasn't uncommon to wake up and find a toe up your nose. We didn't have anything like duvets or eiderdowns, it was just sheets and blankets to keep us warm, and when it got really cold mother would lay old army coats over us to stop us freezing. There was certainly no central heating. Our way of life played a huge part in ensuring I'd keep my feet on the ground as I grew up and became successful. I know a few people, for example, who have left home in Ireland and before you know it they've lost their accent and are pretending they aren't from Dublin at all. That just isn't me. I'm proud of my roots, identity and heritage.

Being a traditionally Catholic family also meant that the boys got every perk under the sun while the girls worked their fingers to the bone learning the ropes of how to be good Catholic wives and mothers. I'm not saying that is right or wrong, just that's how it was. The boys definitely got preferential treatment, especially those who earned wages. It also meant church. To me church also meant money, as I was an altar boy from an early age and when we officiated at weddings we would get a tip; after the ceremony the best man would slip us some money, which could be as much as a crown or even a ten bob note – a fortune to us. Of course, I wouldn't be allowed to keep my new-found wealth as it had to go into the family pot just like my elder brothers' wages had to.

At that time, though, we had a canon who ruled the roost in the parish – Canon O'Callaghan – and my mother disliked him intensely because she thought he was a conman. She was right. He would come to us after each wedding and make all the altar boys give him the tips they had received from the best man, saying, 'This will be for the orphans at Christmas.' We all knew it was a ruse and the very first time it happened I went home to my mother and told her that I'd been given a half crown, but it had been taken off me by the canon. My mother was not happy to say the least and told me in future that it would be OK to lie and say that I had not been given anything, even if I had. So there was my mother encouraging me to lie to a man of the cloth.

Canon O'Callaghan came from a well-heeled background as his family was well known throughout Ireland for its success in the leather business, with a shop in the city centre and they owned plenty of land too. So this kind of behaviour was very suspicious and we looked upon him as a mean, avaricious feller. He certainly made the most of his flock's deference to the church by creaming off these tips from people who weren't prepared to tell the odd white lie to keep what was rightfully theirs. Mother wasn't having any of it. In many ways she was ahead of her time as she saw through the priest clear as day. The canon was prone to knocking on the door with a bucket, claiming to be collecting for something like the parish Christmas party, even though it was July. My mother would open the door and if he tried to come in she'd put her foot in the door and make sure he could not enter. There would be a Mexican stand-off while he tried to entice her to give some money for whatever cause he'd invented this time and she refused to both donate or let him cross the threshold into her domain. There weren't many who would stand up to the church in this way, but my mother was one because, despite her deep religious conviction, she was very suspicious of the men who ran the church in our parish.

To sum it up, one day the canon knocked on the door of our house. My mother opened the door and said, 'What do you want?'

Now, as I've said, all bar one of us Conroy boys had a shock of very distinctive red hair, which on this occasion would cause the canon a problem, rather than us, as he mistook another couple of lads for us.

'Your boys are all up at the schoolyard playing in the playground,' Canon O'Callaghan said, referring to the fact that we'd often climb back over the fence of the school to utilise the space to play in once it had closed and locked its gates for the night, which was strictly against the rules. The church was next to the school and he was saying that he'd seen all of us boys there and that he was going to report us to the authorities and we would be in so much trouble and all this and that. He was really laying it on thick and clearly enjoying himself, on a roll. As it happened we were actually in the back garden playing and my mother called over her shoulder to us, 'Ollie, Lar, Donny, Vincent, Michael, Peter, Paul, Terry,' and we all came marching through, one by one, to stand behind her in a tableau. The look on his face was priceless.

'Now, tell me,' said my mother sternly, 'which of my boys was it you saw?'

The canon just turned and walked away. Mother closed the door and murmured, 'You old gobshite, you...'

Cabra was an area where people did not own their own homes, had high unemployment and in which everyone was strapped for cash, but that's not to say life in our street wasn't actually great. It was. Not least because we didn't really know any different. We led simple but very fulfilling lives. And for the astute among you what that means is, as one of the youngest in our family with plenty of older siblings to do the majority of the chores around the home, I got to play football pretty much all day every day when I wasn't in either school or church. In fact, from a very early age pretty much all I did was play football. It was just the natural thing and it seemed as if there was always a game going on right outside my door. Games weren't really organised, they just broke out sporadically whenever a ball was produced, seemingly from nowhere, and word would get around like wildfire. Kids would appear from all over the place and a game would commence, building up a head of steam until night fell or our mothers called us in for tea.

Because the streets of Cabra were traffic-less – no one could ever even dream of owning a car – we were able to play outside from first thing in the morning to late at night. It would be anywhere between ten and 20-a-side at times. The games were fluid and who took part was dependent upon when they were needed to help their mothers, especially at the weekends. It was essentially playground football out on the street. Rough and ready, a free for all; our street versus the street from round the corner. No tactics, just play and play and play. The street and its football was our life.

There were certain issues though. The street was quite narrow – far narrower than a football pitch, of course – so our 'pitch' was long and thin. Then to make it even narrower still there were pavements on either side, which you had to try to negotiate if you had the ball at your feet or you were trying to make a tackle. So there was an element of difficulty and danger that meant you had to have your wits about you, especially when 30 or 40 other boys would be trying to hack you down, kick your ankles or dispossess you in some other fashion – legal or not.

The laws of the game of football were rarely enforced – in effect there was no such thing as a foul, it really was the survival of the fittest – but this didn't bother us. It was simple – you got kicked, then you got up and played on (a bit like playing against certain full-backs in the late 1960s, you might say!). Even though there weren't really any rules, we were essentially a pretty fair lot. Even so, almost every day you'd go back home at dusk with cut knees and this led to a fearful routine in our house which I bear the scars of to this day.

Because the street was roughly tarmacked you would end up with grazes on your knees or elbows which had tiny specks of gravel embedded in them. You weren't allowed anywhere near a doctor or a hospital as that would be far too time consuming what with the travelling and the interruption of family life due to the hours you would be waiting (some things don't change). So returning home with such battle scars meant my father – seizing the opportunity to 'help' my mother, who would not want her endless routine of washing, cleaning and cooking to be interrupted – would take it upon himself to act as the surgeon and extract the alien particles from my body. Assisted by my uncle Gerard (after whom I'd been named, incidentally, so he'd probably got it in for me for having renounced his name for my chosen Terry), who would be enlisted to hold me down, dad would bathe my knee. Now this sounds like it should be soothing, but far from it. It was only about ensuring that the wound was clean.

This fastidious treatment took the form of first hot water and then a bread poultice (a gauze containing boiled pieces of stale bread) being applied to tease out any possible infection. Obviously my father's degree in medical science stood him in good stead with what many of you might think is a bit of a quack's remedy… at least that's what he would tell this six-, seven- or eight-year-old boy, who, each time he felt the feared, scalding hot bread poultice applied to his gaping flesh wound, would scream in agony, struggling for escape from my uncle's firm grasp while simultaneously being told by Doctor Conroy that it was good for me… I still have the scars to this day, although now you'll have spot them amid those left by my multiple cartilage operations, which look far more impressive. To be fair to my father, while painful, it was actually effective. I never did get an infection. It's arguable, of course, whether this was because of or in spite of the poultice.

Despite all that, the biggest problem by far for our band of footballing brethren was being chased away by certain neighbours, who weren't so keen on our lengthy, impromptu games taking place on their doorstep. Sometimes a game would have to stop because we'd kick the ball into a garden and the neighbour refused to give it back to us. There would only be one ball around at any one time as they were expensive things back then and we would play with it until its leather became so threadbare it became misshapen or, worse, it burst. Having it withheld by an irate neighbour was a fairly common occurrence.

Every so often the neighbours would get so annoyed that they would call the police to disperse us. Now they'd more often than not be the posh neighbours as they'd actually have phones with which to summon the Garda to deal with the miscreants creating havoc outside. There was a particular sergeant, I remember him well, called Sergeant Bradley, against whom we would have to pit our wits on a regular basis. We called him 'Soap' for some reason and I don't actually know why as it doesn't relate to any particular incident I can recall, but Soap we called him. He used to come round on his bicycle with his clips in his trousers. He'd either have been called by someone or else would be on his rounds which he did maybe once a month down our street.

Now he wasn't a very nice man and was a constant thorn in our side. I suppose you could say we were the same for him as he was intent on catching us doing something wrong. Often word would reach us before he turned into the street – someone would shout 'here's Soap!' and we'd scatter in all different directions, up the side entries and the back passages behind the houses. He would particularly target somebody that he thought was slow who he could catch and he'd chase them on his bike, trying to grab them by the scruff of the neck to apprehend them. If he caught them he would take them down to the station and they would actually be charged and brought up before the judge. Apparently there was a heinous crime of 'playing ball in the street' which said miscreant would be guilty of.

We got fed up of this, so one day when Soap turned up, threw his bike down and started to chase one of the 'culprits' of this hideous injustice known as football, some of the lads grabbed his bicycle from where he'd dropped it, wheeled it down to Christ the King school, which was only a few yards down Annaly Road, and somehow hoiked it up on to the roof. This led to the fabulously comic moment of Soap arriving back at the place where he'd dropped his bike to find it gone, doing a brilliant double take and then hunting up and down the street, bike clips still round his ankles (and there's little funnier in the fashion stakes), until he spied it atop the school. This just made him angrier than ever. I swear fumes were blowing out of his ears! When you are eight years old it ranks among the funniest things you've ever seen. More often than not we got the measure of poor old Soap.

Then one day a few years later – I think I was 11 at the time – this feller in a suit came into the street and beckoned me over to him saying, 'Excuse me, can I just ask you something?' Now, being a helpful, happy-go-lucky kind of kid I went over to see how I could help this man, who I assumed was looking for directions to find a neighbour or something. Far from it. As soon as I got within arm's length he grabbed me, put my arms behind my back and said, 'Right, you're done, sonny, for playing football in the street.' I'd been arrested by a plain-clothed copper. It was a sneaky change of tactics from the Garda which I did not appreciate. I got taken down to the station and charged and then sometime later I had to go, along with my father, who was not at all happy at having to take a half day off work, over to the Children's Court on the south side of Dublin, near Dublin Castle, where I went up before the judge in a court of law. I remember it so well. The judge said to me, 'Gerard Anthony Conroy, you are charged with playing football in the street, how do you plead?'

Well, I'd been caught red-handed so I couldn't say anything else but, 'guilty'.

Luckily for me as a first offender my punishment was not a fine, but a probationary period during which I must not get caught playing football in the street again.

My father, being the guiding light of my life that he was, said some very wise words to me on the way home from that particular episode. Again, I remember them as clear as day. 'Terry,' he said, turning to me sternly. 'Next time make sure you don't get caught.'

The other illegal activity which I was involved in as a boy was betting. I was what they call a 'runner'. Now this was entirely my father's fault. He loved a bet, and so did my elder brothers, which was all right for them as they were over the legal age for gambling of 16. I was only about 12 at this particular time, but I would be despatched down to the betting shop, a couple of hundred yards away, past the school and the church (to which I deferentially doffed my cap as I passed just in case 'He' was watching) to place my father's bet. Now, you might think that this was bad form for him to be sending his son out to do his dirty work for him, but he had a perfectly valid reason. The family had just acquired a television in 1958 and Saturday afternoon meant horse racing, so dad would be stuck in front of the TV watching the racing, sending me down to the bookies to place bets on the horses he could now see right before his eyes. It was perfect for him. The two ladies in the betting shop, Peggy and May, weren't supposed to accept money from under-16s, but they knew I was placing it on behalf of my father, and that it wasn't my own, so they took the bets. Not that I was often sent back to collect the winnings…

Perhaps the most remarkable thing was that when my teachers at Christ the King school got wind of this, their reaction was not one of horror, but to ask me to go and place bets for them during lunchtimes. So, I got a good Catholic Irish education as well as upbringing.

I will always believe wholeheartedly that street football stood me in great stead when it came to developing into a professional player. I began to learn how to keep the ball under close control, fighting the multiple enemies of opposing players, pavements and neighbours getting in my way to win through. At least the street wasn't cobbled, which would have added to the difficulty. Equally, I learned to protect the ball as, once you got hold of it, you always felt that with so many playing you really needed to keep hold of it, because if you lost it to the other side it could be a very long time before you got a touch of it again. To retain possession I learned to play one-twos with the pavement, beating my man by flicking the ball against the raised kerbstone and running round the other side of him to get it back. Playing on the park as we did during the summer months was so much easier after this, although once you begin to play one-twos with human beings you do learn quickly that they don't necessarily return the ball to you as faithfully as a pavement does. It was a great grounding and those games on the street helped me develop my skills and an awareness of where players were in relation to me, again making playing a more traditional organised game with just the 22 players on a full-sized pitch all the easier when I graduated to playing youth football. I don't think I am by any means alone in having honed my early ball skills in this way. Most lads of that era will tell you a similar story, I imagine, along with mentioning that there were far fewer distractions in those days too. Very few people in Ireland had televisions even in the mid-1950s and even then there were only two channels – the BBC and ITV – as RTE, the Irish TV channel, didn't come into operation until 1961. So there wasn't a lot to watch.

Football was so natural to me and that was also because my entire family was also obsessed with the game and playing it. Ollie, as the eldest boy (he was 16 years older than me), set the trend in relation to football which Lar, Donny, Michael, Peter and I would then follow keenly. Ollie played as a junior for a youth club in Dublin, progressed to the League of Ireland as a left-winger with Drumcondra, a team based on the north side of Dublin near Cabra, and won representative honours for the League of Ireland, playing against the Football League (or as we called them the English League). At the age of 20 Ollie came to the attention of Wolverhampton Wanderers, who at that time were just about the biggest team in England under the management of Stan Cullis, having won the FA Cup in 1949 and only missed out on the First Division title the following season on goal average to Portsmouth. Wolves had a scout in Ireland who said that the club wanted to sign Ollie as a full-time professional. However, things didn't work out for him. Ollie was the main wage earner in the family at that time as he was working in the print industry as a machine minder, quite a responsible job. Also, the great thing about playing in the League of Ireland was that you were paid to play. So you supplemented your working wage with earning money at the weekend playing the game that you loved. What a wonderful life! Another issue was the fact that breaking into a team which at that time in the very early 1950s boasted the likes of Billy Wright, Denis Wilshaw (who would later sign for Stoke City), Jimmy Mullen and Irishman Sammy Smyth was a significant challenge. Could Ollie risk everything for his dream?

It would be almost exactly the same decision which would face me 15 years or so later, although the circumstances of the family had changed by then. Who knows whether Ollie would have made it either at Wolves or moved on to another club in England, but he never regretted it and stuck to printing as his way of life.

Printing was a line of work which my father loved and he ensured four of us Conroy boys followed him in. Ollie led the way as usual, although he in turn was following in my father's footsteps. Dad was very keen that we each had to have a trade. Printing seemed the obvious choice given that dad could both get us in and show us the ropes. You actually had to go through a formal training course and pass an entrance examination in order to be accepted into the Graphical Union (the printing union) and thus become a fully-fledged printer. Of course, having dad meant that five of us all passed the exam no problem; Ollie, Vincent, Peter, Michael and myself.

Dad had got himself into the industry initially as a lad, but then had met my mother, whose brother had a printing works which used to produce pamphlets and letterheads, that kind of thing. They also used to produce the Irish football coupons, a kind of package which you tore off the edge from to reveal the names of three clubs, and if you matched that week's results then you had the chance to win money.

Given the wages Ollie was earning from both printing and football, moving to England would have probably not led to him receiving any kind of pay rise, so the risk was just too great. It was a family decision too, not just Ollie's. He didn't go. Decision made and offer rejected, Ollie continued to star in the League of Ireland for many years, providing more inspiration for me.

It's strange thinking about my experience of Ollie's footballing career now. I'd see him disappear off each Sunday morning with his boots to go and play (League of Ireland games were all played on a Sunday then), but then we often wouldn't know how he'd got on until that night. In fact, I can always remember on a Sunday night – this was in the days before TV, mobile phones or the internet – we would get the match reports on a Sunday evening courtesy of Radio Ireland. Imagine that… even though Ollie was one of our family, if his team had played away down the country somewhere we had no way of knowing the result until it came on the radio on the sports news between half past six and quarter to seven on a Sunday evening. I can distinctly remember being seven and eight years of age huddled round the radio listening to the reports of how my brother's team had got on.

My father was passionate in his support of us all in our footballing careers and he was particularly proud of Ollie as his first born making it into the League of Ireland. Most people in Dublin would know of Ollie Conroy as the crowds that attended the games were colossal. They often included me, from eight or nine years of age, proudly watching Ollie when he was playing in Dublin. This experience also introduced me to the peculiar dynamics of a crowd. Now, dad's eyesight wasn't great and he sometimes struggled to see across the pitch at games. Let's say his judgement would sometimes be a bit clouded. I remember he'd be shouting things at games and they'd be way off what was actually happening. 'Ref, he's offside,' Jack would shout, and I'd be thinking to myself the feller was onside by at least ten yards. But it was his way of having an input and supporting his boys at a game. It may be that having worked as a printer for many years his eyesight was now struggling to make it past the distance he would spend much of his working day looking at blocks or paper just a few inches away from his nose. In any case, he sometimes struggled to even identify his own sons out there on the pitch!

I remember another occasion, this time a few years later when I was playing for the Home Farm seniors aged about 16, when dad again got involved from the sidelines. We were playing University

College of Dublin one Sunday. Most of the university team were students, but some were people who worked at the college. They were a tough side and always brought along a decent number of supporters, so on this particular morning the touchlines were packed with fans, several deep. I was getting some fearful stick from the UCD supporters as they could see I was a threat to their team. Midway through the first half I picked the ball up deep and ran at their midfield in the centre of the pitch. I beat a man and was bearing down on their defence, midway inside their half, but I touched the ball just a little too far ahead of me and this huge central defender came in all guns blazing, throwing himself into the tackle. He was going to reach the ball first, but was determined that in his follow through he was going to take me with it.

Now you simply weren't allowed to pull out of challenges in those days or you'd be taunted all the more and maybe even dropped. It wasn't in my nature either, so I charged in to the tackle too. But as we were about six feet apart I was tripped from behind and instead fell with my head going towards the ball just as this fearsome hulk of a defender was about to whack it. We collided and I went down, although I'd had time and the sense to raise my hands to protect myself and the defender actually only made contact with my palms, which smarted a bit, but I was otherwise OK. From the touchline, though, it looked like the defender had deliberately kicked me in the head. My father was not happy. He ran on to the pitch and joined in with the general melee which was going on around me, lying prone on the deck. My dad was only 5ft 9in and about six stone wet through and I looked up to see him standing in front of this massive defender, wagging his finger and saying, 'You can't do that to my son,' and then he threw a punch at him. This centre-half could have wiped dad out by blowing him over. From my vantage point this looked like one of the bravest things I'd ever seen and it really brought home to me how much dad wanted us to succeed. Blood, they say, is thicker than water and that day I saw that in action. I was very proud of him. As proud as he was of me.

It wasn't just my father, though. Countless fellers around us when I was younger and in the crowd watching alongside dad would join in with singing and hurling abuse at some player or other. It was funny and not meant nastily, and it gave me an understanding of just why crowds should be pretty much ignored when you are out there on the pitch – which is a good job given some of the abuse hurled at me by supporters up and down the length of England during my time with Stoke City.

Of the six Conroy brothers, five of us would play in the League of Ireland, only Peter didn't quite make it that far, although he was a very good amateur at the level below. Michael, an inside-left, was very prominent with Shelbourne, winning the FAI Cup in 1960, defeating Cork Hibernians 2-0 in the final. That was a very proud day for the entire family as Ollie was also in the Shelbourne side that day – the entire left wing was staffed by Conroys! I remember the feeling at the end of the game as everybody celebrated. I was by now 13 and I wanted to be part of that success. I wanted to be a professional, in fact I had already decided I wanted to go further and play in England.

I had now joined Home Farm, the famous youth football club based in the north of Dublin which over the years has produced the likes of Johnny Carey, Liam Whelan, Joe Carolan, Ronnie Whelan, Richard Dunne, Darren O'Dea, Owen Garvan and Graeme Kavanagh to name but a few who have gone on to make excellent careers for themselves. It was a natural progression for me as it was also my closest junior club, as well as being the best. We could actually walk there, although that was mainly to avoid paying the bus fare which we couldn't really afford on a regular basis. At the age of ten in 1956, then, I was playing competitive football in an Under 13 league. At that age my lack of size was made all the more apparent when up against some of the giant 12-year-olds I would face, although I could beat them for skill and pace almost any day of the week. This turn of events ratcheted up people's perception of me from a street urchin footballer to one who should be taken a bit more seriously.

This new-found status also meant being allowed to have my first pair of football boots – a huge investment on behalf of my parents in such straitened times with 12 hungry mouths to feed. My mother, though, was determined I should have them and took me to Dublin's Daisy market on the south side of the city, two bus rides away. The boots were second hand from a stall and, although they were leather, there were nails protruding through the end of the one boot. Despite this mother said to the stallholder, 'Sure, I'll take them,' paid two and six (12 and a half pence in today's money, but a fortune to us Conroys), and I had to overcome the hardship and agony of having a nail digging constantly into my foot. In fact I was simply in awe of owning my own pair of leather boots as they were a real rarity in our street. Hardly any boys had them. I fully appreciated the commitment my parents were showing to me in procuring such status symbols and this was a very proud moment for me. The reality, though, was that after every game or training session I had bloody feet and toes. I didn't care. I had my own boots, where previously I'd had to wear old-style canvas pumps (we called them 'runners') to play in which had no grip or protection at all.

Predominantly the Home Farm under-13 team was made up of boys who I had grown up with in and around Cabra and six of us progressed over the next five years up to youth level together. We knew each other's game inside out and were a very tight group. Billy Newman, Eddie Ryan, Richie Mulhall, Brian Carolan (Joe Carolan's younger brother), Jimmy Ginnitty and Noel Robinson were my pals. Three of them would go on to play at League of Ireland level – as did I – and Billy Newman won one international cap for Ireland as a left-half. We were a talented bunch.

There was one thing which nearly got me into trouble, though. Once you were a Home Farm boy you weren't supposed to play for anyone else on the weekend, not even Gaelic football for your school, which is traditionally what Irish lads would learn to play. Representing your school up at one of the many pitches at Pheonix Park was considered a great honour and I wasn't bad at the game. I just wanted to play sport and I also didn't want to let anyone down, so when in the weekly Home Farm team meetings the coaches asked us if anyone was due to play for their school on a Saturday morning I, like many other boys, kept my hand down. This was, as far as I was concerned, another example of where a little white lie couldn't hurt anyone (and would get me what I wanted) as in fact I was more often than not representing my school at Gaelic football on a Saturday morning, before meeting up with the Home Farm boys to play for them in the afternoon or on a Sunday.

Conversely, at school they would be asking us if any of us were going to be playing 'that foreign game' at the weekend. Again this was met with stony silence from yours truly. Either party would have banned me from playing for them had they known what I was really up to. I could only keep it up for a season when I was around 12 or 13 years old, though. After that football won out easily. Of course, to keep up the subterfuge I had to fastidiously clean my boots between games otherwise I'd have been rumbled.

Playing for such an auspicious club as Home Farm meant we got to do things like go on tour. Now for a 12-year-old lad this was incredibly exciting. We went to England and it was a real adventure. This was Easter 1958, not long after the Munich disaster. We travelled over to Blackpool and watched the home team play on Good Friday and then saw Manchester United at home on Easter Saturday. Both games were actually against Preston North End which meant I got to see legendary winger Tom Finney playing on two occasions. Preston won the first game 2-1 and drew 0-0 at Old Trafford, with a team featuring two future United managers; Tommy Docherty and Frank O'Farrell. The tour was arranged and funded by Manchester United in order to excite young Irish talent like us to seriously think about joining them. It was a fantastic experience and I loved it.

Every other club in Ireland wanted to beat Home Farm as we were regarded as the best team, the Manchester United of Irish youth football if you like. Sometimes we even got accused of being posh. Now, while nothing could be further from the truth I can assure you (I had no idea what a prawn was let alone that you could put it in a sandwich at that age), the level we were being judged at was most likely that we only had the one nail protruding from our boots, while our opponents would have many. While we might have holes in the knees of our trousers, our opponents might not have any backside in theirs at all. You can see now why we were considered snobs!

A man called Billy Bean, who was also a bookmaker, was Manchester United's scout for the whole of Ireland. He had a network of people who would recommend youngsters to him and then Billy would pitch up to run the rule over them before offering them a trial 'over the water' at United. If you were good enough and impressed at that trial you might then be offered an apprenticeship at the age of 15. So this was the aim of all of us. Billy was often to be found at Home Farm as he knew that was where the cream of the talent generally graduated to, so there was a well-worn path from our club to Old Trafford. It was the route which Liam Whelan and Johnny Giles had taken and United's youth policy was resulting in the Busby Babes sweeping all before them in the 1950s and much of that was and continued to be based on Irish talent, including the likes of Tony Dunne and a chap from north of the border called George Best, who was about six months older than me, but in the school year above. My friends and I wanted some of that, thank you very much. For every lad United took on from Home Farm some money, a set of balls and some training gear or playing kit would appear, which kept the club happy and well-equipped, fuelling those posh boy rumours even more.

Some of the lads I played with on the street also progressed through the ranks to play League of Ireland football, although many played youth football, but when they reached the age of 18 they felt that work was more important or somehow lacked that final drive to go on and make it in the professional game. I would often play against them and would chat to them after games and realise that where they were maybe happy with their lot, I wasn't. I had all the ambition and all the focus that you would ever need to go on and make a success of a career in football. In this way I was maybe quite different from some of my brothers too. We all had talent and all played football to a good level, but I seem to have been the one blessed with the determination and single-mindedness to make the break away from the League of Ireland and become a success in England.

Despite this, I know that my parents were hugely proud of all of us boys and how we performed on the football field, whatever our ability and drive. I have a fantastic picture taken of all six of us Conroy brothers dribbling a ball towards a camera in a very staged but wonderful shot which my father took of us in the late 1950s. You'll find it in the photographic section of the book. It's one of my fondest memories of my family and a picture which I know made my mother and particularly my father so proud of their boys.

3

A Wing and a Prayer

FRANKLY, growing up in this environment and with my family background meant there was only one thing I was ever really going to do and that was play football. It was all I ever wanted and all I ever dreamed of or strove for. Everything else I did was a means to an end. I had tremendous focus and belief. Thankfully that was also allied to enough natural talent to get me noticed.

I was lucky, then, not to have been born first as the fate which befell Ollie (not that he resented it at all) could easily have happened to me. Instead I found my way through the youth football ranks in Dublin into achieving my dream by earning a move to a First Division club in England. Me, a young lad with flame-red hair and wafer-thin legs from Cabra.

Here's how it went.

I was small even at the age of 14 and there were quite a few lads who were as talented as me, but a lot bigger, who were being picked up at the age of 15 by English clubs to move over and become apprentices. I was jealous. I wanted their success. I wanted to go and try my luck and I knew I could do it. At trials, though, I was always being told I was too small.

I think my father realised that at that age I had a chance to be at least as good as Ollie and Michael and he wanted to give me as much support as he had given them on their roads to success. He also knew I was very focused and he'd educated me in football right from a very early age. I remember he once told me all about this incredible footballer called Neil Franklin, who it turned out was a Stoke City legend as a ball-playing centre-half who won a record 25 consecutive caps for England in an era when it was very difficult to get picked more than three or four times in a row due to the selection panel chopping and changing the team so much. So I knew all about Neil before I'd even heard of another legend of the game, Wolves's Billy Wright, who followed him as England's centre-half. Another Stoke great I was aware of, this time through my forensic reading of *Charles Buchan's Football Monthly* magazine, was Freddie 'Nobby' Steele. Freddie was a superb centre-forward who played for England and still holds the Stoke club record for most goals scored in a career, even though half of his playing time was interrupted by the Second World War. So I knew a bit about Stoke.

I was always a right-winger, though, and as far as my father was concerned there was only one player that he could ever conceive of me learning all about – Stanley Matthews. I had first come across the magic of Matthews when I listened to the 1953 FA Cup Final between Blackpool and Bolton on the radio. It was that famous match when Blackpool, inspired by Stan, came back from 3-1 down to defeat Bolton 4-3 with a last-gasp goal set up by Stan for Bill Perry to slam home. I was just six at the time and this was awe-inspiring, stirring stuff to my ears. I knew by then too that Stan Matthews had begun at his hometown club of Stoke City and was now reaching the end of his career, so everyone wanted him to win that elusive FA Cup medal. And so he did, although those people who thought Matthews, at 38, was nearing the end proved to be more than a decade out. He would eventually return to Stoke aged 46, inspire City to win promotion back to the First Division in 1962/63 and thus provide me with a platform on which to strut my stuff on the very same wing in front of the Boothen End at the Victoria Ground only a couple of years after the great man had retired following his last appearance for Stoke in the First Division at the grand old age of 50 in February 1965. When I met Stan after moving to the Potteries he would tell me how he still thought, on reflection, that he'd retired too early. Incredible.

When I got to know him I found Stan was so good to people. He was generous with his time, loved the city and did everything he could to help. You'd occasionally hear people say that he could be mean, but I found completely the opposite. In fact I found him warm. Often people also say it's best not to meet your heroes so you can't be disappointed. I'm delighted to say that when I met Stan he only went up even higher in my estimation because, despite all his vast array of achievements in the game and in life, he remained the same humble feller from Hanley. Everyone else viewed him as a superstar, but he didn't see it that way himself. He was, after all, a knight of the realm, having received the honour upon his retirement, but instead of glorying in that title he would put everyone at ease, saying, 'Call me Stan.' He had no airs or graces at all. I thought he was fantastic, particularly when it came to promoting the club and the city in his capacity as president of Stoke City.

Back in 1956, just three years after listening to that famous cup final comeback on the wireless, I got the opportunity to actually watch the great man play. Stan was selected to play for the Football League against a League of Ireland XI at Dalymount Park. The home of Bohemians FC was also the home of Irish football before the arrival of Lansdowne Road (or the Aviva Stadium as it is now known) and was so close to my home that you could hear the roar of the crowd if you stood out in the back garden.

Before the age that I was allowed to go with my father to the game, I remember doing just that as a young kid, closing my eyes and dreaming of scoring a great goal. Now I was going to see Stanley Matthews himself play at Dalymount; this was one step closer to my dream. The expectation leading up to the game was huge for me. I was going to see the ultimate hero in my backyard and Stan's impending appearance got the whole city talking in anticipation. There was hope of dishing out another hiding like the one the Republic's national team had dealt to England when becoming the first non-Home country to win an international on English soil in 1949. People still told tales of captain Con Martin, Tommy Eglington and their team-mates who had triumphed 2-0 at Goodison Park to rack up a famous victory, one which would not be repeated until Ray Houghton's famous header clinched victory in the opening match of the Euro 88 finals.

Even better, Stan would be wearing the number seven – my number. He was a right-winger and so was I. He was a godlike figure in the game and someone who I wanted to emulate. Little did I know that in some ways I would actually achieve that by donning the red-and-white-striped shirt of Stoke with a number seven on its back just like Stan had. Funnily enough that number seven seems to follow me around. I'd worn it as a kid and when I came to Stoke I was given the number seven shirt. I was the seventh son, although, as my family are at pains to point out, not also of a seventh son, so I can't claim any special powers from that particular fable. I also lived at 7 Beechwood Close in Trentham, Stoke, for 35 years during my time in the Potteries. So seven followed me around for quite a while. I like to think that all began with my association with Stan Matthews that September day in 1956.

It was a fantastic game, which ended in a 3-3 draw. Stan starred, despite being over 40 years old. Because he played on the wing I got to see him in action quite close up as we stood on the side of Dalymount Park and I was able to study his languid approach to a full-back and then the incredible burst of speed and dip of a shoulder which would invariably leave his man for dead, allowing Stan to get a cross in for his forwards to attack. Even at that stage of his career he was compelling to watch. Seeing him in the flesh was quite an experience.

I don't think it had a huge impact on my own playing style as I was always quite a natural player who played to my strengths, but it certainly had an effect in that when it came to the time that I knew Stoke City were interested in signing me I knew who they were, where the city was, quite a bit about the history of the club and that led to me being even more interested. Whether this all be the gods or fate, I don't know, but I do sometimes have reason to think that I was drawn to the club, or maybe, just possibly, chosen to go there.

Even today Stan stays with me. Each home game at the Britannia Stadium sees me lead a tour around various parts of the ground for the match sponsors and their guests. We always finish up in the Stanley Matthews Suite, which is devoted to the story of Sir Stan. It boasts photographs and memorabilia telling the life story of this most remarkable of men. It is the most interesting part of the tour. I always spend the most time there talking about his life, career and achievements. It's a fascinating subject and captures the imagination of the guests, whether they are from Stoke or have never visited before in their lives. They all want to know more about Stan, especially the younger generation who think life began when the Premier League was created in 1992. It helps communicate the rich heritage of both the club and the area too. If you haven't visited and spent some time in there soaking up the genius of Stan then please do come and be my guest.

We still remember Stan each year on the home game closest to the anniversary of his birth. This year, 2015, we celebrated 100 years since Stan was born with a very special day at the Britannia Stadium. Stan's name has become so closely associated with the city that we forget that he achieved all this global fame in an era when there was little TV, no internet and no mobile phones. Astonishing when you think about it. It fascinates me that Stan's name was so powerful, particularly abroad. The legend still keeps on going.

One thing that does get my goat, which I'm going to take this opportunity to have a little moan about, is the fact that Stan was once blacklisted by the United Nations. Can you believe that? This was because he was a white man who went into South Africa during the apartheid years to take football to black, underprivileged townships. But to the United Nations it was merely the fact that he had visited the country at all during their embargo which led to his name being sullied. What a terrible indictment on the political classes who sit in judgement upon us that is, isn't it? I find that appalling. Here he was trying to give these people some hope and joy in their lives during an incredibly difficult period – that's all. In fact the people in South Africa loved him. I always remember that many years earlier he'd actually been on a similar mission to Ghana during a close season sometime in the 1950s and played for the Hearts of Oak club in Accra. After that game he was crowned 'King of Soccer'. There's a Pathe newsreel film featuring the story, which has some incredible footage, not least of the locals' reaction to this incredible man; another testament to the kind of work which earned Stan his knighthood, alongside his pure footballing ability.

So maybe it was written in the stars that I would sign for Stoke City, but when I was still only 15 I had a problem. I didn't really look like an athlete. There were all these big, strong lads and then weedy little me; white as a sheet and if you turned me sideways you could mark me absent. I was that thin. In fact my father used to joke that when he was watching a game and I sped across the halfway line I used to disappear for a split second against the whitewash. I saw boys heading off for trials and apprenticeships and I began to think that no one was ever going to come for me from across the water in England. So I got my head down and determined to make my name in the Irish game and attract attention that way.

Then I had my growth spurt. Over the 18 months from 16 to 17 years old I shot up almost half a foot to 5ft 10ins. Suddenly I wasn't so small. With that growth came strength to add to my determination. And I managed all this without losing any of my speed.

By this time our Home Farm youth team had been together five years and we were fantastic, an exceptional side. We were national champions and youth cup holders. Each of us now had to decide how we were going to continue our career as we were going to be too old to continue to play for Home Farm juniors come the new season when we'd no longer be under-17s. One option was to go on and play for the Home Farm senior team, which played in the League of Ireland B Division, featuring the reserve teams of the main clubs who played in the top division such as Shamrock Rovers, Shelbourne, Bohemians and Dundalk. The manager of the senior team approached the manager of the youth team partway through my final season as an under-17 and asked if I could play for him. A compromise was reached which I was very happy with as it saw me playing for the senior team on a Saturday and then turning out for the youth team on a Sunday morning, so I was playing two games each weekend. I loved it.

Many of the reserve teams in the League of Ireland B Division featured old pros who were on the way to the end of their careers and they were often hardy, grizzled defenders against whom I would be asked to play. I was getting a bit of a reputation at this stage and they were often determined to stick it to the up and coming kid. There were no holds barred as they tried anything to stop me, while I tried to waltz my way past them using skill, pace and guile. Thankfully I had the assistance of one team member in particular who promised to protect me. This was our goalkeeper

Tony Swan. I remember we were playing in Tullamore, down in County Offaly, right in the centre of Ireland. I was playing inside-left, dropping into midfield, picking up the ball and running at people. This opposing defender was giving me a bit of stick. I could smell the alcohol on his breath from the night before, so I'm fairly sure he was still the worse for wear. Anyhow, he kicked me all over the place and when he brought me down for the fifth or sixth time Tony ran from his goal into the opposing half of the field where I lay prone with the defender standing over me, span the feller round and knocked him clean out with one punch. It was a salutary lesson in survival and pitching in to support your team-mates – us against them.

Playing for the Home Farm seniors was a fantastic education and prepared me for the next move which was to make it up into the League of Ireland First Division. My burgeoning reputation brought me to the attention of Shelbourne, a north-side-of-Dublin club based at Tolka Park, and also the club for whom my brothers Ollie and Michael had played so successfully. It just seemed to be a natural progression for me to follow in their illustrious footsteps and carry on the Conroy association with Shelbourne. But I also had another contender for my services, Shamrock Rovers, the Manchester United of Irish football. They were based on the south side of Dublin, miles away from us. We used to joke that if you went over there you'd get a nosebleed. There was a traditional rivalry between the clubs and I was part of that, supporting Shelbourne and despising Rovers.

In 1964, by the age of 18, I was three years into my apprentice-ship as a machine minder in the printing industry at James Ardiff and Sons, earning £2.50 a week, and ready to make the move upwards in my footballing career. The owners of Shamrock Rovers were the Cunninghams, a very successful family. Joe was a renowned businessman and his wife Mary ran the football club they bankrolled. One night there was a knock at our door at number 50 Annaly Road. It was their chauffeur and he asked me, 'Would you like to come for a ride in Mrs Cunningham's car?' I looked out and there was a Bentley parked outside.

Now a car in Annaly Road was fairly rare, but to have a Bentley in the road was unheard of and instantly drew crowds of kids looking at its shining metallic paint and beautiful curves. My father gave me permission to go and I got in to the back seat of the car to find leather seats and a drinks cabinet. Also in the car was Mary Cunningham, chair of Shamrock Rovers FC. She introduced herself and asked me to take a ride with her on which she proceeded to tell me all about Rovers, the club's history and their plans for the future, which included me. All the while I was thinking, 'I can't sign for them. I'd be looked upon as a traitor in my community. I can't join Shamrock Rovers.' But Mary wasn't done yet. She offered me a large bar of Cadbury's chocolate and said, 'If you sign for Shamrock Rovers I'll also give you a £100 signing-on fee.' Now, this was more money than I'd ever dreamed of – and the opportunity to sign for the Manchester United of Irish football. At the time there was a rule that anyone under the age of 21 had to have the agreement of their parents in order to sign a contract with a professional football club in Ireland. I had to discuss things with my family in any case, so I asked her to drop me back home so I could talk with my father. Her parting gambit was, 'Don't forget, Terry, Shamrock Rovers is the place for you.'

I talked it over with my father until late in the night and his attitude was very much that it was my decision and that the family would support me whatever I chose to do as they knew Shelbourne would also want me, although there wasn't likely to be a signing-on fee of that kind of size on offer. I was still undecided, though, and this was partly due to the fact that over the years I had heard a lot about how players in the League of Ireland were actually badly treated by clubs. For example they wouldn't get paid on time. It put me off and I decided to wait for now and see what else came along. I was picking up youth caps for Ireland by this stage, so I knew I was doing well and that I would be being watched regularly. One night another knock came on the door at home and it was a scout for a Northern Irish club, Glentoran, who went by the name of Tommy Hunter. Tommy was a lovely man and he told me he'd watched me numerous times and had told Glentoran manager Billy Neill that they had to sign me. I was impressed by the fact that he'd obviously come all the way down from the north to see me play. I also knew that my ambition to get to England would be better served by playing in the north. The standard of football was higher and consequently the English league teams would scout more players from that league than the League of Ireland.

Home Farm didn't want me to leave and told me that I was making the biggest mistake of my life. This, in part, was a desire to hold on to me, but was also partly because Glentoran were based in east Belfast, a wholly Protestant area, although the club was open to both religions. The Troubles were brewing, turning nasty and becoming headline news; even so, I was determined and I signed for Glentoran in December 1965. I actually negotiated a £600 signing-on fee with a weekly wage of £6 plus bonuses. It was the one good business decision I managed to make in my life! Mind you, most of this new-found wealth went directly to my mother in order to contribute to the family coffers.

Dublin is predominantly Catholic, but there had been a couple of lads who had broken into our team at Home Farm who were Church of Ireland, the Protestant church. So I had a basic awareness of the religious divide, but very little real experience of it. Certainly there were never any issues that I had witnessed in my life. To me Protestants were like aliens from another planet as I'd met so few of them, but what I knew was that those I had met looked the same as me, played football the same as me and wanted to win the same as me. So I had no problem with them. There was no suspicion on my part and I didn't really think they were any different to me. Often, in fact, I had no idea that someone was a Protestant until someone else, usually an older person, took pains to point out to me that they were not Catholic. This would be done in hushed tones, 'Sure, he's Church of Ireland, you know.'

I had heard of the issues that were going on in the north, but it had always felt like it was a world away. Now here I was in the mid-1960s heading to Belfast, where the problems were all too real. I had an awareness of people like Michael Collins, the freedom fighter who had helped create a southern republic earlier in the century and also Edward Carson, the Anglican Unionist who effectively created Northern Ireland. I knew a bit about the Easter Uprising of 1916, the Civil War and the arguments about pro- and anti-treaty. So I wasn't totally naïve about religion and politics, but all I wanted was to play football and win trophies.

There was a logistical challenge of course. I had signed for a football club whose home ground was over 100 miles away. This was overcome by getting the train from Dublin into Victoria station in Belfast. It would take up to two hours. Sometimes I couldn't get back home after midweek games so manager Billy Neill and his lovely wife Lily would put me up in their house in the Seaview area of Belfast, feeding me with a slap-up breakfast before I made my way down to work on the early train the next morning. Billy was a Glentoran legend. He'd been there man and boy as player, then as coach and now manager. He was also part-time, though, working in the shipyards by day then heading to the training ground. So when I stayed at his house he would be up with me and the lark and on the same smoke-filled half-past six bus to take him to work, while I headed to the station to catch the train back down south. I had a busy schedule, especially as I trained twice a week in the evenings with a junior club in Dublin I had an arrangement with, but it became the norm. It meant I was on my way. I loved it.

Once I arrived in Belfast I began to experience some of the low level antagonism that being a Catholic meant you were bound to receive. I was called a 'Papist' plus various other unprintable names, but it was all just cat-calling to me. I do remember one game which tested me, though. This was the time I played for Glentoran at Distillery, which is a predominantly Catholic club based in County Down, between Belfast and Lisburn. At one end of the pitch hung the Tricolour flag and underneath it stood the home supporters singing the Soldier's Song, the Irish freedom song and national anthem, while at the away end stood the Glentoran supporters singing 'God Save the Queen', holding aloft the Union Flag. It was a very odd day; the people on my side were the Brits and the opposing fans were the Irish. This was pretty strange to me.

The other issue I had to face was the fact that the demands on my time which Glentoran placed began to eat into my working hours at the print works. Fortunately for me I had a staunch ally in shift manager George Goodson. He was a football lover and a member of the Junior Football Council of Ireland. He was very proud of the fact that I was making my way in the game and moved heaven and earth to help me as he felt it reflected very well on the firm, which I suppose it did. He often covered for me when I had to nick off early to catch the train in order to make the kick-off up in Belfast for a midweek game. One of the managers at the print works was Jem Ardiff, a member of the owners' family and also a staunch Republican. So he wasn't happy when I signed for Glentoran, and took pains to tell me I was selling out and taking the Queen's shilling. He would have been even less happy if he'd known George was letting me go early to be able to play for them and not docking me any of my wages.

My debut for the Glentoran reserves was the week before Christmas 1965 and then on Christmas Day I found myself playing in a cup final, the prestigious Steel and Son cup. We defeated Larne reserves 1-0 and I found myself travelling back home having played two games and carrying a winner's medal. This was great as far as I was concerned!

I soon got the call to make my first team debut. In fact it was actually the next day that our brand new home phone rang and the club secretary from Glentoran asked me to travel up as I had been selected for the game on 27 December as they had some injuries in the first team squad. I played against Bangor on the right wing. We won 3-2, I scored a goal and the headlines in the *Belfast Telegraph* the next day read 'Glentoran find a new star'. I was a fixture in the side from then on through the next 15 months until I left. I can still remember scoring that day. I beat two players and smashed the ball from 25 yards into the top of the net past the keeper. It was a beauty, if I do say so myself.

That goal cemented my place in the team which included goalkeeper Albert Finlay, full-backs Harry Creighton and Billy McKeag, midfielders Arthur Stewart (who went on to play for the Derby County team which lifted the Second Division championship under Brian Clough in 1969), Billy McCulloch, Eamon Byrne (who also came from Dublin to play in the north and was my minder both on and off the pitch) and Walter Bruce. The right-winger was Eric Ross, who went on to play for Newcastle United, but was more notable for the fact that he played in black-framed glasses. The centre-forward was a bustling, huge 6ft 4in lad called Trevor Thompson. Charlie Macdonald, a Scot, and

Bobby McAlinden, a big pal of George Best's, completed the line-up.

I remember about eight lads, including my brothers and a few of dad's friends, came up to see my home debut a couple of days later, just before New Year. They drove up and stopped near the Harland and Wolff shipyard, where the *Titanic* was built. Of course as soon as they arrived, being good Irishmen, they were straight into the first pub they found. As soon as they walked in, though, my brothers got that instinct that they were in the wrong place. They weren't welcome in this pub. It was Protestant and, equally importantly, my brothers were not regulars. Now, as I've said my dad was quite naïve and ready to see the good in everybody. He was also oblivious to the deafening silence which had greeted their arrival. He went up to the bar and ordered some beer. Hearing the strong southern accent was a giveaway. The atmosphere bridled even further. As they sat down at a table Michael said, 'Dad, we really shouldn't be in here.'

'No, they are a friendly bunch in here,' dad replied, completely missing the staring eyes and cracking knuckles of the wild-eyed locals. As the barman delivered their pints he offered some sage advice, 'Gentlemen, perhaps it would be a good idea if you move on.' My brothers couldn't get out quickly enough, while my father was still trying to down his pint as they dragged him through the door. He did like to think the best of everybody, although they never went back to that pub on the other occasions they came up to see me play.

That season, 1965/66, Linfield were regarded as being invincible. They were the local rivals of Glentoran and I distinctly remember the first derby I was to play in at Linfield's home, Windsor Park. During the build-up I was told by some of my team-mates about a feller Linfield had in their team called Isaac Andrews. He was a tigerish midfield tackler a bit like Billy Bremner. 'He'll have your card marked,' they told me. 'He's a hardman, a staunch Linfield man and he hates Catholics. He's gonna do you.' I had no great fear or trepidation over this as I'd learnt to handle myself. I took things in my stride, even when it came to playing in big games. Anyway, we warmed up before the kick-off of my first Belfast derby and the stands were packed, the sell-out 25,000 crowd was baying, wanting Glentoran blood, and Isaac Andrews trotted over to me as we were kicking in and offered me his hand, saying, 'I wish you all the best, Terry, good luck today.' I thought, 'What a nice feller this Isaac Andrews is. Not at all like the lads were telling me. They were having me on.' They'd built up this picture of Isaac for me and here he was a pussycat.

Contrary to what you're thinking Isaac Andrews didn't then proceed to return to type and kick me all over the park. I never had a problem with him. Sure, he was tough, but I was used to that and didn't have a problem with it at all. In fact over the years I've often found that the press are happy to build certain players up to have some sort of fearsome reputation which then turns out to be bunkum. In fact some of the hardmen of football are actually some of the nicest people in the game. I got on famously with John Giles, for example, even though he would kick you all over the place during the 90 minutes you were in opposition. But come the final whistle you were all friends again. Hard but fair was definitely the mantra back then.

That season we ended up winning through to the Irish Cup Final and again we faced Linfield, but this time at our home, the Oval, on 23rd April 1966. Despite the home advantage the tickets had been shared between the two clubs so there were just as many Linfield supporters as there were Glentoran. All my family came up for what was, thus far, the biggest game of my career. It was up there with Ollie and Michael's appearances for the Shelbourne cup-winning team in 1960 as far as an occasion goes in my family. We won 2-0 and I scored both goals, two of 24 I got that season. The first was a left-foot snap-shot which beat the keeper low down, while the second saw me control a high ball and plant a shot high into the left-hand corner of the net. I was playing inside-left in that team, rather than wide right, which really developed my left foot, that had been much the weaker of my two until that point, so was scoring more goals than I would have done as an out and out winger.

It's funny how things stick in your mind, but, with the clock running down and the majority of the 25,000 fans in the crowd disappointed at the result, I remember the referee ran past me and said, 'Terry, I'm about to blow the whistle. When I do I suggest you get off as quickly as possible.' He'd noticed that the Linfield fans were baying for my blood. Of course it didn't help that I was known to be a southern Catholic as well as having scored the two goals which clinched the cup for bitter rivals Glentoran. As soon as he blew I ran for the protection of the dugouts as the fans invaded the pitch. It was the first Irish Cup Glentoran had lifted in 15 years and a very proud moment for me. It also meant that we qualified for the European Cup Winners' Cup the following season. We drew 1-1 against Glasgow Rangers in the home leg, thanks to a famous last-minute goal by Billy Sinclair, before losing 4-0 away. Rangers would go on to the final and only lose to a single injury-time goal by Bayern Munich's Franz Roth, so it wasn't a bad showing on our part. Playing at Rangers' beautiful Ibrox Stadium only fuelled my desire to make the break into the big time more. Little did I know how soon that would happen.

I was by now just turned 20 and I knew my chance had to come soon or I would go past the age at which anyone in the English leagues would take a chance on me. As it happened fate was once more conspiring to help me.

4

Potteries Figure

DO events conspire together? Are things sometimes written in the stars? Certainly I had no idea about many of the occurrences which led to me signing for Stoke City Football Club until many years after they came to pass, when people told me their version of the various happenings. Piecing it all together I believe it happened something like this.

Unknown to me a gentleman by the name of George Eastham, the manager of Ards, another Northern Irish team, was retained by Stoke City to be their eyes and ears in that part of Ireland. Now this wasn't the George Eastham who by then had signed for Stoke following his participation in the England squad for the 1966 World Cup, it was his father, known as George senior. But because of the association the Stoke manager Tony Waddington was constantly phoning up George senior and asking him if there was anyone over in Northern Ireland that he should be looking at signing. George would give him a report and on this particular occasion, early in 1967 when I'd been playing up there for about a year, he told Tony that there was this ginger-haired kid who was made for the kind of team that George knew Tony was looking to build, one based on rugged defence but flowing attack. Waddo, though, got caught up in something else, which turned out to be the signing of a certain Gordon Banks, the world's greatest goalkeeper, who he prised from Leicester City in March 1967 and so consequently he forgot all about me. Can't think why…

In the meantime a friend of mine called Michael Keenan, who'd played with me for Home Farm, had a father who often travelled to and from the UK importing cattle on behalf of Irish farmers. He always stayed in the hotel right beside the station in Crewe, which just so happened to be Tony Waddington's place of residence. By that I mean both the town of Crewe and the bar of the Crewe Arms. With John Keenan spending at least two nights a week there over a period of a month or so concluding various deals, he came across the Stoke City manager in the bar on numerous occasions. They got chatting and John told Tony all about this kid in Ireland who had grown up with his own son and who was a brilliant prospect; a lad called Terry Conroy.

It was serendipitous, but even then the penny didn't completely drop for Waddo.

It took one more intervention to get things moving. In early March 1967 Glentoran were drawn against Derry in the cup at The Oval, our home ground. We drew 2-2 and the replay was the following Wednesday up in Derry. That was all that was on my mind as I left the dressing room to head home after the game. I was intercepted by the Glentoran club secretary, a man by the name of Billy Ferguson, who said, 'Terry, I'm glad I found you. Would you mind coming into my office please. There is somebody who wants to meet you.' So I walked in to find a man wearing a beautiful cashmere Crombie coat, a little pork pie Tommy Trinder hat and a cravat. Thinking back he reminds me now, although the series wasn't going at the time, of Arthur Daley, the wide boy character in the ITV series *Minder*, played by George Cole. He was a dead ringer for him. He held out his hand and introduced himself to me, saying, 'Hello. My name is Vic Buckingham, the manager of Fulham Football Club.' I knew that Fulham were a First Division club, who boasted England's World Cup-winning left-back George Cohen among their ranks, so this was a very exciting development.

'I want to sign you,' Vic said. 'We've agreed terms with Glentoran for the transfer fee of £10,000 and all that remains is for you and I to discuss personal terms. Fulham is the club for you. I want to build the future on youth and you are our future.'

Vic obviously thought he was selling me my dream on a plate and in many ways he was, but I actually had some major doubts, mainly around the fact that London was such a big city and I'd feel lost there. Even though my life's ambition was to become a professional footballer in the First Division in England and this was on offer to me there and then, I still felt reticent. It was strange; as if someone or something was trying to tell me to wait, not to jump in right away.

'Mr Buckingham,' I began. 'Thank you for the offer, but I'm going to have to go home and discuss this with my parents, I hope you understand that.' Vic said he did and that he'd look forward to hearing from me very soon. I could see that Billy Ferguson was also eager as there was £10,000 going a-begging here.

I headed home with all these thoughts whirling around my head only to be stunned when I got to Victoria station to find that in the *Belfast Telegraph Green 'Un*, the Saturday night results paper, the headline shouted 'Conroy signs for Fulham'. Apparently it was a done deal. This only served to make me more unsettled.

I arrived back home and told my father all about what had happened, saying, 'Look I'm not really that keen, but I don't want the chance to slip by.' I would be going back up to play in the replay the following Wednesday and had promised to give my decision then, so I had a few days' grace to mull over what to do. It was a dilemma.

George Eastham senior also read the *Green 'Un* that night. Thankfully he got straight on the phone to Tony Waddington and said, 'Look, Tony, this boy is brilliant. He's going to sign for Fulham, but he really is perfect for you. You've got to sign him.' Finally Waddo was galvanised.

So on the Wednesday morning I made my way up to Belfast in readiness to join the team on the journey across to Derry for the cup replay.

The train arrived at 11am and I was met at the station by Billy Ferguson, who told me that there was snow on the pitch at Derry and the game had been postponed, so I could head straight back home again. I was just going through the ticket barrier when from out of the shadows this voice called me. 'Terry,' it said. 'Can I have a word?' It was George Eastham senior, who had been lying in wait for me in readiness to pounce when I arrived at the station, but had then been forced to hide to keep away from the club secretary. I recognised George as we'd played against Ards on several occasions during my time at the club.

'There's someone I want to introduce you to, Terry,' said George. 'This is Tony Waddington, the manager of Stoke City Football Club.' Then out of the shadows came a second figure, this time Waddo himself. 'Hello, Terry,' Waddo said. 'I came all the way over here to see you play, but the game has been postponed so would you mind if I travelled back with you on the train to Dublin? There's something I'd like to discuss.'

The penny didn't drop immediately, but as we settled in for the journey back south it became apparent that Waddo had come to Ireland to convince me to join Stoke not Fulham. His only problem was now that he hadn't actually been able to see me play, he was going to have to rely on the recommendation of George Eastham senior. Waddo had a silver tongue and he turned on the charm all the way home. He could be very persuasive and he started off by saying, 'Look, Terry, you won't be signing for Fulham, you'll be signing for Stoke City. It's the place for you. I'm building a young side at Stoke and you are going to be part of it.' Almost exactly the same words as Vic Buckingham, but they were delivered in a very different way. Somehow you wanted to be with Waddo. He was such a charming man, not like Buckingham. He was incredibly convincing and added to that was my deep knowledge of the club, something which of course he had no idea about. I was sold.

What I had no idea about was that this was actually the classic old-style illegal tap-up. Waddo hadn't even spoken to Glentoran at that stage. He proceeded to clinch the deal by accompanying me home, ingratiating himself with my father, with whom he spent that night knocking back half a bottle of whiskey. By the time that was done he had my father eating out of his hand. 'Whatever Terry wants to do is fine by me,' he slurred. We ordered Waddo a taxi to take him to the airport to catch the late plane back over to England and he was at pains to let me know that even though we hadn't actually talked about what I would be earning it would be plenty. I didn't need to worry about it. This seemed to satisfy my father, although he was three sheets to the wind at the time. I, on the other hand, was not so sure. 'What about Glentoran?'

I asked. 'They are expecting me to give them an answer about Fulham tomorrow.'

'Leave them to me,' said Waddo, falling into the taxi. 'I'll sort everything out for you.'

And he did. The very next morning Billy Ferguson rang me up all excited. 'Terry,' he said. 'You won't believe this, but another club has come in for you.'

'Have they?' I offered sheepishly.

Billy was too excited to notice my apparent complete lack of surprise at this turn of events and continued on, 'Yes, Tony Waddington, the manager of Stoke City, wants to sign you. We've agreed terms, so you have a choice to make now. Let me know what you want to do.'

I'd already made my mind up, although the final clincher, if one was needed, was the fact that the club had signed World Cup-winning goalkeeper Gordon Banks just the week before. Stoke City was indeed the team for me. The fates had conspired to make it so. I was off to the Potteries.

The deal was done between Stoke and Glentoran – £10,000, the same fee, plus a further £2,500 if I played more than ten first team games for Stoke and a further £2,500 if I won an international cap, so Billy Ferguson was happy and in the end Stoke paid £15,000 for me. I'm pretty sure Vic Buckingham was livid, although I left Billy to make that particular phone call. Fulham were relegated at the end of the following 1967/68 season, not returning to the top flight until the 21st century, so I made a good call there!

They say first impressions matter most. Well, my first impression of Stoke-on-Trent was not good. 'God almighty, they haven't got round to clearing up after the war yet,' I thought to myself as we drove into the city. Honestly it was. Even growing up in inner-city Dublin hadn't prepared me for this industrial wasteland, full of chimneys, smoke and grime. I genuinely thought that the city hadn't been tidied up in the 20 or so years which separated VE Day in 1945 from TC Day, the day I arrived in Stoke in 1967.

I arrived in the city, accompanied by my father, just a week after first meeting Tony Waddington, in order to sign my first professional contract. It was a very proud moment and I still have that document to this day. In fact I've made it available to you via the photographic section of this book. There you'll see that I was earning the princely sum of £30 a week (a good wage in those days, and £15 appearance money in the first team). It was a bit of a wrench leaving home, as I was the first member of the family to move overseas, although judging by the number of Irish bars that have popped up across the globe I was merely following in the great Irish traditional of emigration. One thing that didn't change was the amount of money I'd have to send home to my mother. A decent proportion of my wages would wing its way back to Ireland and this allowed my parents to extend the house, adding a purpose-built bathroom for the first time, giving them proper amenities. That was a real achievement as far as I was concerned. It showed me how my success could contribute to making life better for my family; another valuable life lesson.

Added to the strange landscape which greeted me, was the oddness of my first night in Stoke. Club coach Alan Ball (the father of the Alan Ball who had won the World Cup with England) had picked us up in a taxi from Manchester airport and he greeted me warmly, but with his foot in plaster, making no reference to it whatsoever. I thought this was strange. Things got odder still when Alan asked the taxi driver to drop him at home in Bolton first and then take me down to Stoke, so we went from the airport near Stockport all the way north to Bolton and then drove back down to the Potteries. Oddest of all was saved for when we pulled up outside the Metropole Hotel in Stoke. I thought there had to be some mistake. Waddo had promised me that I'd be looked after well, but this shambles of a place was a two-star hotel at best. You could tell that because you could see the two stars through the hole in the roof! It really wasn't great. I think I was pretty much the only guest in the hotel and I remember after eating my tea at about 8pm I thought I'd pop out and take in a film as I loved going to the cinema.

For those of you who know the town of Stoke, the Metropole Hotel was situated where Bourne Sports is now on Church Street, a few hundred yards up from the site of the Victoria Ground. So I came out on to the street and walked around the block of downtown Stoke; up Glebe Street, round by the King's Hall and back to the hotel again. No cinema. This was 1967 and there was no cinema in Stoke. It was like I'd stepped back 50 years. Not only that, but when I got back to the hotel there wasn't even a TV in the lobby or bar. I went up to my room thinking, 'What am I doing here?' But at least it gave me the opportunity to get my head down at the earliest hour I'd hit the sack since I was a child. I would be ready to start work completely fresh, bright and early – on my first day as a full-time professional footballer.

But the strangest thing of all occurred when I heard a knock on my door the next morning, rousing me from my slumbers. While I was still wiping the sleep from my eyes this friendly Irish voice shouted through the door, 'Morning sir. Was it seven o'clock you wanted calling, or eight o'clock?'

'Actually neither,' I replied, slumping back down thinking I'd been woken far too early. 'It was nine o'clock.' At least I could have a lie in now, so I put the pillow over my head.

'Well, apologies, but it's nearly ten o'clock,' he said. 'My mistake.'

With that, I leapt quickly up, splashed water on my face, threw on some clothes and ran all the way to the ground with knots in my stomach at the twin thought of being late on my first day and of meeting all my heroes from my Charlie Buchan magazines; Gordon Banks, Dennis Viollet, Harry Gregg, George Eastham, Roy Vernon and Peter Dobing, what an introduction to life as a professional footballer.

Funnily enough, though, my worries at the goings-on thus far soon disappeared because I hit it off with the people at Stoke City right from the off. My digs were great. They were in Lime Street, just a minute's walk from the ground and even closer than the Metropole, so I could have a nice, planned lie in before getting up and heading off for training. They were found for me by Cliff Birks, a lovely man, who was the club's chief scout and who looked after all of us young lads. After that very first training session Cliff listened to my moans about the hotel and immediately took me across the street, promising me he'd got the very place for me to stay. We pitched up and met the lovely landlady Kate Cope and her husband Joe. The Copes took me in and looked after me for four years until I was able to get my own place. Another lad,

Micky Bloor, who was from Welshtown in mid-Wales, also moved in to the digs at around the same time. He was a Welsh schoolboy international and we formed a little band of brothers who got on famously. We had the time of our lives there for the next four years. Kate was like a surrogate mother to us, keeping us well fed and doing our washing for us in return for our rent.

I was like a pig in muck. I could wake up at 9.40am, have a shave and some breakfast and still be at training for 10am. It was the next best thing to home and I settled in very quickly. This process was made all the easier by the social club, which was right opposite the ground and so also just a minute or so's walk from my digs. It was a haven for us. We would be in there most nights drinking, although probably not what you are thinking. I didn't drink alcohol at all and my preferred tipple at this time was Dandelion and Burdock. Soft drinks were the order of the day all round. Not a drop of alcohol passed my lips until I was about 25, such was my dedication to football as my career. We would meet a lot of local people in the social club who became friends. The people of Stoke-on-Trent are very homely and it says a lot that approaching 50 years later I still live in the area, am married to a Potteries girl and love oatcakes. I'm now a local and I feel part of the furniture. The only thing I don't have is the accent!

In fact, the only thing I struggled with in those first months in Stoke was that thick Potteries accent and the unusual dialect. When I first heard the immortal phrase 'Tha canstna kick a bow agin a wow' I was utterly bemused; lost for what on earth this bizarre and unintelligible nonsense was. Now I'm the first to admit that even after 50-odd years in England my accent is still a thick Dublin brogue, but at least I use proper English words! Half of what I was hearing was a completely different language, let alone an accent. I couldn't get to grips with it. My landlady Kate was very heavily Potteries in her speech. 'I conner' and 'Denewst' she would say. I'd look at her in bewilderment.

It took me a while to learn that these two phrases meant 'I can't' and 'Don't you know?'. While why anyone would want to say 'You can't kick a ball against a wall' was beyond me. Everyone was calling me 'Duck' too. 'Well played, me Duck' or 'Are you going up Hanley, Duck?' I just didn't understand that this was an everyday expression of conviviality, rather than a comment on me looking a bit like Donald, Huey, Dewie or Louie.

Genuinely, it felt like I was learning a new language. Kate's husband Joe worked at the Michelin plant in Stoke and being working class he also had a very broad Potteries accent. At times I just kept nodding and saying 'yes' when maybe I probably should have been saying 'no' and vice versa! But eventually my ears got attuned and I began to pick things up. Nowadays it doesn't phase me at all.

My new team-mates were superb and helped me settle in quickly all the more. John 'Josh' Mahoney, a Welshman from Cardiff, was just a few weeks older than me and had signed the day before me from Crewe. Josh was to become my bosom buddy and we got on famously right from the off. We were joined at the hip, pretty much inseparable over the next decade while we shared in the team's triumphs and disasters. Being quite a gregarious soul, going into the dressing room packed with senior players wasn't too scary for me. Of course, among them was the imperious and peerless Gordon Banks, at least that's how I saw the man they called 'the Banks of England'. But as I got to know Gordon, I realised what a down-to-earth, normal feller he was. He was a lovely man, but had a winning streak in him. He hated losing and could get quite worked up about it, especially if he felt he had fallen below his own very high standards.

Arguably the antithesis of Gordon was experienced striker Roy 'Taffy' Vernon; the only man I know who could keep a lit cigarette going while taking a shower without any problem at all. Taffy also liked a bet. In fact he loved gambling on the horses, and this would eventually become his downfall. I was present the fateful day which finally saw his addiction cost him his position at Stoke. As a senior player, and a very talented one at that, Taffy was expected to set some sort of example, especially when playing in the reserves, as he mostly was at the age of 30 when I joined. Roy had captained Everton to the First Division title in 1962/63, top-scoring with 24 goals to boot. He'd also won 32 caps for Wales and appeared at their one and only World Cup finals in Sweden in 1958, when the team incredibly made the quarter-finals and only lost 1-0 to Brazil, the eventual winners.

Taffy had a beautiful left foot and was about ten stone wet through, probably because rather than eat he would chain smoke at all times, developing this incredible method of keeping a tab going while showering by shifting it round his mouth to keep it outside the water as he washed. This particular day, though, we were playing in the reserves at West Brom and Roy clearly had better things on his mind than reserve team football. The Hawthorns was quite modern then, especially in that it had a television set in the visitors' dressing room. As soon as we arrived Taffy switched it on to *Grandstand* on the BBC, so he could settle down and watch the horse racing. Following a tip-off, he'd bet £1,000 at 5/1 on a horse called Torpid. He'd tried to get me to put a wedge on too, but I'd only risked £5, which was a sizeable amount of my weekly wage at this point. The only problem was the race was due off at 3.05pm, while our game was due to kick off at 3pm. So Taffy, who was captain that day, came out and warmed up, did the toss, then disappeared down the tunnel to go and watch the race. We were left with ten men until he emerged a few minutes later with a huge smile on his face. Torpid had won. Unfortunately word got back to Tony Waddington, who couldn't countenance this and moved Taffy on, first to Halifax Town on loan and then by releasing him.

Waddo wouldn't tolerate disruptive influences and the only other player who had those sorts of tendencies during my time at the club was a dashing, enigmatic, aggressive turmoil of man named Calvin Palmer. When I arrived Calvin was the midfield dynamo of the team, well-established, suave and dangerous. He was like a coiled spring waiting to go off. You just never knew where you were with him, which was unsettling for a young pro like me. One day he'd be nice as pie, the next he'd blank you as if he'd never met you before. He had this attitude that if something didn't suit him then it wasn't right. He was a fiery character and he'd say things just to be disruptive, giving Waddo headaches. Many fans loved him as he was so combative; he always fought tooth and nail for the cause to the very end. He was a very good right-sided player too, having joined the club in 1963 from Nottingham Forest, after something of a fall-out there. You just felt that Calvin was on the edge all the time and that something could happen at any minute.

Sure enough, it did. Right at the end of that 1966/67 season in which I joined the club, a fight broke out between Calvin and another brute of a man called Maurice Setters in the gym under the Boothen End during a five-a-side game. Setters had joined Stoke from Manchester United two years earlier and had been on a collision course with Palmer throughout that time. They hated each other and this was a fearsome set-to. They kicked ten bells out of each other. The fight eventually got split up and Tony Waddington was forced to formally discipline the pair of them. Typically, though, Waddo tried to keep the peace by getting them to apologise to each other, but Calvin was having none of it. As far as he was concerned he had done nothing wrong and the scrap had all been Setters's fault. He refused to say sorry and so Waddo ended up excluding him from that summer's end of season tour to America, although the manager did slip Calvin around £1,000, no small beer then, to go on holiday to Spain with his family. That was Waddo all over.

We all knew then that this pretty much signalled Calvin's last chance at Stoke and sure enough he was gone before the end of the following season, sold to Sunderland in February 1968 for £70,000. A rebel he may have been, but in the portion of the 1967/68 season Calvin did play in for Stoke he scored four goals in 23 appearances, including the winner at Southampton in what turned out to be his last game. It was typical of the man that he should sign off like that. Setters, meanwhile, was also out on his ear, carted off to Coventry City in November 1967, so Waddo shipped both of them out as a result of that fracas. Maurice would eventually manage Doncaster before joining Jack Charlton's Republic of Ireland revolution as assistant manager for many years, so in many ways he bookended my professional career in the game as you'll find out later.

Setters had taken a dislike to me when I arrived, or I've always thought so, but he was probably just the kind of bloke who would test a new boy by having a go at him and seeing if he could take a rise out of you. He wanted to see if you would get irked and try to respond physically, then he'd have you. I would never rise to anything like that and I wouldn't call it bullying, more of a test, or an initiation. Not like they did at Wimbledon in the 1980s, that was a different gravy entirely. This was just an old school introduction of the new boy to who was top dog in the dressing room. I didn't like that much, but it didn't really bother me and it wasn't a problem for long as it happened. Those two were the only men who didn't greet me with warmth and a handshake at Stoke and they were soon gone. The happy family which was to become Stoke City FC for the next decade was beginning to take shape.

One thing that made a huge impression on me in my first years at Stoke City was that the sense of humour which I'd grown up with in Ireland translated so well into this group of people – players and supporters alike. Indeed the sense of humour that the people of Stoke-on-Trent have is remarkably similar to mine. Once they knew I was Irish the jokes would come flooding thick and fast:

'Hey Terry, did you hear about the Irishman who went Riverdancing?'

'No.'

'He drowned.'

Things like that cracked me up, I loved it. I now know that the people of Stoke-on-Trent are among the greatest and most caring on God's earth. Did I mention generous and warm? It was simply the best decision of my life to join Stoke City and come to live in the Potteries. I've never regretted a second of it. I learned all this by getting to know many of the regulars at the social club, where we spent many of our evenings as it was only just round the corner from our digs. One of those was a feller called Neil Baldwin. Now, if you've seen a BBC drama called *Marvellous*, which was shown in late 2014, you'll know about Neil. If you haven't seen it, get a copy on DVD. It is a wonderful, life-affirming, heart-warming story about a man with learning difficulties who, through the most pronounced case of having a positive mental attitude you could ever come across, became the kitman at Stoke City under Lou Macari in the 1990s. It features hilarious stories revolving around his motivational techniques like wearing a chicken suit while sitting on the bench or putting on the players' underwear, one over another, while the team was playing at Tranmere, to then take them off one by one to reveal the identity of the lucky owner of the undies that were at the bottom of the pile to great hilarity after the game.

I knew Neil 25 years before this as, being a loyal fan, he'd always be in the social club. Often we would invite him back to our digs to carry on the party. We had a lot of fun and Neil loved it. He became part of our group. Most nights there would be ten or 12 of us and there was a great community spirit among and around us. This didn't stop the fans telling us when we'd been rubbish – even the great Gordon Banks wasn't immune from comments like, 'Well played Gordon, but you should have saved that shot, son.' When it came to the annual darts competition, if Neil was playing you'd need to wear headguards and body armour as his accuracy left something to be desired and the dartboard would be the last thing he'd hit. We also used to boost Neil's ego by writing things like 'Neil forever' or 'I love Neil' on bits of paper and pinning them on unsuspecting people, then point out to Neil how everyone was supporting him and wanted him to win the darts. He was made up.

Neil's amazing ability to persuade you to do what he wanted is legendary around the Potteries. Even many years later I still fall victim to it. Many is the time that I've come out of the Britannia Stadium to find Neil leaning against the railings outside the club shop and players' entrance, where he sets up camp each matchday.

'How are you, Neil? How are you getting home?' I'd ask.

'I don't know,' would come the hopeful reply.

'Oh, go on then, I'll run you home,' I'd say, caving in to the inevitable.

But the funniest story revolves around the time Neil got involved in a pantomime which we put on at the social club back in 1970. About six of us young players got together and wrote *Cinderfeller*. Myself and Micky Bloor were the Ugly Sisters, while big Terry Smith, our centre-forward, was the Fairy Godmother. Josh Mahoney was in the show too, as was Neil and his friend, Ken Green, who played the title role. We rehearsed for a month before putting on the show for one night only on a Monday evening. Neil was the star turn as the character you would know from traditional tellings of the Cinderella tale as Prince Charming, but we called him Prince Barmcake. He only had one line, which was to come on with Cinderfeller's shoe when looking for his 'princess' and say to the Ugly Sisters, 'I suppose you know why I am here.'

We'd kept things to a minimum for him, so as not to give him too much to learn as that was one of the things Neil struggled with. The problem was that Neil couldn't say the word 'suppose'. He just couldn't. However how hard he tried it wouldn't come out right. He'd say 'suspose'. No matter how much we rehearsed he could not say this line. So, in the end we relented and left it in. On the night he came on stage with the place rocking. We were just using this little stage in the corner which could only fit about three people on it and the rest of the place was jam-packed with fans. Neil, speaking very deliberately in an effort to say the offending word correctly, brought the house down by getting it wrong. The crowd loved him. It just fuelled Neil's growing self-belief all the more, even back in the late 1960s. Not long after this he'd run away to join the circus as a clown. Seriously, watch the show on DVD. It's all there.

Just in case you have the thought that any frankly utterly unbelievable story you might hear about Neil isn't the gold-plated truth, because it generally is. For example Neil was made a Freeman of the City of Stoke-on-Trent, alongside Gordon Banks in May 2015, there is now a Facebook campaign to have him knighted and some wag has spray-painted a graffiti picture on one of the canal bridges in Stoke-on-Trent which depicts the Queen knighting Neil, who is dressed in his chicken suit. You couldn'er make it up, as I'd by now learnt to say in my best Potteries dialect.

I suppose in many ways I should consider myself fortunate that I had this fantastic, close group of people around me and a wonderful family at home who would regularly come over to visit me and to see me play. If I were to compare my experience to that of George Best, an Irish contemporary of mine, albeit from the north, I'd say we were complete opposites. George was actually rejected by his local club Glentoran at the age of 15 for being 'too light'. Manchester United's Northern Ireland scout Bob Bishop had a different opinion and famously sent a telegram to Matt Busby saying, 'I think I've found you a genius.' He was right and what followed saw Bestie turn into the first rock and roll footballer with some incredible performances between the ages of 19 and 25.

I have every sympathy for George because he didn't have that close-knit support network like I had. He had no guiding light or role model to look up to. This meant that when temptation beckoned he could spring after it full throttle. I knew George reasonably well, even after our playing days, when we'd occasionally meet on the after-dinner speaking circuit. He had no regrets at all about his drinking or womanising (as the papers liked to call it). He'd had many heady days in the glorious 1960s when he was considered the fifth Beatle and all that. But George and I were very different people. I'm a homebird. My family are everything to me. I didn't drink and smoke, although I did do the occasional spot of clothes modelling and boasted some fearsome sideburns, which made me stand out all the more. In fact I used to like to think I had good fashion sense, and if you want proof of that visit the photographic section of this book for evidence. Some of you may think the photo of me leaning nonchalantly against a farm cottage is more of a 1970s crime against clothing rather than an example of my superb fashion sense, but I beg to differ!

By the age of 27 George had left Manchester United, after successive managers became frustrated with him. I felt that was a waste, although he never agreed with that when we discussed it. Despite various attempts to make a comeback, most notably at Fulham and then in America, George just couldn't control himself enough to return to the level of performance as a top athlete which he and his fans demanded. You always think that life could have turned out better for George, but he always insisted that he'd enjoyed every moment.

I was never like that. When I was 18 the lads at Home Farm would go out drinking of a Saturday evening. I would go with them, but I'd be on soft drinks only, while they'd be knocking back Guinness and then chasing the girls. I was really there just to socialise with my mates. Not that I wasn't interested in girls, because I was, but I was more reserved and not fuelled by the drink, so I didn't get up to any of the shenanigans that they did. For me, there was always something more important than just drinking. I had an aim and I knew even then that drinking would impair me, although there wasn't the medical evidence around as there is today. It was more that I'd heard stories of Irish lads who had ability at 16 or 17, but who then fell by the wayside due to booze. You'd hear people say, 'If only for the drink he'd have been a great player.' I wasn't going to let anyone be able to say that about me.

I actually had a girlfriend when I joined Glentoran and as part of my decision to commit to the club up in the north I told her we had to finish as I just wouldn't have time to fit her in. It wouldn't have been fair to her given my hectic schedule during that period. I was that focused and wouldn't let anything interfere with my football. It may sound clinical, but that was the way I was thinking. I had to give myself the opportunity of being what I wanted to be, and maybe that was the crucial difference between me having a long and successful career in the game and those who had been offered apprenticeships at 15 and who I'd watched depart for England with growing jealousy. Many of them didn't make it due to the temptations that crossed their path. So you could say that at least Bestie had many great years before he fell off the wagon.

For this reason I never acquired the taste for drink. I didn't touch a drop until I was 25 and even then I'd just have half a lager or sip on a glass of champagne if Waddo brought a bottle in for us to share after a game. Now, this completely belies the image my manager tried to build up for me when I first arrived at the club. He was determined to make some capital out of signing this flying Irish winger by bigging me up to the papers and local radio, so at my first press conference he built this image of me as being stereotypically Irish. All the visual signs were there; I had this shock of red hair, was developing pretty tremendous sideburns and was chirpy, so Waddo didn't have any trouble selling me as someone who loved the craic. However, he also told everyone that I only ate steak and loved nothing more than a pint of Guinness after training. Now, I wasn't really a red meat kind of guy and, as I say, I was teetotal. Not only that but Waddo hadn't mentioned to me that he was going to do this, so I was stumped and could only really just nod to confirm this duff information as I wasn't prepared for it!

That wasn't the end of the clichés, though. Waddo then told everyone what a wonderful singer I was 'in the great traditions of Irish balladeers' and the next thing I knew he was getting me to stand up and sing the Irish folk song 'Danny Boy'. Now I am not a bad singer, but I'd never sung in public before except at church. I was extremely nervous as I stood up and launched into the song. Fortunately I don't have a bad voice so I carried it off, but Waddo didn't know that. It was swallowed hook, line and sinker by the press and the next day these stories appeared about the hell-raising, carousing Irish winger who had just joined Stoke. I suppose they were looking for another George Best figure, although the truth couldn't have been further from these images which Waddo had painted!

What was true was that he ordered Kate Cope to feed me up on steak and eggs as Waddo was worried about how anaemic I looked. My pale, white legs were a constant source of concern for him, so I was put on this high protein diet. I never did touch Guinness, though. In that sense I am the least stereotypical Irishman you will ever meet.

After I'd been at Stoke just three short months I got my first taste of what was to become a regular occurrence, the close season overseas tour. We'd just finished 12th in the First Division in the 1966/67 season, although I'd only played a few games in the reserves. Waddo kept to his word, though, and involved me in a fantastic trip to America where Stoke City were to transform into the Cleveland Stokers. This was the trip to the States which Calvin Palmer was excluded from as he refused to apologise to the manager for his scrap with Maurice Setters. It came about because there were moves afoot to really break football as a sport in the USA. Up until now it had been looked upon as a minority pursuit for kids rather than a professional sport. For the summer of 1967 the USA (United Soccer Association) League invited various European clubs, including Wolverhampton Wanderers (Los Angeles Wolves), Aberdeen (Washington Whips), Den Haag from Holland (San Francisco Golden Gate Gales – doesn't that one trip off the tongue) and even my old club Glentoran (Detroit Cougars), to come over and represent a city in a 12-team league, split into two divisions, with the top team in each division meeting in the final. We were sponsored by the Cleveland Indians baseball team, under the patronage of their owner Vern Stouffer, and would be spending almost two months in Ohio as the Cleveland Stokers.

I was so excited to be going on this trip, all the more so when on the way to Heathrow we went via Wembley to take in the

1967 FA Cup Final between Spurs and Chelsea, which was a great experience. The trip certainly proved to be an eye opener. It all kicked off from the very minute we touched down on US soil. Bear in mind I had never been anywhere other than England and Ireland, so what happened as we got off the plane was mind-boggling. We were met by a series of dignitaries and were lined up in our club blazers to shake everyone's hand. As we finished the polite introductions we were due to clamber aboard a coach to be taken to our hotel in downtown Cleveland, but this sheriff took a shine to me as he had heard me talking and realised I was Irish so offered to take me in his car, which turned out to be a huge Cadillac. So there I was on a personal tour of Cleveland from the airport to the hotel with the sheriff, who proceeded to don a huge Stetson and bite off the end of a massive cigar before lighting up as we cruised around with the top down on the car. This was the life. Welcome to the good old US of A! As we travelled the sheriff told me the reason why he had offered me the lift. I was Irish and his name was Shannon, like the river. You see there's always something to talk about with us Irish!

We stayed at the Pick Carter hotel in downtown Cleveland and I was dropped off there in regal style to find that the rest of the squad were already in situ. In fact I walked in to a sight which was to become a pretty permanent one over the coming weeks; Maurice Setters and Roy Vernon were at the bar. But this wasn't just any old bar-room, it was like a Wild West film set with straw and sawdust on the floor and a long bar, which they sat at one end of while the barman pushed frosty, frothy mugs of beer down it from the other. It was actually an Annie Oakley Wild West-themed bar, she of gun-toting cowgirl fame. You could guarantee that while we would go shopping or out to see the sights during our spare time those two would be perched on those particular barstools throughout the entire stay. This was the summer of love, with thousands of hippies famously taking over most of San Francisco, and here we were in the United States, the most exciting place I'd ever been. Not a time to be stuck indoors as for as I was concerned.

About 6,000 people bothered to attend our games, so we weren't that popular given that Cleveland is a city around the same size as Stoke-on-Trent; 350,000 people. Football just wasn't their sport, really. We had a fabulous time, though. We were playing our 'home' games at the Municipal Stadium, a 78,000-seater facility, which would have these few thousand fans lost somewhere in it. It is incredible to think that the baseball team and the Cleveland Browns American football team both regularly attracted full houses to this same stadium. It is located on the shores of Lake Erie, with Canada facing you across the water, so although the weather was hot during the summer it wasn't the intense heat that some of the US faces. It was a challenge all the same. Our first game was against the Chicago Mustangs, who were actually Cagliari FC from Italy. We drew 1-1 and went on to win five and draw four of our first 11 games. Over the course of the campaign, Peter Dobing scored seven goals and Roy Vernon two. I managed to play a handful of games without making too much impact, but Dobing, George Eastham and, somehow, Roy Vernon, managed to get selected for the all-star team at the end of the tournament.

With one game to go in the league season we just needed to win the final game against Sunderland (aka Vancouver Royals) in order to win our division and qualify for the final. That would bring us both footballing success and the reward of a week's holiday in Fort Lauderdale paid for by our benefactor Vern Stouffer. We felt confident as Vancouver/Sunderland had nothing left to play for. Especially after we received an approach from a couple of the Sunderland players saying they wanted to have a 'chat'. The ringleader of Sunderland's renowned rabble-rousing likely lads at this time was the mercurial ball-playing midfielder Jim Baxter, whose left foot was the stuff of legend. He could do anything with it. Unfortunately the one thing in life he couldn't do was pass a bar. Jim loved the good life, and that mostly meant a drink or two. When he took the field, though, he was incredible, untouchable at times. He also liked a laugh and on this occasion it was to be at our expense.

Our former central defender George Kinnell and Jim were cousins, now both playing together for Sunderland and, it turned out, had been trying to find ways of making a few dollars. George, being an ex-Stokie, met up with our nominated representatives Roy Vernon and Maurice Setters the evening before our game that would decide if we would go through to the final to make us the kind of offer you just can't refuse. They proposed that their team 'wouldn't try too hard' against us to allow us to win comfortably. In return we would 'donate' a proportion of our winnings to their drinking fund. That was the plan. All of our squad accepted the terms on the quiet and next evening went into the game in a confident frame of mind. However, it was soon evident that we were the ones caught out, as Baxter demonstrated what a world-class player he should have become. He scored two and created the other in a 3-1 defeat that put paid to our hopes of qualifying. If he wasn't trying that night, I would love to have seen him on song. We were well and truly had by the pair of them.

The defeat cost us the opportunity to take on the Los Angeles Wolves for the ultimate championship. Instead Washington Whips (Aberdeen) qualified for the final and our American adventure had come to an end without any silverware... or a visit to Florida.

Football didn't take off in the States for many years, despite the likes of Pele, Franz Beckenbauer and even our own Gordon Banks trying their luck there. It just isn't in their culture. Even now with the success the team has had at World Cups and the likes of Stoke City's Geoff Cameron playing in the Premier League it doesn't really rival their traditional sports of baseball, American football and ice hockey. We tried, though. And it was great fun.

It wasn't long before I did win my first medal as a Stoke City player, although bizarrely it wasn't for playing for Stoke.

I'd left Glentoran in late March 1967, three-quarters of the way through the 1966/67 season. Glentoran went on to win the Irish League that year under new manager John Colrain and I was given a winner's medal as I'd appeared in enough games. In September 1967 they were then drawn against Benfica in the first round of the European Cup in 1967/68, the team featuring the giant striker Eusebio which would go on and lose the final to Manchester United as the Red Devils became the first English side to lift the coveted trophy. Glentoran only went out on away goals after two draws, 1-1 at home and 0-0 away against the Lisbon giants, so I missed out on a little bit of history there.

It was around that time, though, that things got more exciting for me at Stoke as I made my debut in the First Division against

Leicester City. It was 6 September and Stoke had started the season with only one win in their first five games. Winger Gerry Bridgwood was seemingly not fulfilling his early promise, so Waddo pulled me to one side and told me I'd be making my debut in a midweek match against Leicester City. He didn't give me much warning, so I didn't have too much time to get nervous and the game went well for me. We were 2-1 up in the second half when a cross broke out of the box towards where I was running in. I set myself and hit it on the run. I didn't strike it cleanly, but it beat a certain Peter Shilton, who had been the teenage prodigy who had usurped our own Gordon Banks from the Leicester goal thus enabling Tony Waddington to steal England's number one, and found the corner of the net. It was quite a bobbly shot, so it isn't a goal that I consider that good. It was, though, a goal on my First Division debut and the winner in an eventual 3-2 victory, so wasn't to be sniffed at. It also signified the fact that I had, finally, arrived in the big time.

5

All Stoked Up

THERE'S no room for complacency in football as I quickly found out to my cost. Despite that debut goal and all the interest which ensued, over the next two years I battled away, making sporadic first team appearances, unable to hold down a regular place. I was still skinny, pale and had this awkward, long-legged running style, like a young colt. The team was struggling in the First Division and we lacked goals. We had David Herd up front. He was a Scottish international striker who had scored 100 goals for both Arsenal and Manchester United, but David wanted balls played through to run on to and with myself (when I played) and Harry Burrows on the wings we were more set up to deliver crosses into a big centre-forward. David was only 5ft 11ins, just an inch taller than little me. He was also already 34 when he joined us from Manchester United in 1968 and was clearly losing his pace, which had been his major asset. He was also injury prone. We actually ended up nicknaming David 'Aladdin' because he was almost always to be found on the treatment table under the heat lamp. So he became Aladdin and his lamp.

Herd only scored 11 goals in his 44 games for us over the next two seasons, although he was an integral part in one of Stoke's greatest ever victories – the day we won at the Nou Camp in Barcelona in May 1969. Yes, that's right, it is often forgotten that Stoke have a 100 per cent record at the Nou Camp, so never mind pundits wondering if Barcelona would be able to hack it on a wet and windy January night at the Brit, Stoke City proved we could do it over at their place with the sun on their backs in 1969. We beat them 3-2. OK, so they were playing the European Cup Winners' Cup Final against Slovan Bratislava in Basel the following week, but I will always argue that their team were playing for the places in the final, although neither this night nor the final would go well for Barca; they lost both games 3-2. They let all their fans in for free, so there were over 90,000 people there to witness our triumph. David Herd scored twice and Harry Burrows netted the third. In fact we led 3-0 at half-time, before a second-half fightback from Barcelona.

The next day we got up to fly from Barcelona to Madrid to travel on to our final game on the post-season tour. It was a very early flight and we then left Madrid airport around 9am with the heat already up to 70 degrees. We were heading for this place called Pontevedra and we'd been told it was only an hour or so on the coach. Of course none of us had heard of Pontevedra and we had no idea where it was. As we drove on this old charabanc bus the heat rose and there were no windows to open to get some air into the bus. 'Is it far, Boss?' came our plaintive shouts towards Waddo seated at the front of the bus. 'Only a couple of hours,' came the reply. 'We thought it was about an hour,' we said. 'Hour or two,' the manager replied. Not far then.

The bus ride went on and the day got hotter and hotter. We started to climb into the mountains more and more, so the coach was twisting round mountainside roads. After three hours of this uncomfortable journey, with no water on board to drink, we finally stopped. This must be Pontevedra, then. Far from it. This was simply the lunch stop. We'd already been going for three hours. At least it was a break and some food and much needed drink and a chance to stretch our legs. Waddo took us into this tapas bar, which had hams hanging down from hooks. They seemed impressive until you looked a bit more closely and discovered there were flies all over them. The locals didn't seem bothered by this. We were. Waddo tried to convince us to eat, but we just got some sandwiches made up and bought some drinks then got back on the bus. We couldn't get out of the place quickly enough.

The coach got going and the afternoon passed by in 90 degree heat and we began to really suffer. Waddo kept saying, 'It won't be long now,' while bringing round the brandy bottle. Most of us had a swig and then, with the heat also contributing to our drowsiness, promptly fell asleep. The manager was deliberately knocking us out with alcohol so that we wouldn't realise how long the journey was taking. So most of us missed the next 12 hours. Yes, a further 12 hours on that coach winding across Spain. We eventually arrived at the coastal town of Pontevedra around 2am the next day. For those of you who know your geography the port lies about 50 miles north of the border with Portugal on the Atlantic coast of Spain, between Vigo and Santiago de Compostela. Quite why we'd only flown to Madrid and then got a bus to take us that 400 miles or so was beyond belief or explanation. Or was it?

The next day when we returned from training, which had just involved stretching our legs to loosen up after the long journey, we came in to find there was an almighty row going on in the foyer of the hotel. One of the directors, Tommy Degg, was shouting at Waddo, 'You will never manage this club again as long as I am a director. This is a farce.' I couldn't believe what I was hearing. Waddo saw us coming in and tried to placate Tommy Degg by saying, 'Mr Degg, shhhh or the players will hear.'

'I want the players to hear what you have been up to, Waddington,' shouted the angry Degg, who then turned to a group of us and asked, 'Do you know what this man has done?'

We all shook our heads. It proved to be a rhetorical question in any case as Tommy continued his rant without really waiting for our response, 'I have just found out from the Spanish agent that we were actually paid to fly from Madrid to the local airfield here in Pontevedra, so you should have flown. It would have only taken about an hour or so from Madrid. But instead the manager saw fit to make you spend 17 hours on a coach because it was the cheap option.'

It turned out that Waddo and an agent called Charlie Mitten, who was an old pal of Waddo's from their days together at Old Trafford where Charlie had been a renowned winger, had pocketed the difference between the money they had been paid and the cost of that tortuous coach journey. Degg completed his rant by spouting, 'They have conned both us and you and you have had to suffer as a result. What do you think of that?'

The sheepish look on Waddo's face told its own story. This was true. We were all flabbergasted that Waddo would pull a stroke like that. But now we'd been able to have a run around we were all feeling fine, so this turn of events was really quite amusing to us. 'Good old Waddo,' we thought. 'He's not averse to having a little touch on the side.' That made him more like one of us. So in a funny kind of way it made Waddo go up further in our estimation, rather than down. It was actually a piece of genius on his part.

I'm sure it didn't help Mr Degg's humour that we lost the game 2-0 the following evening, although as it was our final game of a long hard season it wasn't anything other than a kickabout as far as we were concerned. But then he could return to Stoke to tell the story about winning at Barcelona, so when all was said and done the whole thing blew over and nothing more was ever said about the incident.

Our problem with scoring goals had seen Stoke struggle in both 1967/68 and 1968/69. In those days only two clubs dropped down from the First Division to the Second and we finished 18th and then 19th out of 22 clubs (in other words fifth and then fourth from bottom) in successive seasons. In fact we only avoided relegation in the first of those two campaigns by defeating title-chasing Liverpool at home on the last day of the season thanks to goals from Peter Dobing and Josh Mahoney. Then we finished six points, but only two places, above the relegation zone in the latter season, which was David Herd's first at the club and ended with the eventful Spanish tour.

I played the day we beat Liverpool to stay up in May 1968, the ninth appearance of my first season. I'd just scored the one goal, on my debut, but I hadn't made a huge impact. At that time I felt I was struggling to get up to match fitness and strength and I occasionally wondered if the manager was thinking whether I would make it or not. I had to prove myself. The pressure was on. Things began to turn around for me in 1968/69, however. It was Liverpool again that offered me an opportunity to lay down a marker. It was the fourth game of the season at Anfield and I scored against a team which featured Lawler, Callaghan, St John, Yeats and the like. It's one of my favourite goals as it was so important in solidifying my place at Stoke. I played a one-two on the halfway line with Harry Burrows and skipped past a lunging Tommy Smith challenge, beating him for pace. Heading towards Tommy Lawrence in the Liverpool goal, I suddenly stopped mid-stride and side-footed the ball past Tommy into the far bottom corner of the goal, opening out my body and hitting the ball with my right foot, when he was probably expecting me to hit it with my left. It wasn't a conscious thing. I just did it.

That goal was the first occasion that journalists started to write about me, which was lovely to read when you woke up the morning after a game battered and bruised following the kicking I would have undoubtedly received at the mercy of whichever full-back I had been trying to torment the previous day. I don't have many cuttings, but I do have that one. It was penned by the *Daily Express*'s Derek Potter, 'This red-haired ghost impressed me at Anfield where he was bundled over the touchline by a massive Liverpool defender. Terry got up, took the return pass and after battling down the wing he flicked the ball past Tommy Lawrence with the outside of his boot. That is flair.'

That goal gave me so much confidence, and I think it gave Waddo confidence in me, too. The 1968/69 season became a defining one for me. I scored the winner in the home game against Manchester City a couple of weeks later, then netted in four consecutive matches over Christmas against Nottingham Forest, Spurs, West Brom and Sunderland. The first goal in that run is another one of my personal favourites. The Vic had frozen over and we were effectively playing on hard-packed, rutted ice that day. Welsh international Terry Hennessey was Forest's centre-half and I skated round him like Robin Cousins somewhere near the halfway line. Peter Grummitt was in goal. Now, I always wanted to beat the keeper by going round him. I didn't like taking an early shot if I was through one on one. I'd rather beat the man as I felt I could do it every time and then slip the ball home. I did this against Grummitt and then tapped the ball home to spark a 3-1 victory. It gave me huge confidence once again, particularly as I had done it in such difficult conditions.

Over the season I made 30 appearances and scored seven goals, but because we were still struggling as a team Waddo sometimes chose to play Josh Mahoney as an extra defensive midfielder instead of keeping with me as an attacking option. This period was a time when Waddo would build what was known as Waddington's Wall, keeping two defensive midfielders back to protect the defence, particularly when it had old-timers such as Tony Allen, Alex Elder and Maurice Setters in it.

The major issue for me that season was a serious injury I picked up against Manchester City at Maine Road towards the end of the campaign. They had quite a cultured left-half called Alan Oakes. He wasn't a hardman at all, but this day he absolutely creased me up in a tackle, causing me to twist as I went down. I felt and heard a snap in my knee. I was carried off and assessed and it turned out to be cartilage damage. It was my first major injury and put me out for five months until the end of August 1969. Waddo didn't have much faith in the surgeons around Stoke-on-Trent, so he would send injured players to see specialists that he knew around the country. I was sent to a hospital in Bristol and stayed there for two weeks, recuperating from my first cartilage operation. These days it's done by keyhole surgery and players are in and out in a day, but I was in bed for a fortnight, with my foot raised up, having had the whole cartilage removed. The number one record at that time was by Thunderclap Newman and it was called 'Something In The Air'. 'Call out the instigator because there's something in the air' went the opening line. This brought huge amusement to my, and all my visitors', faces when it come on the radio; me with my foot raised up to head height. Every day the record was played and we'd laugh about it. It actually helped a lot. The battle to get fit was a long process and I started the following season behind everyone else, so was in and out of the team until just before Christmas.

As bad as that injury was, it was nothing compared to the fate which befell a colleague, a 25-year-old reserve team goalkeeper named Paul Shardlow. I was there the day in October 1968 that Paul collapsed and died during a training session on the pitch over the back of the Victoria Ground. Paul had played a few of the games over in America when we'd been there the previous summer to give him some experience and give Banksy a rest. This particular day we were warming up for training in pairs, doing a few stretches and jogging around. As we worked Paul just collapsed, without any sound. It was a heart attack and he was effectively dead before he hit the ground. He couldn't be revived, despite desperate attempts. It was such a shock and quite surreal. To think that someone so young and so fit could have serious heart problems was disturbing. That we knew him so well was incredibly upsetting. It turned out that Paul had a defect in his heart, which was what caused his death. At that time there were no regular tests on players to spot conditions such as this, unlike now. Waddo did get us all checked out afterwards and we each got a clean bill of health, unlike poor Paul.

Clubs weren't set up for medical concerns or injuries in those days. If you got a knock in a game on a Saturday and it wasn't that serious you'd be sent up the North Staffs Hospital on a Monday morning to see the nurses there to get some treatment. I remember there was a Madge Harrison and a Pat Mellor who looked after us, but there was no special treatment just because you were a footballer. We were expected to wait in line with the general public. You'd get some physio treatment and then head back down to the Vic to report for training. It was pretty archaic, although that soon changed when the club appointed their first physiotherapist, Fred Streete, who would go on to be the England team's physio for many years. He arrived in 1969, which gave us relief from the tender mercies of our first point of treatment on the field; coach Frank Mountford and his famous bucket of icy water. Frank had no medical qualifications at all, and also very little sympathy. He was a Yorkshireman who had moved down to Stoke-on-Trent as a young lad when his father got a job in the mines here. He had a dry sense of humour and we loved him, but he could be pretty rough when he came out on to the pitch to 'treat' you. His gruff bedside manner left something to be desired and he certainly didn't have MD after his name. He had a sponge and could offer you a pretty rough massage. That was it.

We loved him, though. Frank was a dedicated, tough, gnarly one-club servant who had made 425 appearances for Stoke at right-half and then centre-half and scored 24 goals between 1946 and 1958, but that only told half of the story. He'd actually been a boyhood goalscoring prodigy. During the war, when he'd emerged into the first team as a baby-faced striker, Frank had scored countless hat-tricks and one season ended up with 29 goals in just over 30 games. When I first arrived at Stoke Frank had his face wired as he'd been in an accident. He also had this massive scar all the way from his ear right down to his chin. It transpired that he and Alan Ball senior had been out drinking one night at a country pub and Alan had driven his car off the road, sending Frank through the windscreen, while Alan broke his leg. This explained the strange shape both of them were in when I first met them. A mystery solved.

Frank was also determined to maintain a tradition which had taken place at Stoke ever since before his days playing in the team. The procedure was that at 2pm before every home game Frank would go up to the boardroom and knock on the door. The chairman Albert Henshall would open up and Frank would ask, 'A bottle of whisky, Mr Chairman, for team spirit?' Albert would then give Frank a bottle of Bell's whisky from his drinks cabinet and Frank would proceed to bring it down to the dressing room and offer us all a tot, saying, 'Team spirit anybody?' As Frank worked his way around the room it went like this. Banksy might have a little tot and then Frank would have a nip. Then Jackie Marsh would have a sip, and so would Frank. When it came to Mike Pejic he couldn't entertain alcohol before a game, far too unprofessional for Pej. This didn't deter Frank, though. Two glugs were soon passing his lips; one for Frank and he didn't want Mike's to go to waste either.

This one for him, one for me routine would go on every game. I occasionally had a sip, as most of us did; purely for medicinal purposes. But whether you had one or not, Frank did. So by the time it came for us to go down the tunnel Frank had supped quite a bit of whisky. He'd take it out on to the bench with him too, taking judicious nips every now and then between roaring out instructions to anyone who would listen. Not that many of us did. I remember this one particular day Denis Smith got injured over the far side of the ground from the benches and Gordon Banks rushed out to Smithy, saw he was hurt and waved Frank on from the bench. Frank gathered up his bucket and sponge and headed out on to the pitch, but ran in completely the wrong direction. Gordon was beckoning him over to the far corner where the Butler Street stand met the Stoke End and Frank was off towards the

Boothen End. Whether those 'warm-up' drops had any part to play in that failure in navigation, who knows.

Frank didn't even have a Boys' Brigade badge, let alone a coaching badge or medical qualification, and yet here he was as first team coach and 'physio' at Stoke City. He was such a lovable character and he'd worked his way up after finishing playing doing every job as he went. Tony Waddington clearly used him to boost the confidence of the players. We had a whale of a time with him and I loved every minute of it. Frank was particularly interested in helping the younger players like me and would be great at geeing you up. There are myriad stories about Frank, but I'll just tell you a few of my favourites.

Tony Waddington never watched a game from the touchline. He believed you could see more from a vantage point in the directors' box on the halfway line, raised up higher. So, ever the innovator, he had a phone installed in order to communicate to Frank down on the bench as Tony's knees were really suffering from all the climbing up and down the stairs to pass messages on. The first game after the phone had been installed, Frank, fuelled by several tots of rum, heard it ring. He picked it up and said, 'Who is it?' Well, it couldn't be anyone else but Waddo, could it now? 'It's me. Tony. Get TC to come wider and take the full-back on more,' or some such instruction. 'OK,' said Frank.

With 30,000 or more in the Victoria Ground making a din I never once heard any instruction from the bench. I could tell Frank was trying to tell me something, but I had no idea what it was. I cupped my hand to my ear to make it look like I was listening and nodded my head, but that was all. Nothing changed, so five minutes later the phone rang again. 'Who is it?' said Frank. 'It's Tony,' said the ever-more exasperated manager. 'I've told him to come wider like you said,' offered Frank. 'Well tell him again,' came the order and we'd go through the whole rigmarole again.

The third time the phone rang Frank had had enough. He picked the whole phone up and slammed it into his bucket full of icy cold water. That was the end of that and for the next game Alan A'Court, one of the other coaches, was designated as the man to answer the hotline. I swear on my life that early in the next home match Tony Waddington rang up and asked to speak to George.

'George Eastham?' enquired the confused Alan. 'Yes,' confirmed Waddo. 'But he's playing, Tony.' So during the next stoppage Alan beckoned George Eastham over from his position on the far wing to come and take a tactical phone call from Waddo. Incredible. The FA soon put a stop to that.

One of Frank's duties on away trips was to get the kit to and from the ground at which we were due to play. Sometimes this was nice and easy as we'd travel by coach from the Victoria Ground directly to the venue. But when we played in London more often than not we'd travel down on the train the day before the game and then take a coach back to Euston station from whichever ground we were playing at. This particular day we'd been at Crystal Palace, whose Selhurst Park ground is in south London a good hour's coach ride from Euston. As usual, the directors had imbibed a few drinks to aid their post-match discussions; our directors were renowned as being among the most friendly and convivial in the league. We eventually left the ground at 5.50pm and were booked on the 7pm train from Euston, so didn't have much time to spare. The Saturday night traffic was building as we drove into central London and Waddo sat at the front ensuring the coach driver used all his driving skills to get us there on time, urging him on at every opportunity. We were really cutting it fine and it looked like we were fighting a losing battle. As we approached another set of traffic lights, they turned orange and the driver slowed, ready to stop, but Waddo urged him on and, against his better judgement, the driver went through the lights as they turned red.

Whoever Sod was, his law was in operation. Hiding round the corner was a police car. Siren on, he pulled us over. The language on the coach was a dark shade of blue as this was the last thing we needed. Waddo somehow sweet-talked the policeman in his usual persuasive way and we were on our way in five minutes flat. The driver would be getting a hefty fine and maybe three points on his licence, but we still had a chance of making that train. To ease the pain Waddo promised him an all expenses paid day out with Stoke City next time we were in London. The driver retorted that he hated football and was a rugby fan. As we approached Euston we still had a chance to make the 7pm rattler. We all had our bags at the ready and when the coach pulled up it was every man for himself. As we were running towards the ticket barriers, we heard Frank shouting for us to help him with the two big baskets of kit. None was forthcoming, so, with a slight delay for a few oaths in the direction of our fast-disappearing backs, he then yelled for a porter. There wasn't one to be sighted anywhere. Instead of either a squad of fit professional sportsmen or a team of professional station porters, Frank was helped by an 85-year-old, who was returning home from his day out in the capital.

As we boarded the train with seconds to spare, we looked around to see the gates being closed just as Frank appeared with the skips. He was stuck. We were on the train home and he wasn't happy. He was shouting all sorts at us and waving his fists. At that moment it was funny, but we dreaded Monday morning, meeting up with Frank to take our punishment. He eventually got the next train, a stopper which didn't depart until 9.10pm, getting in to Stoke at 11.30pm. His choice words at the next training session are, not surprisingly, unprintable.

One final story about Frank. We beat Olympiakos 2-1 in a pre-season game in Athens in the summer of 1971. We were staying in this big hotel and Frank wouldn't go out on the town with us, he'd prefer to stay in the bar drinking with some of the many Americans who were staying there. We were in town for a few days and Frank took great pride in laying down a marker for Great Britain against the 'Yanks' as he called them. Well, the night after we'd played the game we players hit town to celebrate and rolled back in about 5am. Sure enough there was Frank still going strong in the bar with one final American just taking his leave. As he headed up the stairs this tough-looking Texan turned to us and said, 'I've met some drinkers in my time, but that Frank sure takes the biscuit.' Frank was cock-a-hoop! He'd won.

On the way home when we got to the airport we were all sitting in the lounge when Frank sidled over and said to a small group of us, 'I've got a dilemma. I've ten drachma left and I don't know whether to have a drink or get something to take home for my wife.' We proffered the sage advice that maybe Mrs Mountford would be the wise choice, but you could see that Frank was torn between turning left to the Duty Free shop or heading right to the bar. He stood there swaying, almost physically being tugged by the pull of these two options, when he finally made a move to go left. Mrs Mountford had won. Then before you knew it Frank had spun round and marched off purposefully to blow his last ten drachma on booze. We were in hysterics watching this play out. That was Frank. One of a dying breed.

One of the other characters that I got to know around the club (we were never short of them) was the groundsman, Len Parton. He was a typical ex-army man; small white moustache, very well spoken, probably the best dressed groundsman in the country. He would be out there forking the pitch in a suit or jacket and tie. You had to compliment him on the pitch when he asked you or you'd be in for it. 'What do you think of the pitch, Terry?' he'd ask. Now Waddo may well have had the fire brigade in on the previous evening to water the pitch as he often did and it would be a sea of mud, but you would still have to answer, 'Perfect, Len. It's a beauty, well done.' Even though it was a quagmire. One trick Len did regularly pull off was making the oblong patch of turf ten yards either side of the halfway line and ten yards in from the touchline the best piece of turf in the division. That would often be perfect, while the rest of the pitch was a bog. This was because most of the directors of both Stoke City and whoever the visiting club was would have had so much to drink that Len reasoned they would only be able to see so far out on to the pitch. He would tell us this theory and muse that if Stoke won at least the visiting directors wouldn't be able to blame the pitch. Job done.

I first met Len, just after I'd joined the club, when I heard gunfire during training. I ducked, but there wasn't anyone shooting at me. More to the point everyone else just carried on as if nothing was wrong. 'What's going on?' I asked. 'Oh, that's just Len shooting the pigeons,' came the reply. They were right. Gunfire was emanating from the Vic, where Len was to be found chasing around trying to shoot the pigeons which were roosting under the roofs of the stands and then covering Len's pristine stadium with their droppings. Len hated pigeons with a passion; loathed them. He loved nothing more than to bag himself a few and then the apprentices would have to collect them for Len to take home and eat them.

Len had a limp, which gave him the demeanour of an injured serviceman, but he refused to talk about his 'war wound', so we had no idea what had really caused this injury. On a matchday Len would be immaculately dressed in club tie, his moustache perfectly trimmed and tapered, and sporting a soft hat. He would be there to greet the visiting team and especially the manager and directors when they came off the coach. This wasn't really his job, but it made an impression on these visiting dignitaries who believed that one of the club directors was greeting them at the door. We could never let on that the man they thought was a director was actually the groundsman. It became a standing joke which we went along with.

This manifested itself one day on one of the rare occasions when Len travelled with the team to attend an away game at Old Trafford. Manchester United was such a glamorous place at that time with the likes of Sean Connery, Rod Stewart and the occasional Miss World in attendance, often at the invitation of George Best. These stars could be found in the players' lounge after the game, so we mingled with them. There was strict security around the lounge, which was maintained by a lady we all knew as Mrs B, who ran the place and wouldn't stand for interlopers. On this day Len, all suited and booted, with a cigarillo going, came into the lounge with us after the game and held court, loving every minute. There was free drink and we knew we'd have about 45 minutes to relax and have a chat before we had to get on the bus. The last group to make it up to the lounge was Bobby Charlton, George Eastham and Gordon Banks, who knew each other so well from England duty. They were chatting away and as they came in Len turned to them and shouted over the hubbub, 'Bobby, Gordon. George, over here, what are you having?' Bobby looked in amazement – it was, after all, very generous of Len to be offering to buy what were actually free drinks! As we left that day Mrs B came over to me and said, 'Terry, I do love it when you boys come and visit as you clearly are a very close-knit group. Even to the extent of one of your directors coming and spending time with you after the game, rather than staying in the directors' lounge.' I hadn't the heart to put her right. Len really did carry off his persona to that degree.

Our goalscoring difficulties meant that the fans were clamouring for a striker. Waddo knew he had to do something and he took action, rectifying a wrong which he himself had perpetrated some three seasons earlier. Prior to my arrival in Stoke a young striker had made a big name for himself by netting goals for fun. His name was John Ritchie and he'd been brought to the club from non-league Kettering Town in 1962. Big John, as he had become known, scored plenty of goals, but for some reason Waddo came to think that he was dispensable early in the 1966/67 season. Despite notching eight goals in 14 games at the start of that campaign, Waddo sold John, amid a huge outcry, to Sheffield Wednesday for £70,000, a record sum for an outgoing transfer from Stoke at the time. Waddo realised he'd made a mistake, though, and so did John. He didn't fare so well in Sheffield, so when he became available in the summer of 1969 for a much-reduced fee of £28,000 Waddo swooped and re-signed him. The manager would often contend that this was all part of the master plan to make a decent profit and still retain the player! I think he was very lucky to be able to do that particular piece of business, but Waddo manipulated the media to ensure his version of events was the one that was told. That coup was important because the supporters were really galvanised by Big John's return as he was very popular.

That summer another striker joined the club, this time from Birmingham City for a club record spend of £100,000. His name was Jimmy Greenhoff and he proved to be the perfect foil for Big John. Jimmy was a nippy forward, who could feed off Ritchie, had an eye for goal and could hit a volley as well as I've ever seen anyone strike one. As our new strikeforce knitted together, I made my comeback from injury to eventually make 31 league appearances, notch two goals and have a great run towards the end of the 1969/70 season, regularly linking up with Ritchie and Greenhoff. I was proving my worth and had become a guaranteed regular, justifying my decision to reject an offer Tony Waddington had received from Millwall manager Benny Fenton when I was still on the cusp of really establishing myself the previous season. Waddo stuck by me and I repaid him.

By 1970 the youth that Tony Waddington had promised me three years earlier that he was going to bring into the team was also establishing itself in the starting line-up. I've already mentioned my colleague in midfield Josh Mahoney, but there was an entirely new, young defence emerging, which would stand us in such good stead for almost the next decade. The great thing was it was exclusively local.

Alongside the one old head in the back four, Alan 'Bluto' Bloor, a sturdy centre-half who was a silent assassin and who had been tough enough to dislodge the teak Maurice Setters from the team, were three other equally brutal and uncompromising defenders. Bluto's partner in the middle was Denis Smith, a lad from Meir at the south end of Stoke-on-Trent, a tough place to grow up apparently. It must have been because Denis played through more injuries and came back from more broken legs, noses, knees, ankles, fingers, hands, shoulders and toes than the rest of us put together. He actually made it into the *Guinness Book of Records* as the most injured footballer ever. If Bluto was silent, Denis was anything but. He was a leader and a vocal one at that. He would go on to become Mr Stoke City, the captain of the club and then forge an incredible career as a manager of teams like Sunderland, Oxford, West Brom and Wrexham. Denis joined the very elite club of managers who had taken charge of over 1,000 games during his final spell in charge at the Racecourse Ground and now works for the Premier League as a matchday observer. You can often hear him on BBC Radio Stoke as a co-commentator too, especially since he and his lovely wife Kate have moved back into the area after so many years away.

Denis was just as much of an assassin as Bluto; a hard, hardman on the pitch, who came from the school of hard knocks which saw him treat every forward as a punchbag, ensuring that he got his retaliation in first. I was just glad I didn't have to play against him. Or Bluto. They were men mountains. Off the pitch Denis was wonderful. He and I got on extremely well together, as I did with right-back John 'Jackie' Marsh. Jackie was a flying full-back who loved to overlap and crack in a shot at the opponent's goal, or get in a quality cross, at which he was fantastic. As the player who would be immediately behind me on the right wing we developed an affinity which would see him either lope forward looking to play me in either directly or via a typically deft flick off Jimmy

Greenhoff, or give me the ball early and then make a run beyond me looking for a return pass himself.

Completing the back four was arguably the toughest nut of the lot, left-back Mike Pejic. Pej was probably the hardest tackler I ever saw and I really learned about that when I finally came to face him when he moved to Everton and then Aston Villa many years later. He knew no pain and was also just about the angriest person I ever came across. Pej had a problem with authority, he won't mind me saying. He often questioned the way the manager chose to approach games and would get wound up very easily. I used to strip next to him in the dressing room each day before training. Pej would come in with a right face on him, having wound himself up on the journey in from his remote farm outside Leek where he lived with his wife Lyn. I'd try and crack a joke. 'Morning, Pej, why the face? Another chicken died on the farm?' This didn't necessarily meet with the desired response. He'd be so grumpy and argumentative, always complaining that the club wasn't as professional as he thought it should be. Sometimes he was right, but that wasn't the philosophy at Stoke City during our time at the club. It was no surprise to me, given his tactical brain and regular contributions to the dressing room debate, that Pej went on to become a highly respected top-level coach, who now delivers training on behalf of the FA. Pej is also now often to be heard co-commentating on Stoke matches for Signal Radio, the Potteries' independent radio station. You can tell he's mellowed a lot as he hasn't threated to kill anyone for weeks now.

Behind them, of course, should any marauding forward be lucky enough to make it past all four with limbs intact, lurked the one and only Gordon Banks. This was some team that Waddo was putting together, a changing of the guard. The all-local back four knitted together beautifully and gave us creative types the platform to play from and they also gave Waddo full confidence to allow his talented attacking players free rein. This particularly helped me. I had the opportunity to gain some revenge on Manchester City by scoring the winning goal the next time we visited their old Maine Road stadium, the winner in a 1-0 victory which exorcised the ghost of my injury there. That was another special goal. I picked the ball up on the halfway line, went past about three players, including Mike Doyle, who would later join Stoke, and slotted the ball home under the advancing keeper. It was rather like Mame Diouf's goal which won the game for Stoke at the Etihad Stadium in August 2014. Sadly there are no TV pictures to prove my claim. Or disprove it, either!

We won three of our last five games to finish in ninth place in the First Division. The good times were here. It was summer 1970. Banksy was heading off to Mexico to become a world superstar thanks to that save from Pele's header and I, at 23, was an established Stoke City first team footballer. But I still wanted more. OK I'd achieved my initial dream, but there was so much more to do.

6

Wing Man

I WAS always quick. Ever since I was a kid, playing street football, running away from old Soap, or dashing down to the bookies to place my dad's bet before the race went off I'd known this. I also had a lot of stamina and even over longer distances when I competed in occasional athletics events for the school I could run most people into the ground. It obviously ran through the family, with four of us playing in the League of Ireland, and yet I'll never understand how this came about, because my father wasn't sporty at all. He couldn't keep up with the goalkeeper. My mother showed no sporting inclination at all, either. Not in any way, shape or form.

I'll always maintain that my grounding in street football was key to my success in the professional game. Even some of the moves made it through to the big time with me. For example, remember that I used to play one-twos with the pavement back on Annaly Road? Well, one of my trademark moves now was a little give and go – normally with Jimmy Greenhoff – which would end up with me having a strike on my right foot from the edge of the box. Jimmy was brilliant at returning the ball to me just perfectly weighted so it sat up and begged to be hit. It's funny how you realise these things come with you through life. It's happened to me a lot.

It was natural for me to look to attack my full-back, particularly if I'd got him isolated. I always thought I had the beating of him, whoever he was. I was confident in my ability to do my job of hitting the byline and delivering a cross for my forwards to convert. That was my role, the classic winger's role. A trick, then head down and go, hit the byline and cross. With the likes of Ritchie and Greenhoff now on the end of my deliveries we were becoming a force to be reckoned with as the pair bagged 30 goals in the 1970/71 season.

Until I sat down to write this book I never really had pause to analyse how similar my style was to the approach that Stan Matthews took throughout his career. I'm not saying I modelled my game on his at all, because I didn't. That fleeting glimpse I had of him in 1956 was wonderful, but I was my own man. What I do believe is that, like Stan, I was an old-school winger, who fulfilled that role in the team and had similar tricks and abilities in my armoury with which to deceive and beat full-backs. We also shared a belief in our own ability to beat the full-back and deliver nine times out of ten. That was a natural thing, rather than anything I worked on.

What's great for me now is that the squad Mark Hughes has built at Stoke City includes similar players; the likes of Victor Moses, Peter Odemwingie and Oussama Assaidi, while he was at the club. All of them love to attack their full-back directly. It's a bit of a throwback and we haven't seen that for years at Stoke. It was my kind of style. I look at any winger and am interested in their initial attacking intent. They should be looking to take their man on, beat him and get a cross in. I never deterred from taking my defender on. I was ready to make a pass to a team-mate who was open and in a better position or play the one-two in order to mix things up, but when it came down to it my job was to get to the byline and whip in a cross for Big John or Jimmy G. It was my first instinct and was my role, my duty – end of story.

When I played out on the left, as I often did, I also had the option of cutting inside and hitting a shot with my right foot, which was the stronger of my two. But the width is the thing which opens up play and all defenders will tell you they dislike being taken on directly and then pushed back towards the byline. In our day this was the norm, there were so many great wingers and I'm disillusioned about the way wing play has gone out of fashion. I feel that coaching solely for possession is not helping.

Ball retention is this mantra which seems to have risen alongside the endless possession statistics which get trotted out in the media and which seem to influence modern coaches and managers. But in my opinion being a winger is about risking losing the ball in trying to create something. Nowadays all too often the so-called winger is forced into passing it backwards or square simply in order to retain possession. That's the prevailing coaching instinct – do not give the ball away. For me it's a negative ploy rather than a positive one as it kills much of the creative spark which these most exciting of players have. Think Matthews or Finney. Their sole reason for being on the pitch was to get to the byline and cross the ball in to the box to create something. That's what they lived for and that's what they delivered week in and week out.

When goals are at a premium and are so important in winning matches surely you would want to spend more time creating situations from which you might be able to score than simply keeping hold of the ball. Perhaps that's a symptom of the fear of failure which pervades the modern game. It certainly wasn't an issue for us when I was playing, although I do also recognise that defensively full-backs are now more astute and wingers are also told to track their opposing numbers back now, double-teaming them and reducing the space they have to operate in. It's a shame because in many ways I think the game is easier to play now than it was 30 or 40 years ago. You might be surprised to hear me say that but there are three key reasons why I believe this. Firstly, there are no knee-high challenges like I used to face week after week when defenders had a licence to kill for the first 20 minutes. They would be trying to nobble you and put you out of the game, or at least keep you quiet. And they'd be doing this legally or at least with the tacit complicity of the referee, who gave them far more leeway than they do today. This meant that defenders felt they had a divine right to kick you. They were professional assassins, if you like.

Cautions are now issued far more easily by referees which means if defenders foul a winger badly they cannot afford to do it again or they'll be sent off, which reduces the physical contact element of the game massively. They cannot get away with the kinds of things that went on in my day and this creates more space and time in which to operate. I would love to have played in that kind of environment.

Secondly, the ball is completely different now and far easier to control than the heavy leather ball with a lace in it which I started my career using. Finally, there's the pitches. The Victoria Ground was a sludge pit. There's no getting away from it. As were many other pitches across the country, particularly during the winter months. I remember the Baseball Ground in Derby and Stamford Bridge, even Old Trafford being pretty terrible at times. I would love to have had the opportunity to perform on the standard of pitches the players are blessed with nowadays. In many ways that era was one for the defenders, while this is more of a time for the attackers.

Being a winger I had many a battle with some of the full-backs of the day – the likes of Leeds' Paul Reaney and Terry Cooper, Ron 'Chopper' Harris and Eddie McCreadie of Chelsea, Spurs' Cyril Knowles and Arsenal's Bob McNab, all tough men who would kick you. Most clubs had full-backs who wanted to make sure you knew you were in for a hard time. Tommy Smith at Liverpool would be constantly in your ear, especially if you managed to beat him. 'Do that again, son, and I'll break your leg,' he'd say, or 'I'll put you in the stand next time.' It was just his way of putting the fear into you, along with his pretty fearsome appearance. I was never really fearful of any individual as I felt confident of my ability to win through. I am a very positive-minded individual.

The one that sticks in my mind, though, was Southampton's left-back Dennis Hollywood. He was a small, squat man. The Dell, then Southampton's home ground, was an experience much like the Victoria Ground. It was a small, tight, intense ground with a thin, red shale track around the raised playing surface. Hollywood had a particular way of dealing with his winger, particularly if he knew you hadn't played at the Dell before. He'd shepherd you to go on the outside so you were getting whitewash on your boots as you sped up the line. He'd let you get half a yard ahead of him so you thought you'd be able to get round him and then he would hit you, sending you toppling off the pitch and on to the track. This would give you grazes and burns all the way up your thigh and wreck your hands as you tried to break your fall. Then you'd end up slamming into the advertising hoarding to boot.

He was great at that and invariably that gravel rash would take you weeks to get rid of as it would be constantly weeping and there was no quick way round getting it to heal like there is now. You'd be bearing the scars for ages. I'm sure that was deliberate, so you would think about the pain and how long it took to get right again next time you were travelling on the coach down to Southampton and you were beginning to think about who you were playing against. It was a kind of psychological warfare as much as the immediate physical one – all designed to intimidate you into not performing. He did it to me and he did it to Harry Burrows too – we still talk about how it stung when we meet these days. Dennis was an evil little shite and he was very very good at it!

Often, though, the challenges would not even be as gentlemanly as Dennis and by that I mean that there would be off-the-ball naughtiness going on. People would rake their studs down the back of your calf or across your ankle, leaving stud marks. The ball was nowhere near you when this would be going on so the referee wouldn't have any clue that it was happening. My calves would be black and blue at the end of every game and not just from the tackles from behind which we received which then were legal and so part and parcel of the game – as long as they got some part of the ball at some point in the tackle of course. Now that's all changed. Back then I had to have massages (albeit from 'expert' masseur Frankie Mountford or bother to go up to the hospital and sit and wait my turn) or take long soaks in the tub to try to get my muscles back into some sort of shape. Once we were into the season the physical demands meant we actually trained less during the campaign, but then we were playing more games, so kept our sharpness and physical fitness through playing matches, rather than endless hours on the training ground.

In fact our training regime sounds quite cushy when you look at it written down in black and white, although I would defy anyone who says that we weren't as fit as the modern players are today. Pre-season was hell. It always is and always will be, but you need to go through it in order to set yourself up for a long campaign. During the season we would do one hard day's training each week up and down the hills at Trentham. Monday would almost always be a loosener (maybe a run along the canal and then a five-a-side), while Tuesday would be tougher, either at Trentham or running round the cinder track at the Vic. For that, you'd have to sprint from the tunnel down to the Stoke End, then jog round to the halfway line on the far side, then you'd have to sprint the rest of that side and all the way along the Boothen End, then jog back to the tunnel. Each lap you'd then add further sprints in until the seventh lap was a sprint all the way around. It was tough and Frank Mountford was a tough taskmaster. He would never let you off and would time you and let you know if you were slacking. Wednesday would often be a day off, or we'd be playing a game, then on Thursday we'd work on tactics, playing defence against attack at Lyme Valley Stadium, where Newcastle Town play, or we'd play reserves versus first team with the reserves playing in the style of the opposition we were to face on the weekend. Then Friday would just be five-a-sides in the gym under the Boothen End. Most sessions were over by lunchtime so our working hours were two to three hours a day four days a week, plus a game at the weekend. Not bad really.

One of the key differences between today's game and my era is that the pace at which today's game is played is mostly high tempo with fewer breaks for rest during a match, but I will always maintain that good players in any era would be able to adjust to the way the game is played in any other. You can't tell me that Matthews and Finney wouldn't be global superstars in the 21st century. They would.

While I'm on the subject of the modern game for a moment one of the things which really annoys me is the prevalence of statistics in the mass coverage nowadays. The vast majority are meaningless. I've already mentioned how possession stats seem to have taken over the world. But they mean nothing. During the first five seasons in which Stoke City were in the Premier League from 2008 I don't think they ever had the ball more than the opposition – in other words their possession stats look, on the face of it, appalling. Sometimes, when playing against the likes of Arsenal, for example, it would be 60/40 or even 65/35 in the opponents' favour. So, if possession is so important, why would Stoke often emerge as the victors in those games, sometimes by 2-0 or 3-1?

It isn't about possession, it's about how you use the ball, how you hurt the opposition, how you score goals and also how easy it is to defend against sides who constantly pass sideways. In fact, if anything can be proved by these stats, then I would suggest that any team which dominates possession as, say, Arsenal do, if they don't win a game then the statistics are in fact pointing out how clueless they are in terms of what to do with the ball when they have it for such long periods. These statistics are presented by TV as the be all and end all, to boost their viewing figures, to give fans talking points, to make themselves look sophisticated. When it comes down to it, though, the game is simple – who can get the ball between the posts and under the bar the most times in 90 minutes. All this bunkum based on stats is nonsense. It rarely achieves any purpose. And while I'm on about it, how come a shot which hits the woodwork is counted as 'on target'? Was the player aiming to hit the post or bar and not score? I don't think so. Sometimes I want to put my foot through the television when I hear people (so-called experts) saying, 'Did you know that Wilshere passed the ball 142 times with his right foot in the first 32 minutes?' It doesn't mean anything.

Then, at the end of the game, you get the interviews. How inane are the questions these days? To a player who has lost, or has missed an open goal, a reporter will ask, 'Are you disappointed with that?' No, Mr Reporter, he's delighted to have failed. Of course, he's disappointed. Us footballers live with disappointment regularly. Conversely, to a player from the team which has won 7-0 and who has scored a hat-trick they will ask, 'You must be happy with that?' I would love to be asked that question. I'd look them straight in the eye and answer, 'No, actually. I'm really upset and disappointed. I didn't fancy us today at all and I had a few quid on the other team to win.' Then I'd wait and see how long it took them to take that in. Then they might stop asking stupid, ridiculous questions and learn to be a bit more original. We don't need reporters stating the bleeding obvious and insulting the viewers' intelligence.

Right, rant over.

The physical and often brutal nature of the game in the late 1960s and early 70s meant that injuries were a very common occurrence. I picked up more than my fair share over the course of my career. In fact I would say that once you start playing at the top level you are almost never 100 per cent fit. You are always carrying some niggle or another, but you'd just get yourself through the 90 minutes, nursing yourself as necessary. Feeling 95 per cent fit was as good as it almost ever got and anyone 80 per cent fit would be considered for selection. If it was a more significant issue you'd get an injection to get you into that 80 per cent or more category. This was a drug called cortisone – a steroid hormone – which was commonplace in professional sports, especially football at the time. It was 'sold' to us as the cure of all ills, but in effect all it was doing was masking the effects of the injury from your brain for about two hours while you played the game. It wasn't a cure at all. In fact playing through the injury with the pain withdrawn was arguably causing more long-term problems as the stresses and strains of competing at the highest level took their toll. That is the problem with cortisone. Over time, if you have that many injections, the drug doesn't disperse out of your system and it coagulates together. This only happened in a minor way for me, but a friend of mine called Tommy Carroll, a Dubliner who played full-back for Shelbourne, Ipswich and Birmingham, then alongside me for the Republic of Ireland, had regular injections in his ankle. Now it is set solid and he has real difficulties with it. Tommy tried to sue his former employers in the end, but didn't get anywhere with it.

Fortunately for my generation, we didn't have the financial imperative of previous eras in which players would need appearance money on top of their basic wage in order to scrape together enough to feed their families. Our wages were very decent, even by 1970s standards. Nowhere near what Premier League players earn these days of course, but good all the same. Our coach Frank Mountford would tell me that in his era of the 1940s and 50s he needed to be on that teamsheet as he'd only be earning around £10 per week. Without his appearance money and win bonus he'd be struggling financially. This means Frank would often declare himself fit and put himself through a midfield battle on terrible pitches (yes, even worse than those we played on) purely because he needed the money.

Often the reason I would be drugged up and sent out would be because the manager knew that my presence on the pitch put the frighteners on the opposition and if they were concentrating on me, maybe by putting two players on me, even if you had a quiet game then it left someone else with more time and space to create chances to score. I can illustrate this point from personal experience. We used to get the opposition's teamsheet in our dressing room an hour before kick-off and if we were playing Manchester United and the name of George Best did not appear we suddenly had a huge lift. We'd be buzzing. Lacking a player of such significance is a huge boost for the opposing players. Conversely if George's name was on the teamsheet we'd have to make plans for him. Sometimes that would be enough to tip the balance in a closely-fought game.

Playing with a cortisone injection was commonplace and may have caused all sorts of longer-term issues, but it wasn't actually a contributing factor to any of my major injuries, which all involved my knees. I ended up having all five of my cartilages out (OK, so humans only have four, but more of that later…). In those days it would take me up to six months to recover and that was only to get back into training. Each one took longer as I had less power in my knees to drive me back to something approaching full fitness. But then once I got back into the mix for selection I'd have to have the cortisone injections to enable me to take the field and that's where the drugs contributed to me having such terrible knees these days. After the game my knee would swell up and I wouldn't be able to train for a couple of days, so I'd lose a bit of fitness while enduring the pain. By the Thursday I'd be able to do some very basic training ahead of a fitness test on a Friday morning.

Then if the boss wanted me to play I'd 'pass' the fitness test no problem, have the injection again and be back in the team come 3pm the following Saturday. Then the whole thing would start all over again. Over my career this became more and more of a problem and I reckon I had over 100 cortisone injections in total, administered by either Doc Crowe or Sandy Clubb. I just accepted that as normal in those days, because it was. Just ask Denis Smith; a lot of weeks he'd be having a fitness test on a Friday morning and, never mind run, he could barely walk down the track. Waddo, though, would be there ensuring that Denis was passed fit. It was laughable, but he knew that the cortisone would sort Denis out so he could play. A couple of jabs and he was jumping around like a two-year-old.

When you were 'fit' you felt untouchable, you wanted the ball all the time and I suppose for about two years from 1970 I had an unbelievable injury-free run and I felt I could achieve anything. I had bundles of energy, I could beat any player who stood in front of me and it didn't matter to me one jot that we were being asked to play three games a week. I never would have conceived of, for example, asking for a rest from any game. Far from it. I was desperate to be in the team. In those days, of course, there was only one substitute, so it was all the more important to be selected for the starting XI as only one man would be on the bench, rather than the seven they are allowed today.

In fact the bleating about too much football being played and needing a winter break does make me laugh. Over the two seasons from August 1970, Stoke City played 127 competitive games in all competitions, including the much-maligned Anglo-Scottish and Anglo-Italian trophies. Remember, back then there were endless replays, with very few competitions having penalty shoot-outs deciding ties. There were even third- and fourth-placed play-off matches for the FA Cup to compete in and we played two in that period, winning one and losing one. That's an incredible number of games. Then you add in end of season tours and pre-season friendlies. And to those who say that playing that number of games reduces a team's ability to perform well and succeed I offer these facts: within those two seasons Stoke City won their first major trophy, the League Cup, and reached two FA Cup semi-finals. Frankly I'd have played more games if I'd had to. I was that up for the challenge. Winning is stimulating and we were on a roll.

Playing at the Victoria Ground was quite an experience. Supporters stood all the way around the ground and the only seats were in the top half of the Boothen Stand, the main stand of the ground where the directors' box was. The stands were all close to the pitch and this made for a spine-tingling atmosphere, especially when we were playing towards the Boothen End, the traditional home end of the ground. But in fact there wasn't really any segregation when I first arrived in Stoke and so there were fans wearing red and white and singing up for us all the way around the ground, with only pockets of visiting fans to be found here and there. Being a winger I became particularly used to playing with the two sides of the ground so close. Both the Boothen and Butler Street paddocks began well below the playing surface so often people's heads were at your knee height. It felt tight and hemmed in as well, which was great when you were doing well and you were being encouraged, but if you weren't they soon let you know about it.

Home games generated a very special atmosphere. People will be used to that which is generated at the Britannia, particularly the atmosphere which propelled Stoke to win promotion to the Premier League and then comfortably retain that status in the first few years afterwards. It was once measured at 122.2 decibels, the loudest in Premier League history. As far as I am concerned that's great, but it only puts the Brit on a par with the Vic when it was rocking. It was a very special place and, with 30,000 or 40,000 people inside, made an incredible sound. It lifted us and contributed to our success.

The danger comes if at any time fans begin to think that Stoke's status is secure. History tells us that we bob between the top divisions far too often to ever feel comfortable and I think that the edginess of fans thinking that something new can be achieved or that something accepted can be taken away from them gives a much rougher, tougher edge to their contribution to the atmosphere of a match. We certainly felt that as players and then witnessed it again in Stoke's first Premier League season when the crowd became a 12th, 13th and sometimes even 14th man at times. That carried forward into our run to the FA Cup Final in 2011 and our European adventures which followed the season after that. When something is fresh and new and exciting then both at the Vic when we were winning trophies and at the Brit during the success the club have had in the last ten years or so, the Potteries fans are a force to be reckoned with.

As great examples, our games against Manchester United in the 1971/72 season when we knocked them out of both cups in replays at the Victoria Ground are perfect. On the night when we finally put paid to them in an FA Cup sixth round replay to clinch a second successive FA Cup semi-final berth, having already taken three games to defeat them in the League Cup, the crowd topped 49,000 – for a game on a Wednesday night. It was incredible. The buzz and anticipation was astonishing. The second largest crowd ever to cram itself into the Vic. Night games at the old ground were very special, often with an eerie kind of Potteries smog enveloping the ground which gave the lights a really special quality as they burned through the gloom, illuminating the pitch and the fantastic play we produced, but all the more so when the opposition boasted the likes of Best, Charlton and Law among their number. That game was exceptional; end-to-end, making the hairs on the back of your neck stand up, with George Best opening the scoring and Denis Smith equalising with a flying header from a corner to take the game into extra time. I scored the winning goal, prodding home in a scramble following a corner.

We were on a roll then, having won the League Cup a couple of weeks earlier. The crowds were absolutely loving this success. They had been starved of it for over a century and were making the most of it while they could. In many ways that was a night that can never be equalled, but for modern fans to be able to get a hold on how it felt then the phenomenal game against Manchester City in Stoke's first season in the Premier League, 2008/09, generated the kind of atmosphere which greeted us that special night in March 1972 and spurred us on to another meeting with Arsenal to vie for a Wembley place.

In the years since retiring one thing I've learned is that this wall of sound often did achieve its aim in that a lot of players who I played against have since owned up to me that they hated coming to play at Stoke. The topic of the abuse that they would face would often be brought up among them in the days before the game, particularly the night before. This got to them more than I'd ever realised during my playing days. John Giles has told me this and several lads from Manchester United have too. They hated the Vic and the prospect of playing there in front of our fans. I think that's a fantastic credit to the club and nowadays it's great to see that this tradition continues, particularly where Monsieur Wenger and his men are concerned. If ever a team has turned up at a ground and been beaten before kick-off it's a series of underachieving Arsenal teams who have dismally failed to make much of an impression at Stoke since we won promotion in 2008. Mind you, their north London neighbours Tottenham have had their moments too.

Where Stoke have always done well is by taking the game to opponents at home. Both in my era and the modern one this has stood us in good stead. The modern phrase is that it's in our DNA. Well, certainly the same kind of up-and-at-'em attitude has pervaded the last decade. For me it's a vital component of a successful Stoke City team, not least because I firmly believe you take the fans with you and Stoke can become a breathless, irresistible force when everything comes together in that way. That intensity and approach has been vital to our modern success. And it was for us back in the 1970s too. It's something we must not lose.

I can give you an example of why from the 2014/15 season. Stoke were struggling in the first half against Swansea, already one goal down after the award of a controversial penalty and hardly making an impact. Suddenly winger Victor Moses went past his man and hit the deck in the opposing penalty area. Some 25,000 voices screamed for a penalty kick. If ever a decision was given thanks to the crowd's input then that was it. There was huge controversy after the game when Swansea manager Garry Monk accused Moses of diving and this was backed up by pundit John Hartson on that night's *Match of the Day 2* programme on the BBC. Replays actually showed that the defender Angel Rangel had a firm hold of Moses's shirt, so there was a foul, but there was no way anyone in the stands around the Britannia was actually appealing for that. Lost in the momentary anger of having the spot-kick awarded against us by referee Michael Oliver for grappling by Ryan Shawcross as a corner came over, there was a collective will to pressurise the official into redressing the balance. It worked. Stoke went on to win the game 2-1. Job done; a wonderful vocal contribution by the crowd to the team's success.

That's not to say that it was always like that. We had plenty of critics among our fans who would get on our backs if things started to go wrong. At times the criticism got to certain players. I remember John Mahoney saying to me at half-time in one game that he didn't want to go out on the left as we were now going to be kicking towards the Boothen End which meant he'd be near a renowned pocket of fans who would ridicule any player who wasn't having a great game. I had it too at times, but as I said earlier I'd learned from a young age to ignore anything which was thrown at me from the sidelines, no matter whether it was from opposing or even my own supporters. This group of fans in the Butler Street paddock were very critical and could dish out stick all right. I experienced this for myself at the start of every season. Due to my Celtic roots and my fair skin I just can't take the sun, so I didn't really go on holidays to simply soak up the rays and get a tan. Far from it. Most of the rest of the boys did and would return bronzed and beautiful for the first home game. So they would run out and then in the middle of the team was pale old me – like a bottle of milk. Over on the Boothen terrace side there was a couple of wags and every year as I ran out for the first home match I could hear them shout, 'Where have you been on your holidays Conroy? The pub?'

What was remarkable was that even among the din of 30,000 or so fans you could hear the criticism coming through. You needed a thick skin all right. Especially as the social sensitivities that temper some of the chanting today didn't exist. For example, I remember at West Ham I'd always get a ribbing about being Irish. For some reason that was the thing they picked on. 'Conroy, you Irish carrot top,' or 'Ginger leprechaun' or 'Go back to the bog, Paddy,' that sort of thing. Nothing too offensive or anything, and almost always meant in jest, but somehow I was always aware of those kinds of things being shouted at Upton Park. Perhaps it went back to the 1972 League Cup semi-final and my challenge on Bobby Ferguson (about which more later), but I always got more stick there than anywhere else. I certainly didn't think it was abusive or even racist. I just let it wash over me and got on with playing the game.

There was at least one person who seemed to like me. I met a girl called Sue at a famous nightclub called The Place in Hanley one night in 1970. She was one of three sisters and had no interest in football at all, which was quite refreshing. In fact, despite having grown up in Stoke-on-Trent, she didn't know Port Vale from Stoke when we met. So it certainly wasn't a case of her being dazzled by this football star. I think that's one thing which has stood us in such good stead over the years; our initial attraction wasn't based on who I was at all. We were just two people meeting and getting along famously. I was in love and I wasn't one for long courtships – back home you'd hear about people courting for 20 years and then finally getting married because they'd somehow realised they were actually the right woman for them – so Sue and I became engaged within 18 months. Things were really going for me.

I had developed something of a persona based on both my playing style and ability and my appearance. I had these huge ginger sideburns, pale white legs, and a shaggy mop of red hair. I was still skinny, though now quite strong. I loved swapping wings and trying my luck against the other full-back. This was relatively rare then as players were supposed to stick to their positions, but Waddo gave us this freedom to roam and I'd swap over to the left and look to cut in and get a shot off on my right foot. If you look at the winning goal at Wembley I chose to go the other way and beat the full-back on the outside, hit the byline and cross deep with my left foot. I could do both and this was because often I would go back to the training ground on an afternoon and work on my left foot, because I knew it was weak. So I'd work and work on it to make myself better – as did the other younger players such as Jackie Marsh, Mike Pejic and Josh Mahoney. I had an appetite to improve, especially when it came to crossing the ball, which is a basic skill that I think is lacking in the modern game. Myself, Jackie and Pej used to practise this constantly and prided ourselves on the quality we delivered in matches.

Sometimes when I evaluate a Premier League game and see the standard of crosses which have been put in by both sides over the 90 minutes it makes me weep. It's one aspect of today's game which is significantly worse than it was when I played. It kills me because the players work so hard to get into a good position, but then the art of crossing lets them down. If Peter Crouch had played in our era he would have been sensational and bagged a hatful of goals each season because of the service he would have received. All too often these days players hit the ball long when they are crossing. The modern ball seems to fly longer and I get so frustrated by overhit crosses.

Then there's the fact that many teams – Arsenal being a good example – don't bother creating crossing situations. They want to walk the ball through a central area, which makes it much easier to defend against. I always think Arsenal are at their most dangerous when the likes of Walcott and Oxlade-Chamberlain get wide and cross for Giroud or even Koscielny to attack the ball. But it seems as if their manager doesn't want to play like that. So, rather than being a dying art I think crossing as an art may actually have died.

Not enough work goes into it anymore. The last great crosser of the ball in the Premier League was David Beckham. He was renowned for going back after training to practise crossing and free kicks, just like we did. He made himself the best in the world at it and created the two goals that won that dramatic 1999 Champions League Final for Manchester United against Bayern Munich that way, plus countless goals for England. It pays off. That's what frustrates me so much about the modern professional. Maybe that's one way in which the riches have changed the game. Perhaps they have stopped players striving within an inch of their lives to be the best they can possibly be and instead are just prepared to settle for good enough. To me good enough isn't. You can always improve.

On the pitch, 1970/71 would prove to be one of my best seasons for Stoke. I scored 14 goals, my best goal return in a campaign, and we had a fantastic FA Cup run which almost brought us ultimate glory. The story of the season really began in September 1970 when we thrashed Arsenal 5-0 at the Victoria Ground. I scored one of the goals and it was voted as Goal of the Month and then third in Goal of the Season on *Match of the Day*. We scored some cracking goals that day. We were so good that even Alan Bloor got on the scoresheet, and that was a rarity. John Ritchie's two goals were belters; the first was a trademark header and the second he created himself by winning the ball off the Gunners' midfield, dribbling round three men, drawing Bob Wilson in the Arsenal goal and slotting it past him left-footed. That performance epitomised our free-flowing football of the period.

My goal was one of my better ones. I received the ball in the outside-right position, played a one-two with the outside of my right foot with Peter Dobing and then hit the return pass first time from about 25 yards out. It flew in. Funnily enough, it was one of those shots which could have gone anywhere, but it arrowed right into the corner. People always assume it was the best goal I've ever scored. For me I don't think it is. I wouldn't put it in my top three. OK, it was a great shot. But it was spectacular more than a huge amount of skill. For me the goals against Liverpool and Nottingham Forest I've already described and the one later this same season at Hull, which I will relate in a moment, are my three favourite goals; mostly due to the level of skill and difficulty which each took. That one against Arsenal I just smacked. Some fly in, most end up in the stand. I got far more satisfaction from those other three. If you want to judge for yourself both those goals from 1970/71 are available on YouTube to revel in whenever you like.

Of course we would face Arsenal at the end of that season in a titanic FA Cup semi-final, but the route to playing the Gunners that bright spring day was full of jeopardy. It really was a classic cup run. Earlier in the season we'd been knocked out of the League Cup by Millwall. They restricted us to a goalless draw at the Vic and then beat us 2-1 at The Den, which was by the way the most intimidating ground I ever played at. Horrible. I scored a fantastic goal in the replay; a throw-in on the left-hand side came to me at chest height on the edge of the box, I chested it down, swivelled and struck it on the volley. It flew in to the top left-hand corner of the net. It was one of those perfect strikes when you hit the sweet spot of the ball and it just zings in. But we lost, after frankly being intimidated out of competing in the game. So when we drew them in the FA Cup third round at home we weren't in any mood to let them repeat their giant-killing feat. We won 2-1 at the Vic and then faced Huddersfield, who were a top flight team at the time. They led 3-1 with 25 minutes remaining, but then Harry Burrows sparked a comeback by scoring and I completed the fightback by netting in a goalmouth scramble. We drew the replay 0-0 after extra time and then won a tight third game at Old Trafford 1-0 thanks to a Jimmy Greenhoff goal. I always think that replay victory stood us in great stead when it came to the following season's League Cup semi-final replay against West Ham which also took place at Old Trafford, but more of that later.

Next up were Ipswich Town, one of the best teams in the country under Bobby Robson. Again we drew at home, but then won a very tight replay at Portman Road, this time thanks to a typically brave Denis Smith header from a corner. I hadn't fancied our chances after we'd failed to win at home, but now we were beginning to think this might be our year. We were in the sixth round, although we'd already played six games, the number most sides have to get through to actually lift the trophy these days! Then when we came out of the hat with Second Division Hull City, the excitement around the city of Stoke-on-Trent was incredible. Tickets were at such a premium, with over 41,000 fans packing into Hull's old Boothferry Park ground. Optimism was rife. We would surely win and reach the semi-finals of the FA Cup for the first time since 1899 and only the second time in the club's history.

Maybe that confidence was misplaced because we were a shambles for the first half of that game. Hull's strikers Chris Chilton and Ken Wagstaff were destroying us and before we knew it we were 2-0 down with Wagstaff having netted both goals. They really were fantastic that day, tearing Smithy and Bluto apart. Snow was bucketing down and their fans were going ballistic as little Hull were heading for the FA Cup semi-final. We were getting hammered by a Second Division team and our tempers were fraying to say the least. This wasn't in our script.

Things changed right on half-time. Harry Burrows played me in with a ball over the top into the inside-left channel. It was incredibly slippery underfoot due to the fresh snow, but I opted to do my usual. The keeper rushed out and I danced around him. On this occasion he would probably have expected me to go to my right, his left, as I was right-footed, so I went the other way, and on that snowy pitch slotted the ball home from a very narrow angle. It's my favourite goal and I have this fantastic picture of me scoring it taken from behind the goal. I never cease in taking enjoyment from that, as it was one of the trickiest situations we'd been in and it sparked an incredible fightback. The momentum was with us.

John Ritchie equalised, touching in a Burrows shot from close range, and then buried the winner to delirious scenes from our fans, who must have thought their Wembley dreams were dead and buried after the start we'd made. I had a major and controversial part to play in that winning goal as well. Yes, I crossed the ball from a tight angle for Big John to head home unmarked at the far post, but I'd received the ball from a long throw taken by Jackie Marsh which shouldn't even have been awarded to us. It should have been Hull's ball. They were so busy arguing about the award with the officials that they lost concentration and we worked the opening for the winner. It was a bit naughty actually. I knew it was their throw, but I picked up the ball anyway and tossed it to Micky Bernard, who took the throw-in quickly and the rest is history. We really got away with one there. It was pretty cheeky and I'm sure Hull fans of a certain vintage still complain about that even today. Much like Stoke fans still remember the ridiculous offside decision which cost us the 1972 FA Cup semi-final replay against Arsenal. In fact I tend to visit the city of Hull incognito when I go to watch Stoke play there these days just in case someone recognises me and takes revenge.

Anyway, we'd done it. We had won through to Stoke's first FA Cup semi-final of the 20th century. After the game we got the train back to Stoke as there was actually a station right outside the ground. This train was packed, Waddo bought us all champagne and also invited many of the supporters who were on the train to join in. The atmosphere was unbelievable. We were on a high and that was one of the most joyous train journeys of my life. It was a very special time as the fans were able to mingle with us and tell us all about the emotions they had been through.

There is one special reminder of that day still around today as a Stoke-supporting couple chose to name their newborn son, who arrived that weekend, after me and invited me to become his godfather. What an unexpected honour that was. This happened because the husband hadn't been able to go to the quarter-final as his wife was due to give birth, so when I played such an integral part in the victory the couple decided to honour me as I'd started the comeback by scoring that first goal. So the lad was named Terry Conroy Weaver.

Reaching the semi-final was massive news for Stoke, and when we came out of the hat with Arsenal (the other semi-final was Liverpool versus Everton) we were confident we could win and reach a first Wembley final. In fact of those three sides we'd have picked Arsenal if we could have done due to the hammering we'd given them earlier in the season. The enormity of what we could be about to achieve hit us and it was understandable then that things got a bit tense among us as the big game approached.

The semi-final was due to be played at Hillsborough, the home of Sheffield Wednesday. In the week beforehand we stayed at a hotel in Buxton to get away from the pressure to train and relax if possible. My room-mate, as ever, was Josh Mahoney. Then there were the usual pairs of Ritchie and Dobing, Greenhoff and Burrows, Eastham and Banks, Marsh and Pejic etc. Josh was a restless sleeper and often took sleeping pills to see him off. The morning before the semi-final saw us playing the usual Friday five-a-side, but Josh and I had overslept and had to be roused by Frank Mountford. We went out to train without breakfast to face the usual flak from the lads. Traditionally Banksy played up front in these five-a-side games so he could pretend he was a great goalscorer and he loved nothing more than sticking one or two in the back of the net. Josh was still feeling the effects of the pills and he and Gordon went into a tackle and got tangled up. It was quite a heavy challenge from both of them considering it was supposed to be a light-hearted five-a-side and Josh took exception to this. He got up and smacked Banksy one right in the face. Waddo stepped in immediately to stop things. When Josh came back to the room he was distraught and utterly embarrassed. He'd been feeling on edge with the approaching game, not that this excuses his reaction. Still, Waddo kept him in the team, although more of that in a minute.

News of this incident never got out to the press at all and we never mentioned it again, not until we had a 30th anniversary dinner in 2002 to celebrate our League Cup victory. It turned out that Banksy sat next to Josh that night and raised the subject for the first time in over 30 years. They apologised to each other and that was that. It hadn't been eating away at them all that time or anything like that but they were able to deal with it, albeit 31 years later.

The first half of that semi-final at Hillsborough was arguably the best half of football that Stoke City team played. We were brilliant. We slaughtered Arsenal. That we only went in at the interval 2-0 ahead was a travesty. It should have been at least four, and we had a couple of great chances early in the second half too. But we didn't take them. Jimmy Greenhoff smashed one over the bar when he could have stayed calmer, taken the ball on a couple of steps closer and then hit it. Josh Mahoney then had a similar chance, although the ball bobbled slightly and Josh hit a tame left-footed shot straight at Wilson. We could have been four up before everything changed. As it was our first goal was a tad lucky. Peter Storey's defensive clearance from a corner was blocked by Denis Smith's outstretched foot and the ball flew into the roof of the net before Wilson could react. The second goal was arguably fortuitous too as Charlie George played a suicidal backpass that left John Ritchie with only Wilson to beat, which he did easily before charging round the Hillsborough pitch with both fists aloft in that famous pose which is replicated in the statue which stands outside the Boothen End of the Britannia Stadium today. We were flying. Surely nothing could stop us now.

Enter Peter Storey. A more unlikely goalscoring hero you couldn't wish to expect. He only scored nine goals in his entire career. Two of them had to be in this game. His first came when a weak defensive header fell to him on the edge of the box. He lashed it into the bottom left corner past Banksy, who had no chance as it took a slight deflection on the way through. There were still 40 minutes to go and we were now in a backs-to-the-wall defensive mode. We had to hang on to reach Wembley. Arsenal ratcheted up the pressure as the minutes ticked away. We could see how slowly time was moving as Hillsborough had a clock up in the corner of the ground (hardly any grounds had clocks in those days) and I will always maintain that it was what did for us that day as it was in our eyeline as we defended. Had we been kicking the other way it would have been behind us, but we could clearly see it. I remember it showing quarter to five and we were still playing. In those days you may have had one or two minutes of injury time in a game, that was all. There weren't any significant injuries in that match and yet here we were still playing when we'd kicked off the half at five to four, so we'd played an unheard of five minutes of injury time.

The whistles from the Stoke fans were deafening and we were almost mesmerised by a combination of this clock and the fact that the referee Pat Partridge hadn't yet blown his whistle. Arsenal were mounting attack after attack and we were repelling all boarders up to this point, but they got given the opportunity to mount one last raid and a series of unfortunate events (as Lemony Snicket might put it) unfolded.

First off, Arsenal were given a controversial free kick when Mike Pejic tangled with Storey. We felt the award should have gone the other way. Had it, then we'd have relieved the pressure and seen out the game, but Mr Partridge saw fit to penalise Mike and George Armstrong lofted the ball into our box, which was packed full of players. We were pretty desperate by this stage and Denis Smith flapped at the ball as he went to head it and it caught his hand. Thankfully Mr Partridge missed that, even though Arsenal's players appealed, and awarded a corner following the scramble which followed. What he'd also missed was the foul that George Graham perpetrated by barging into the back of Gordon Banks, who dropped the ball as a consequence, leading to that scramble. Banksy went ballistic at the referee, probably also hoping to waste time, but Partridge was always going to let Arsenal take the corner, so we got organised.

But not very well it appears as three Arsenal players could have headed the cross that came in. Frank McLintock did, and it arrowed towards the corner of the net where Josh Mahoney had little option but to dive and push it round the post. It was actually a great save. The only problem was, of course, that Josh was an outfield player. Penalty. Deep into injury time. I don't blame Josh for that handball. If he hadn't done it then McLintock's header would have gone in, so at least he gave us a chance. In fact if you watch the game back on YouTube you can see in the aftermath of that incident, while Arsenal's players are celebrating as if they'd scored, I am patting Josh on the back to console him and then I give him a little cuddle. I knew he was disconsolate. We'd been together for so long by that stage that I really felt for him and I knew that if the penalty went in Josh was going to get a really hard time.

Storey was Arsenal's penalty taker and he was always going to score. Banksy barely moved as it was stroked into the back of the net and that was it. We'd been pegged back with the last kick of the game – our Wembley dreams confounded. The dressing room was like a morgue after the match. I have had a few disappointments in life, but nothing has ever really come close to that. I'm normally very phlegmatic and positive, but that game is still even today constantly on my mind. It was a feeling of utter desolation and disbelief and there were a few tears as we'd come so close and blown it. Remember, we'd drawn, not lost. But it felt like we had.

One thing which always puzzled me about Hillsborough was why Waddo chose to drop Jackie Marsh and selected Eric Skeels at right-back instead for that game. Jackie was the cast-iron first-choice right-back at the club and wasn't injured at all. Instead he had to be satisfied with being substitute, although he never got on in either game. I was playing inside-left, too, with Jimmy Greenhoff playing slightly deeper than normal. So Waddo had changed things about a bit, although to be fair it had worked, given our fantastic first-half display. We hadn't seen the game out, though, and we were never in the replay, which the Gunners won 2-0 at Villa Park four days later. There was no possibility of lifting us for that game and we never really turned up. Our minds were still dwelling on the 'what ifs'.

Arsenal, of course, went on to clinch the double that season, defeating Liverpool after extra time in the FA Cup Final. A few years later I met Frank McLintock, their captain, when I was on holiday with a few of the lads and our families and he confided in me that the day after we'd stuffed them 5-0 at the Victoria Ground their manager Bertie Mee had brought them all in for training. They'd proceeded to have one humdinger of a team meeting during which a few home truths were told. It cleared the air after what was a pretty terrible performance and they then went on this incredible run which saw them lose just four more matches before the end of the season; 32 games and only four defeats, not bad. So I'm going to claim that we helped Arsenal win the double in more ways than one. Frank laughed when I told him that.

We had come so close to winning the FA Cup. It hurt. We only won three more games that season. Recovering from the disappointment was going to be difficult as we'd never been in the hunt for major honours before and didn't have any experience to draw on. The only way to exorcise that ghost was to pick ourselves up and go out and try and win something the following season.

That is exactly what we did.

7

Wembley Way

EVERYONE always used to say about us, 'Stoke City are the second oldest league club, but they have never won anything.' This really used to annoy Tony Waddington. The manager would use it to motivate us before cup ties. 'Come on,' he'd say. 'We can show them we can win this thing.' Equally, the disappointment of the defeat in the FA Cup semi-final the previous season had to be put behind us and what better way to do that than having another great campaign, packed with cup action. That's exactly what we did. In 1971/72 we would play 21 cup ties overall between the second round of the League Cup at Southport in September and the third/fourth place play-off in the FA Cup (yes, such a thing existed back then, although it was the last ever season of it) when we lost on penalties to Birmingham.

I didn't play in that opening League Cup tie at the Fourth Division minnows as I was injured, but sitting in the stands I felt that they gave us a really good game. Arguably it was one of the toughest en route to Wembley. I can remember our opening goal, which was scored by Alan Bloor. It was a real rarity from Bluto, which is why it sticks in my mind. Haig Avenue that night was packed to the gills with over 10,000 fans, even though it only holds around 6,000 these days. It was a small, intense ground and we played quite nervously, only winning thanks to a late Jimmy Greenhoff goal after Southport had equalised. I was a terrible spectator and this game made me really nervous as it obviously wasn't one we should be losing and for much of it we seemed in danger of falling at the first hurdle as we had done against Millwall the previous season. Not being able to have an input was also frustrating, but the lads got us through and I then played every game in what turned out to be a cup run of epic proportions.

Next up were Oxford United, another potential banana skin. The expectation is always on the top-flight team on these occasions and we came away happy from their rickety old Manor Ground, which had a vicious slope, having hung on for a 1-1 draw, courtesy of another Jimmy G goal, as we knew we'd win the replay, which we duly did 2-0, thanks to goals from John Ritchie and young substitute Sean Haslegrave. Those two games took place in October 1972 and we were also putting together a decent run in the league, too. I scored winning goals against both Huddersfield and Sheffield United and we also beat both Spurs and West Brom either side of a 1-1 draw at Old Trafford in the next round of the League Cup. John Ritchie scored that night, with Alan Gowling equalising late on. We were beginning to get the measure of United by then and, after a goalless draw at the Vic, we defeated them in an epic second replay, also at the Victoria Ground after Waddo won the toss of a coin to decide the venue. We won 2-1 thanks to goals from Ritchie and Dobing.

Both of those games saw over 40,000 cram into the old place to witness yet more special nights as we saw off a team containing Best, Law, Charlton, Kidd and Sadler – the heart of their 1968 European Cup-winning side – and tricky Welsh winger Willie Morgan. We felt they were vulnerable defensively, though, as the likes of Steve James, Tommy O'Neil and Francis Burns struggled to cope with our attacking play, despite the fact that United were actually top of the First Division table at the time. United were always the scalp you wanted to take and that season we would knock them out of both cups.

We were really beginning to flow and the same feeling was developing which we'd had the year before – this could be our year. Our play all stemmed from training, in which Waddo would run five-a-sides and purr at some of the skills Jimmy G, Peter Dobing or George Eastham would show. It was one-touch, silky stuff, which was realising his personal vision of blending youth and experience, skill and steel. It always surprised me that this same purveyor of the beautiful game, or as he preferred to call it the Working Man's Ballet, would tolerate some of the appalling stick our defenders would give to talented attackers come Saturdays. It was an unbelievable juxtaposition. Our back four would kick their own mother, but Waddo turned a blind eye to these X-rated tackles and accepted it as what was necessary in the context of the game at that time in order to let his free-flowing attackers play.

I was honoured to be playing on the same pitch as old-stagers George Eastham and Peter Dobing. I used to gaze around occasionally, spy them and think, 'This is where I want to be.' Our football was wonderful to be involved in and both senior players were inspirational in their own way. As a lad I had learned all about George's fall-out with Newcastle in 1961, which had led to the breaking of the wage cap and allowed us to earn decent money by the time I came into the game. He was a truly noble individual. By 1971 George was spending his winters in South Africa as he was coaching at a club called Hellenic. He'd then return to England in mid-autumn to add his craft and vast experience to our side. The manager also wanted to give him the chance to coach in England, as Waddo was beginning to see George as the natural successor to himself when the time came.

George was a lovely touch-player and his reintroduction to the team in late October 1971 was very timely. It gave us a great boost and in the middle of the following month he made his first significant contribution to our League Cup campaign. George was introduced to the second replay against Manchester United as a half-time substitute by Tony Waddington and, despite the fact he had just turned 35, proceeded to change the course of the game. George Best had put United in front just before the interval, but our own George came on and stroked the ball around, prompting the likes of myself and Jimmy to flow forward at every opportunity. The comeback victory was secured by Big John's goal two minutes from the end of a tumultuous tie. That it came from a George Eastham cross says everything about the old feller's contribution, although his best was to come at Wembley itself.

Our captain was Peter Dobing, who had joined Stoke from Blackburn just after City had won promotion to the top flight in 1963, so he'd been at the club for a long time. On his day Peter was a wonderful footballer who could beat players with ease, being blessed with a great turn of pace and a lovely body swerve. He could also play a quick one-two with you and be gone like a flash with a defender left trailing in his wake. He did have his fair share of off days, though, and had become one of those players that a section of fans liked to pick on and moan about, which I think was partly why Waddo made him skipper, giving him a vote of confidence.

I remember he scored a hat-trick which won a crucial game against Leeds 3-2 during our relegation battle of 1967/68. There was a mixed reception to this feat, which seemed strange to me as I was just a youngster at the time and quite new to the team. But it became obvious that there was a significant minority who liked to batter Dobing at every opportunity, even though on his day he was superb. Peter should have played for England at the very highest level (although he did earn under-23 caps before arriving at Stoke), but he lacked that element of ambition and total dedication to his career. Frankly, if you'd offered him a fishing rod and told him you'd pay him £150 a week then he'd have taken his boots off and gone down the lake straight away. He loved to spend time in the countryside, hunting, shooting and fishing. He was also often to be found smoking a pipe in order to relax. Peter was very quiet as a captain, but he led us in his own way because we all respected him and looked up to him for what he was capable of producing.

The two strikers who had joined us in the summer of 1969 – John Ritchie and Jimmy Greenhoff – had become a major part of our success, but they were chalk and cheese. For example, if we won then Jimmy was happy to have contributed to the team's success, whether he'd scored or not. But even if we'd been victorious, Big John would be as miserable as sin if he hadn't scored. Come Monday morning when we came back in for training he would have a face as long as a motorway. He was desperate to score, a born goalscorer. I particularly remember after the first game at Old Trafford, which ended 1-1, even though John had scored he'd also had a goal ruled out unfairly. He was spitting feathers about it. He wanted to make an official complaint to the authorities. He kept on about how it was so unfair all the while we were getting changed and on the bus back to Stoke. The rest of us were cock-a-hoop we'd drawn at Old Trafford! As he matured as a player John was also becoming more adept at making an all-round contribution, rather than simply scoring goals, especially when it came to his partnership with Jimmy G. The pair were perfectly suited and brought out the best in each other. Big John's touch was so good in his early 30s that his relative lack of pace became irrelevant. For me he should have been in the England squad at that time. He was that good.

Of course Gordon Banks was our true England superstar, but I remember one story which cracked us up no end. We'd travelled down to London for a game at Spurs on a Friday afternoon. We always stayed in the Russell Hotel and from there in the evening we were able to go for a walk or maybe see a film in order to relax before the following day's game. Gordon, George Eastham, Josh Mahoney and I wandered out into Russell Square and came across this street artist, who had drawn a picture of Gordon, making that famous save from Pele's header, in chalk on the pavement. Except it didn't actually look anything like Gordon at all. We stood there looking at it and cracking up. It was nothing like him. So Gordon thought he'd have a bit of fun with the artist and approached him and said, 'Excuse me, who is that?', pointing to the drawing. 'It's the great Gordon Banks,' said the artist dramatically, dismally failing to recognise that the man asking him the question was actually the great Gordon Banks himself. I had to intervene. 'Is he anything like this man, here?' I said, indicating Gordon. 'No, not really,' said the artist, still oblivious to the fact he was talking to Banksy himself. We were in fits. No wonder the drawing was so bad.

These team jollies, or bonding sessions as we preferred to call them, were commonplace under Tony Waddington's inspired leadership. In fact you never knew when some opportunity might come his way and we'd be told to report with our passports and clothes for three days because we were heading off somewhere sunny to play and make a few quid for the club. You'd have to rip up your plans for the evening, square it with your wife (even if it was her birthday) and report on time to travel. This used to wind Pej up no end. We'd all be thinking that this was the life, a few days in the sun, all expenses paid, while he would build up a head of steam, getting all het up and moaning about having to go away yet again.

There was a very high-profile fan called Fred Tinsley, who had sold his business for about £8m in 1970, who loved to be associated with Stoke City. He was based in Switzerland and also frequented the south of France. He had a penny or two and a lot of influence and for several years in the 1970s he organised friendlies against teams like Marseille and Monaco for us. We'd stay in Monte Carlo or Nice, so we were living the swanky life while we were away. The weather was fantastic and the huge casino in Monte Carlo had a certain calling after we'd played at the stadium in front of Prince Rainier and the like. It was just what Fred wanted, getting him in with the jet set and showing off 'his' team. We weren't allowed to call him Fred, though, we were supposed to call him 'Major', so he could keep up appearances. So, of course, we made sure we 'forgot' this each time we saw him. 'Hello, Fred,' we'd all say one by one as he greeted us off the coach as it arrived at the ground. 'It's Major,' he'd say through gritted teeth. Later he took to trying to get us to use the French word 'majeur'. Fat chance!

There was one particular evening which summed up the fun we had with Fred during those trips. He had arranged dinner for us in a bistro after the game. I remember it had blue and white plastic tablecloths, so it wasn't exactly a Michelin starred restaurant or anything. There were around 20 of us including the players and staff. Pej was still fuming from having had to come on the trip in the first place and decided that he didn't want anything that was offered. When the starter came and it was melon he asked the waiter if he could have something else. 'Prawn cocktail, monsieur?' the waiter offered. Pej accepted and when his starter arrived it caused a domino effect and half of us opted for that as it looked tasty. Then the main course came and it was steak. I joked that it was the horse that I'd lost a bet on the previous day and this set Pej off again. He requested chicken, as he preferred white meat anyway. So again the domino effect occurred. Finally dessert was ice cream, and Pej wanted fruit salad, as he was always conscious of his diet. Again half of us changed our mind and followed Pej.

Now, it turned out that Fred had pre-booked the Prix Fixe menu and all these extra options were not included. Pej had gone

Welcome to the world – Gerard Anthony Conroy

The four Conroy youngest boys – with the cherub Terry second from right.

The eight footballing Conroy brothers – if only sponsorship had been available then. We'd have made a packet!

The Conroy boys plus mum and dad

Receiving the Sir Stanley Cup from Carlton TV's Gary Newbon in very auspicious company of a galaxy of stars, including Shilts, the victim of my weight prank

A standing ovation from a packed Waddington Suite for the Boys of '72

Stoke City Old Boys Association. Denis Smith trying to steal the limelight as usual by showing off yet another war wound.

The 1970s lads getting back together

Walking out at the Britannia Stadium on the 40th anniversary of the League Cup win…

…with all the boys…

…and taking the applause from the Boothen End.

A warm welcome from those crazy Norwegian Stoke supporters at the airport…

…which continued for the full four days of our stay…

…and took its toll on us all. This picture took 24 takes to get right!

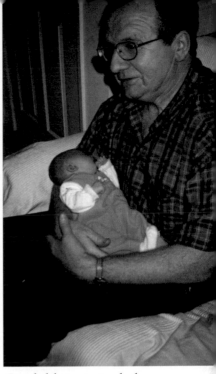

My three wonderful daughters, from the left Sinead, Niamh and Tara – the problems I had with them growing up! Only joking, I never lost a minute's sleep. Sue did, mind you.

Grandad duties start early these days

My three wonderful grandchildren, from the left Estella, Lola and Rafa – Rafa is shaping up to be a midfield dynamo

A typical Conroy family Christmas

Myself with the beautiful Sue

With my very good friend John Devine – a star with Arsenal, Norwich, Stoke City and the Republic of Ireland. Here I am trying to get a game on a Saturday during my tour of the ground by hanging my shirt up in the home dressing room at the Britannia Stadium

A La Carte. Where the meal had been budgeted at about £100, when Fred received the bill he exploded. Bearing in mind he was a multi-millionaire, he wouldn't give a door a bang he was so frugal, which I suppose is how rich people stay rich. But here he was with a far more expensive bill than he expected. He wasn't happy, but it cracked us up and that little moment of triumph was particularly special for our anti-establishment left-back. It was the most vibrant I'd seen Pej on one of these trips in ages. He'd beaten the system, he'd won. It brought an end to our jaunts to the Med, though.

There were plenty of other offers to fly round the world and play, though, spreading the gospel according to Stoke City to places such as Greece, Spain, New Zealand, Australia, Cyprus, Morocco, Israel and even Tahiti. We knew this collectively as Stoke City's Magical Mystery Tour (after the track on the Beatles' 1968 album *Sgt. Pepper's Lonely Hearts Club Band*, which was incredibly popular among us). One such trip saw us visit Ghana, an emerging football nation back then. It followed our victory over Millwall in the FA Cup in January 1971, the start of our long road to the FA Cup semi-final that year. When we came in the next Monday morning there was a hand-written notice on the board which Waddo had left for us which read, 'Report at 7pm this evening. Departing Manchester airport for Ghana.' So if you had any plans you had to rip them up. This irked Pej, as usual. He overreacted and went off on one. 'Ghana? I'm not going there.'

But he was on the coach at 7pm along with the rest of us, who had all had to square things with our wives, although they were quite used to it by this stage. It was five degrees of winter frost below zero when we left Heathrow. Then when we landed in Accra, the Ghanaian capital, at about midnight the heat and humidity hit us the second we stepped off the plane. We were going from one extreme to another. Not only that, but as we walked through the airport we saw lots of local women with bare breasts, many of them with babies breastfeeding. This really wasn't what we were used to at all; a completely different culture. I found it fascinating.

We arrived late that night, or rather early in the following morning, at our hotel, which looked fairly run down, or was it unfinished? I'm not sure. I remember Harry Burrows and Alan

Bloor were rooming together next to myself and Josh Mahoney and as we unpacked our things we heard this kind of strangled scream come from next door. It was Bluto. He was the quiet man of the team, barely speaking a word at times, so we knew this was something serious. We rushed next door to discover that Bluto had a lizard on his bed. It was huge. Waddo rushed in next and Bluto turned on him and ranted, 'Look at that thing! It's dangerous here. What kind of place have you brought us to? I'm not staying in this hotel. You can stick your tour.' With that Waddo called the hotel manager, who simply picked the lizard up, put it on the floor and stood on it. 'It's no problem now, is it? It won't come back to hurt you,' pointed out Waddo to the open-mouthed Bluto.

But after word got around we all packed our bags and there was a mass exodus which saw us sitting in the foyer in protest until another hotel was found and we were transported over to it to get some rest.

We were due to play the champions of Ghana, a team called Asante Kotoko, on the Wednesday. So thankfully we had the Tuesday to train – which turned out to be no more than a light jog and ten-minute five-a-side game – and then relax before the match, which we lost 3-1. It was certainly a warm-weather training trip with a difference. No Dubai for us in those days.

The night before the game Jackie Marsh, John Farmer and a young Scouse centre-half called John Moores, who went on to have a good career with Shrewsbury, had caught a taxi into town, saying to the driver, 'Take us to the nearest nightclub.' The car pulled up outside this place and the three of them got out; Jackie and John Farmer from one side and John Moores the other – into a sewer, an open ditch which was invisible in the dark. He was in it up to his knees, ripping his trousers and gashing his shin. Now Jackie and John were responsible lads, so they did the thing that every young feller in his early 20s would do. They put John Moores back into the cab, gave the driver some money and told him to take him back to the hotel where he'd picked them up. Then the pair of them trotted off to enjoy the nightspots of Accra. When Mooresy arrived back at the hotel with his knee gushing blood he was spotted by Tony Waddington, who asked, 'What happened there, John?'

'I fell into a hole, Boss,' came the reply. Somehow they got away with it.

That story also reminds me of the day the manager himself got caught in a bit of a hole, although this one was of a metaphoric variety as it involved an airport (Charles de Gaulle in Paris), his luggage and the baggage carousel. Waddo had reached the carousel while it was still empty and so sat down on it. The only thing was he hadn't heard the beeping which precedes the carousel starting up and just after he'd sat down it jerked into action, taking him off guard and throwing him on to his side with his feet off the ground, being carried along as the first bags appeared behind him. It only lasted about five seconds before he managed to gather himself together and haul himself off, but we'd all seen it happen and were howling with laughter, particularly as his legs scrabbled around in mid-air hunting for the ground as the carousel gathered speed.

There is one other story I remember from our tours abroad. This one came as we were heading to the south of France once again to play Monaco. The night before the flight we stayed at the Holiday Inn near Heathrow airport. Jackie Marsh and Josh Mahoney always had a little bit of devil in them and liked to play practical jokes to pass the time. Tony Waddington had had a drink on the way down and looked dishevelled, his tie skew-whiff. Taking advantage of the manager's lack of focus (let's be kind) Josh signed in to the hotel as Mr Billy Pig. About ten minutes later the receptionist called Waddo over and told him that the list of names he had sent ahead did not tally with the names which had now checked in. So Waddo went down the list of names that the receptionist showed him; 'Marsh, Conroy, Smith, Pejic, Bloor, Pig, Ritchie, Greenhoff… hang on… Pig?!'

'A Mr Billy Pig, sir,' the receptionist confirmed to Waddo.

'Billy Pig?!' Waddo cried. We were collecting our luggage and making our way over to the lifts to go to our rooms, so we heard the commotion break out. Waddo gave the appearance of the whirlwind television presenter of the day Magnus Pyke as he whirled his arms around holding the offending list containing Mr B. Pig and let out his trademark, 'ay, ay, ay' utterance of disbelief.

Then came the coup de grace as Waddo's whirling came to a stop and he gathered himself together and admonished the receptionist by saying loudly, 'We don't have any player called Billy Pig. You've signed in the wrong guest to our list.'

And with that he stormed off, leaving us in fits and the receptionist open mouthed at this turn of events. It was typical of the fun which we had on our trips.

Having seen off Manchester United, in the quarter-final we were favoured with a draw against mid-table Third Division side Bristol Rovers, the lowest-ranked team left in the competition. Over 33,000 packed into Eastville and we put on a fabulous show for them. My goal in the 64th minute put us 4-0 ahead, Jimmy, Denis and Micky Bernard scoring the first three. We then relaxed and Rovers scored two very late goals, but we were never in trouble. We were headed for a second semi-final in the calendar year of 1971, although little did we know that it would be well into 1972 before it was settled.

The first leg against West Ham was played on a typical Stoke-on-Trent foggy night. It was 8 December 1971 and we felt we had to get a lead to take back to Upton Park. A two-goal victory would give us a cushion, but we needed to win. So, when we went a goal up early on thanks to Peter Dobing things looked set fair, but we didn't play well and first Geoff Hurst smashed in a penalty and then, in the second half, Clyde Best, West Ham's strong, leggy striker, scored to win the game 2-1 for the Hammers. There were big question marks hanging over us as we came off the pitch that night. Were we as good as we thought we were? Could we produce when it was needed? Had we blown another semi-final?

This time, however, the format of the competition came to save us. The semi-finals were two-legged affairs and we still had the opportunity to go to Upton Park and win. There was nothing else for it. Before the return leg the following week we went down to Grays in Essex to spend a couple of nights in a hotel there so we'd be fresh for the game. We trained well and the feeling grew that we had a chance. Waddo, ever the optimist, was telling us it was effectively only half-time and there was just one goal in it. So we actually took the field just one week after being so devastated with a spring in our step, ready to take on the challenge of winning away from home. We were fantastic that night and got back on level terms when I crossed for John Ritchie to take the ball down at the far post, spin and smash the ball home right-footed. This West Ham team was packed with legends. Bobby Moore was the captain, Billy Bonds and Frank Lampard (father of the modern day Frank Lampard) were also in defence, the young Trevor Brooking was in midfield, while on the right wing there was a feller called Harry Redknapp.

As the game fizzed from end to end, very late on Harry became embroiled in a tangle with Gordon Banks and Mike Pejic, who left the ball to each other and Harry nipped in. Gordon brought him down and a penalty was given. Gordon is very sensitive about that moment and will argue until he is blue in the face that it was Pej's fault. Pej maintains to this day that Gordon never called. It's funny when they meet because we always bring up that subject and watch the argument play out yet again. It causes lots of laughter.

It wasn't funny back in December 1971. There were just two minutes to go and it looked as if all our hard work had been undone and our dreams were about to be shattered for the second time in eight months. Geoff Hurst just had to do what he did so well from 12 yards, and had done at the Vic in the first leg, and score from the spot and West Ham, not Stoke, would be heading to Wembley.

This, though, was where Gordon Banks stepped into his own. He is the first to admit that a rush of blood had caused him to fell Redknapp to give away the penalty, so he felt he had to make amends. The tension in the air as Hursty spotted the ball, then walked back outside the penalty area in order to take his usual lengthy run-up and smash the penalty goalward was unbelievable. Most of the West Ham players couldn't look and I saw Micky Bernard turn away. I was struggling to watch this ultimate gunfight at the OK Corral, but I'm so glad I did. Hurst raced in on his run up, causing a huge wind effect as he passed us at thunderous speed, and, catching it perfectly, thumped the ball goalwards. Gordon dived to his right, but the ball flew more centrally and somehow Banksy adjusted himself in mid-air, flung up a strong left hand and fisted the ball over the bar. It was a phenomenal, miraculous save given the pace the ball was travelling and the micro-seconds Gordon had to see the ball and react to make the save. For my money it was a better save even than the one against Pele in 1970 which made him a world-famous household name, but then I would think that being an Irish Stoke City player, wouldn't I?! Hurst smacked that ball so hard I'll maintain to my dying day that when I saw Banksy's hand after the game it had the perfect impression of the word Umbro imprinted upon it by the ball. No word of a lie. Leprechaun's honour.

That unbelievable save not only kept us in the tie, but meant that we felt we could go on and win; this was our year after all. Again the format of the competition saved us. Away goals did not count double, so the fact we'd only won 1-0 at Upton Park but lost 2-1 at home didn't count against us. It was off to Hillsborough, scene of our devastating semi-final failure the previous season against Arsenal, for a replay. We were determined not to have that happen to us again. It turned out to be an absolute turkey of a game and there was barely a shot on target in 120 minutes of football. We were heading for a fourth match in this epic semi-final.

Waddo once again won the toss, although this time he had to choose a neutral venue. So he picked Old Trafford, which had become such a happy hunting ground for us. By this time it was 28 January 1972, seven weeks to the night since we'd kicked off the semi-final at the Vic and this epic tie got the denouement it deserved. It was played in a deluge of a rainstorm with the pitch a sea of mud. It contributed to a pulsating match, which really kicked off after 20 minutes when I was sent through in the middle of the West Ham box, chasing down a through ball which I felt was there to be won. Coming out of his goal was West Ham keeper Bobby Ferguson. We arrived together and in the challenge my right shin connected with Bobby's head, laying him out cold. I had a free kick given against me and the West Ham players went mad, claiming I'd 'done' Bobby, which I got a lot of stick for in the press afterwards too. It certainly wasn't intentional. Goalkeepers are extremely brave to go diving in at the feet of forwards and these kinds of things can happen. Bobby wasn't fit enough to continue and for some strange reason Hammers boss Ron Greenwood chose to put Bobby Moore in goal while Ferguson was fixed up, leaving the Hammers temporarily down to ten men.

Now this was both one of the strangest and weirdest decisions of all time and a fantastic boost for us; the best defender and captain in the world being taken out of his main role and asked to don the gloves. We were simultaneously flabbergasted and delighted at this turn of events. All the more so when the next controversial moment arrived. As I've said the pitch was dreadful and when, a few minutes later, West Ham took a throw-in deep in their own half in the right-back position I chased it up just in case something happened. It did. Young right-back John McDowell tried to pass to Tommy Taylor, his defensive partner, but fluffed his kick, leaving it short. I nipped in and in his panic McDowell brought me down. Penalty. The third spot-kick of the semi-final. Now, we had plenty of experienced penalty takers in our side – Jimmy Greenhoff, John Ritchie, Peter Dobing, myself – but none of them were called Micky Bernard. So quite why Micky ended up taking that spot-kick I have never managed to work out. But for some reason he placed the ball on the spot, ran up and side-footed just about the worst penalty I've ever seen in my life right at Bobby Moore. Thankfully it was so bad and the ball so greasy that Moore couldn't hold it (I think he was so surprised at how terrible it was). The ball rolled back out to Bernard from Moore's save and Micky couldn't miss from five yards to put us 1-0 up.

West Ham, like the class side they were, fought back brilliantly once Ferguson had returned between the sticks and Moore could come out again. First Billy Bonds lashed in a superb effort from distance which deflected in off Denis Smith, then Trevor Brooking slammed a cracking volley into the corner of Banksy's net. West Ham were now ahead 2-1 just before half-time, but there was more swash and buckle to come as almost straight from the kick-off we went forward and Peter Dobing lashed in a goal equally as good as Brooking's from the edge of the box. It was 2-2 at half-time and I remember trudging off with my shirt soaked through and mud everywhere thinking this could end 5-5. It was an attacking, flowing game, with chance after chance. Quite how there was only the one goal in the second half I don't know. Perhaps the heaviness of the pitch, the incessant rain and the sheer length of the tie itself affected us, but there would be one more moment which would settle the contest and once again I was involved.

Jackie Marsh crossed deep from the right-hand side and John Ritchie went up for a header, but the ball was cleared. I saw it dropping towards me out of the glowering Manchester sky, this swirling orb of white, like the moon. It was arcing perfectly for me and I struck it sweetly from 25 yards. It hit a huge patch of mud right in front of Ferguson and, instead of bouncing up as he might have expected it to, zoomed across the surface and into the back of the net under his despairing dive. 3-2 to Stoke. That was the most exuberant I've ever been after scoring. I stood there and waved my arms around like a windmill. Funnily enough, writing about that moment has given me cause to remember how I came up with my goal celebration in the first place, or should I say how it was suggested to me. Huston Spratt was the *Sentinel*'s photographer and once he took me aside after a game and told me that he needed me to be more demonstrative when I scored, so he could get a great picture. 'Come on, give me something to work with, Terry,' said Huston. So I began to put both of my arms aloft when I scored. It was about as demonstrative as I was prepared to get; none of this sliding on my knees, using the corner flag like a microphone or cartwheeling for me. I'd more than likely injure myself trying something idiotic like that! So when that volley went past Bobby Ferguson I really let rip, putting my arms above my head and whirling them around. Rock and roll.

There were still 40 minutes to go, though, so I had no idea at that point that it would prove to be the winner. But it did and when the whistle went hundreds of fans came racing on to the pitch and mobbed me. I remember going up to Gordon and hugging him. He was caked in mud, but he was the most jubilant in that moment that I ever saw him. His face told the story of the realisation that he had helped this great old club to reach Wembley. Banksy had played countless times at the old stadium, including once in a losing FA Cup final for Leicester, but this was special for him as it was for all of us. I was all the happier for him that he'd pulled us out of the fire with that save in the second leg. Certainly, without Banksy's genius we would not have reached the final.

That semi-final was one of the most titanic this country has ever seen or will ever see, certainly the longest. It lasted 50 days, or 420 minutes of game time if you prefer (in between the ties we actually played six league games and one FA Cup tie). During the tie the lead changed hands five times. Amazing.

The city went mad. Everyone wanted to go to Wembley. There were queues round the block at the ticket office. In fact I remember coming out of the social club one frosty Saturday night in February at around 11pm. It was freezing and we stopped and stared as we saw this line of fans setting up camp in readiness for the morning when the cup final tickets went on sale at 9am. There were people in chairs, sleeping bags and wrapped up in five layers of clothing huddling down for the night. The camaraderie in that queue was tremendous and the whole thing struck me as incredible. There we were going home to the warmth of our beds and these supporters were queuing up on a freezing night just so they could secure a precious ticket. These are the kinds of fans who keep the game of football alive up and down the land, not just at Stoke and I was so pleased for them.

Reaching the final changed things for us in that we were asked to do loads more personal appearances and even got the chance to cut a record when Tony Hatch and Jackie Trent, the Potteries' premier pop stars, approached the club with a song they'd written called 'We'll Be With You'. This was to reach number 34 in the charts, although if you listen hard you'll spot that you can't hear my dulcet tones at any point on the record (which you may be glad of). I was away in Ireland when the final recording was made, although I did attend the earlier rehearsals. I did hear that at that final recording Jackie Marsh was told to mime, so at least you can hear me as much as him and I wasn't even there. Of course, the team walks out at the Britannia Stadium today to the strains of 'We'll Be With You', which is a lovely nod to the success of 1972 and I always join in singing it, which is ironic given that I wasn't able to be on the record itself.

My trip to Ireland on that occasion was to play for the Irish national team (of which more later), but it does remind me of the many trips I and the family made back to Ireland to take a break from top level football, particularly at the end of a season. We would head down south to a place called Dunhill which is right in the south-east of the country, near Waterford. It became a place we would visit regularly and spend many happy days. I first visited Dunhill in 1969 after a neighbour of mine, Bunny Fullam, a famous League of Ireland full-back in the 1950s and

60s, who travelled regularly down to Dunhill, told me about it. He took me down first of all and in those days before motorways the journey should have taken about three hours, but the way Bunny drove took twice as long, although as one of life's great characters Bunny made the journey endlessly entertaining. The village was tiny, consisting of one pub and a shop (both owned by local character Jim Hamey), a school and the village hall; perfect if you want peace and quiet, which I did. In Dublin I was known so if I had spent all of my eight-week summer break there it would have been a whirlwind of meeting up with people. Down in Dunhill was hurling country. They had no idea about football, especially the English First Division, so the locals didn't have a clue who I was or what I did, which was great.

Life was laid-back and relaxing, if a little spartan. That first year my sleeping quarters were simply a mattress on the floor of the attic of the pub. Hardly the Burj Khalifa in Dubai! But I loved it. Jim hardly spoke and he had a housekeeper, Mary O'Brien, who looked after everything for him. Mary lived in a little picture postcard cottage next door to the pub. Jim eventually came to his senses, realised what a gem Mary was and they married in the early 1970s. Perhaps not surprisingly in such a community, life revolved around the pub. Jim was a great organiser and every night there was some competition or other; darts, cards, music – the pub was packed out. People would even come down from Waterford city to enjoy the craic. They aren't the only outsiders to enjoy Dunhill's hospitality. Dunhill might have been a sleepy little village, but back in 1963, when American President John F. Kennedy and his wife Jackie visited Ireland, the First Lady, for some reason, ended up spending an evening in Dunhill, being entertained by the local drama group. There's photographic evidence to prove it!

There were plenty of other characters in Dunhill, but one who will live long in my memory was Willie Doyle. For those of you who watched ITV's Heartbeat in the 1990s Willie was a bit like the character Claude Greengrass, played by Bill Maynard. Having met Willie in Jim's pub where he would often hold court all evening, never having to stand a round himself, I was fascinated by this village celebrity so I went to see him and found that he lived in a ramshackle old cottage with a menagerie of animals. There were old mangles lying around and bicycle frames hanging on the wall. It was a treasure trove of junk. He was incredibly clever in so many ways. I always remember him pontificating about wealth one night and he said something along the lines of 'the millionaire gets there by car, the average man by train and the poor man by foot, but they all get there in the end.' You'll find a picture of Willie, holding one of his many animals, in a photograph in the photo section of the book. He was one in a million.

Amazingly, Jim never drank in his own pub. That takes some doing for an Irishman! This meant we had to roam elsewhere and we had a few wild nights in pubs out in the countryside. We had such a good time that I went on and on about it when I got back to Stoke and the following year Josh Mahoney came with me to Dunhill. We spent about five weeks just lazing about. It was heavenly. Jim was a big racing man, so we would head off for a day at the races, visiting courses across the midlands of Ireland and the west coast. Of course we got to know pretty much everyone in the village and as they came to understand what we did they would follow our progress at Stoke, so, by the time 1972 came around, about 25 members of the Dunhill Stoke City Supporters' Club came over to watch the second replay of the semi-final at Old Trafford, the first live football match most had ever seen. In fact it was the first time most had been out of Ireland. They drank Manchester dry on that famous night. Needless to say they returned to the UK to attend the final and that was even better.

I introduced my parents Jack and Esther to Dunhill early on and my brothers and sisters also came to love the place, acclimatising easily to the slow pace of life. We went back pretty much every year for most of the summer and our three girls have fond memories of the place, while many of my nephews and nieces have had the same wonderful experience. I will be taking the opportunity to head back to Dunhill to show off my book and relive those great days and can't wait to get back. It was a fantastic place to relax away from the pressures of football.

We warmed up the week before the final with a 4-1 victory over Hull City in front of almost 35,000 at the Vic to reach the FA Cup quarter-final once again. Our confidence was so high we won very comfortably. I scored, as did John Ritchie and Jimmy G grabbed two. There was never any danger of Hull causing us the kind of problems they had the previous season at Boothferry Park. Then, to prepare for Wembley, we headed down to the capital and spent almost the entire week at the Selsdon Park Hotel in quiet, leafy Surrey, rather than at the Russell Hotel which was right in the centre of London. I never had any nerves in the build-up to the big occasions, quite the opposite in fact. We were all chomping at the bit to get out there and play in this showpiece cup final at Wembley. We couldn't wait. Our training was sharp, especially the five-a-sides. We were quite relaxed and on the Wednesday night Waddo took us out to a party at Tony Hatch and Jackie Trent's mansion, packed with pop stars and nubile young things. But Waddo trusted us not to have too much to drink or get up to anything which would upset things. We'd all been through far too much together to risk that. Waddo knew there wouldn't be any abuse of his trust. But it is remarkable to think that just three days before the most important game in Stoke City's history we hit a party full of starlets. It did relieve the boredom of sitting around the hotel, which would really have grated otherwise and we emerged unscathed that night. We also went to the cinema one evening to while away the time. It was all quite relaxed and as the weekend drew closer we began to focus on the game.

Chelsea, as favourites, might have felt a bit more pressure. The competition was only just 12 years old that season and it was just beginning to take on significance. When Stoke had reached the final in 1964, losing to Leicester City 4-3 on aggregate, the two legs were played on each of the clubs' grounds. The final had been moved to a one-off event at Wembley in 1967, so was still relatively fresh, but there was no doubt that this cup was one worth winning. Everyone was taking it seriously. Chelsea had lifted the trophy in 1965 and had battled past Spurs in the semi-final this time round 5-4 on aggregate. This Chelsea team, featuring the likes of Hudson, Cooke, Bonetti, Harris, Webb and Osgood had won the FA Cup in 1970 and then the European Cup Winners' Cup the following season.

On the four weekends leading up to the game I'd been asked by the *Sunday Mirror* to contribute an article a week to the paper by way of a preview. I worked with a journalist called Vince

Wilson and the first three pieces were all fairly anodyne, about my childhood in Dublin and how I joined Stoke. For the last one Vince asked me to come up with something a bit more sensational, even if I had to make it up (perish the thought, dear reader). So I came up with the idea of Mr X – who was trailed as the one player at Chelsea who I absolutely despised. The headline was 'Conroy can't wait to see the anguish on Mr X's face when he picks up his loser's medal'. Now, I have never before revealed who my mystery Mr X was, but I can tell you now that I was thinking of their talismanic centre-forward Peter Osgood. I felt he was arrogant and cocky and in the article I went on and on about how I couldn't wait to see Mr X suffer. I got £1,000 for those articles, but that went straight into the players' pool, which was then split evenly between us afterwards, including our royalties from our chart success.

I never thought anything more of the Mr X thing as it was just a bit of harmless paper talk, but come the day of the game, as we stood in the tunnel, I was berated by various Chelsea players – for example I knew John Dempsey and Paddy Mulligan very well through playing for the Republic of Ireland with them – asking me who Mr X was. They'd all read the article and had been fretting all week about which one of them was this hated, despised figure. That cracked me up. I had really just concocted this whole Mr X thing for the papers and here they were worrying about it. They were even running a book among themselves on who it might be, although I never told them. It just shows you the power of the press.

There were 97,852 people at Wembley on 4 March 1972, the largest crowd ever to watch Stoke City play. We walked out to fulfil both our dreams and those of our fans. We might have been the underdogs, but we fancied our chances, even though we'd actually lost our last seven matches against Chelsea in all competitions.

The game couldn't have started better. Just four minutes had gone when we won a throw deep on the left-hand side, right down by the corner flag. Peter Dobing could lob the ball a reasonable distance, although he was no Rory Delap. He threw the ball as far as the edge of the six-yard box but Peter Bonetti fisted it away. It was turned straight back in by Eastham, though, and before Bonetti could really recover he was having to throw himself at the feet of Denis Smith to smother a shot and get straight up to block from Greenhoff. From that save the ball lobbed up perfectly towards me. I threw my head at it about 15 yards out and watched as it looped into the unguarded net. Then I leapt as high as my legs would take me into the air in celebration (I did have most of my cartilages then). It may be the most important goal I ever scored in my career, but to be honest it really wasn't anything to shout about. I just threw my head at a loose ball and it lobbed in. Right place, right time and I knew that it was a crucial way to begin such a vital game.

In fact when I looked up at the scoreboard, which had only just been introduced at Wembley then, I saw the words 'Conroy 4'. That stunned me. I had scored at Wembley. My name was literally up in lights, my dream utterly fulfilled. Roy of the Rovers stuff. The only problem was we had almost the whole game still left to play. I was in something of a daze for quite a few minutes after that and only came round when Jackie Marsh literally shook me out of it; 'TC, wake up and get your tackles in,' or words to that effect. My concentration had gone for those few minutes, transfixed by that scoreboard.

That final was tough to play in. The Wembley pitch sapped the strength out of your legs and the tackles were really flying in. Some of the challenges Mike Pejic put in were X-rated and he got booked quite early on, as did Alan Bloor. Osgood could put himself about a bit and he too got booked for flattening Denis Smith, which was always a brave thing to do. He then left one in on me as well and I squared up to him. Now, this wasn't very bright on my part as Ossie could handle himself and I couldn't. I was just enraged by his challenge and in that moment I was glad that I'd nominated him as my Mr X. I will say, though, that many years later when Peter was a guest of honour at a function at the Britannia Stadium which I hosted, he proved to be a charming, accommodating and relaxed gentleman, so maybe it was only in the heat of battle he showed these tendencies.

We had players who could mix it too and one Pejic tackle led to Paddy Mulligan getting injured and that played into our hands. Dave Sexton shuffled his back four and as soon as I saw that they'd moved Peter Houseman, a winger, to right-back I went over to our left wing to attack him. We had licence to do that ourselves in those days, so I did. Despite Chelsea equalising just before half-time through a scrappy Osgood goal, which he actually managed to score while lying prone on the ground – some achievement by Mr X – we still fancied ourselves. The beauty about our dressing room was we wouldn't shout and scream and lay blame on each other. We stood together as a team and found a way to win. Waddo, positive as ever, just told us to go out and play as well as we had in the first half. So we did. We had a goal disallowed and John Ritchie also had a header cleared off the line.

The winner came in the 73rd minute and it was such a great goal. We'd played keep-ball in the centre of the park for a few moments before Peter Dobing swung a lovely ball out to me in acres of space on the left. Houseman had gone walkabout, so I was up against David Webb, one of the centre-halves, who'd come out to meet me. I beat him on the outside and chipped to the far post, where I knew Big John was waiting. And so he was. John nodded down for an unmarked Jimmy Greenhoff to hit a peach of a volley. Somehow Bonetti saved it, but only pushed it out about five yards from goal. The two old-stagers Dobing and Eastham raced in to prod home, George belying his age to just nip in ahead and lift the ball over the despairing dive of Bonetti to put us ahead and become the oldest scorer of a winning goal in a Wembley cup final, aged 35, to boot.

That goal was perfect as far as I am concerned. Even though I don't sit and watch the League Cup Final on DVD often myself I can still picture it clear as day. Get the ball to the wide man (me), who beats his defender, hits the byline and crosses deep to the big man (Ritchie) to knock down for the little man (Greenhoff) to shoot. The fact that Bonetti saved, but two of our players reacted quickest to scrap over who was going to score, just put the icing on the cake as far as I was concerned. That goal says everything about what we were trying to do as a team. It was a great way to win the final.

There were still 17 minutes remaining, so it wasn't quite all over yet. It was heavy going as Chelsea put us under a lot of pressure, although they didn't create a clear-cut chance. I was called upon to make a lot of runs down towards the corner flag to waste time and try to keep the ball there, away from danger, so I ran myself into the ground for the cause. There was one heart-stopping moment, though, when Mick Bernard left a backpass short in the very last minute and Banksy charged out to foil Chris Garland, taking man and ball simultaneously. It was another tremendous contribution to our cause by the England custodian. When the whistle went I just felt relief flood through me. We'd won. I sat down on the turf and thought, 'Thank God I don't have to run anymore.' Then a few seconds later the adrenaline kicked in. We'd won – wahey! I was suddenly cock-a-hoop, up and around and jigging all over the place like an Irish Nobby Stiles on our lap of honour.

By the time we'd got off the pitch after having a great time with the wildly exuberant fans for a long spell after the game I leaped into the bath only to be interrupted mid-cleanse by a man in a sheepskin coat carrying a microphone – reporter Brian Moore, who proceeded to interview me while I still continued to soap myself and sup champagne from the famous three-handled cup. It is one of the more bizarre and farcical moments from my career. That it is recorded for posterity on YouTube only serves to embarrass me and give my kids and grandchildren reason to play it over and over again. First off Brian asked me the usual question of how I felt after winning. I came up with the following immortal response, 'Fabulous, Brian. It's proved a lot of people wrong as well, so we're glad about that.' Then when he asked me about George Eastham, I'd obviously warmed up a bit and replied, 'He's fantastic for a feller of 45, isn't he. He keeps telling everyone he's 35, but really he's 45.' Finally, I signed off when asked if we were going to have fun tonight with, 'Oh absolutely, and tomorrow and Monday and Tuesday.'

In his interview Waddo was far more erudite and was quick to point out that no one could say anymore that Stoke had won nothing in their history. He'd managed to lay that ghost to rest.

That evening's celebrations took place at the Russell Hotel, our London home. It was a fabulous night, with a banquet with our wives and families and a disco until late, although the achievement didn't really hit home until the following day when we headed back to Stoke-on-Trent. We returned on the train, but unbeknownst to us Waddo had arranged for us to get off at Barlaston to the south of the city and board an open-top bus (albeit one of the most ancient charabancs you've ever seen) and tour through the city to the King's Hall in Stoke, where a stage was set up in front of thousands of waiting fans eager to celebrate the first trophy in Stoke City's history. What a fabulous afternoon that was, edging past tumultuous crowds through Meir standing next to Denis Smith and seeing the ultimate hardman go misty-eyed as the enormity of what he had been part of achieving sank in as he passed his boyhood home. It had a huge impact on Jackie, Pej and Bluto too; the four local lads were beside themselves with the realisation of what they had done. There were people everywhere, hanging off lampposts and out of windows as we toured through Longton and Fenton and up to Stoke. We took turns to hold up the cup to huge cheers from the crowds. It was fantastic, a truly wonderful experience.

That was pretty much the end of the season for me as I got injured (another cartilage problem) against Leeds before the next big game, the FA Cup semi-final, again against Arsenal, but this time at Villa Park. Defeat after a replay again made us reflect on having finally tasted success and enjoy the glory of winning at Wembley all the more. Even to this day people come up to me and tell me that they were there and how it meant so much to them and that's great to hear. To have brought that amount of joy into people's lives is a wonderful thing, especially as the people of Stoke-on-Trent had been starved of success for decades. I actually look upon it now as a success more for the club and the city and its wonderful people than as a personal achievement, even though I did score one of the goals.

To complete a fantastic year, I got married on 13 May. So I'd scored a goal in a winning Wembley final and got hitched. Could life get any better?

8

Land of Smoke and Glory

ACTUALLY I haven't been totally honest with you. That fairy story of 1972 was interrupted by the total nightmare that was my wedding to Sue. Not that the act of getting married was the nightmare, you understand, but as this tale unfolds you'll understand why Sue and I cannot think of what should have been the happiest day of our lives without a wry smile, even though it is now 43 years later.

When we planned our wedding for Saturday 13 May 1972, the weekend after the end of the 1971/72 season, we didn't have many dates available to us. Sue's mother Eileen was worried about us getting wed on that date as she had always been quite superstitious and she was worried something bad would happen. Looking back now, I suppose I should have taken more notice of her fears, but I'm not at all superstitious. I didn't believe in all that palaver about black cats and walking under ladders. What could possibly go wrong on a wedding day? The date was booked six months in advance and all the usual chats with the priest went accordingly. We were excited about the forthcoming festivities as were all our family and friends.

Then the nightmare began. I was seriously injured just three weeks before the big day; a cartilage was torn and needed removing. Knee trouble was to develop into a constant theme throughout my career. On this occasion I was sent to Coventry. No, I don't mean nobody would talk to me, although Sue wasn't best pleased at this turn of events. Coventry City FC's medical man was Tom Sargent, who was a specialist in knees. When I first met Tom I told him I was due to be married soon and he assured me that he would guarantee I would turn up on the day. Thinking back, Tom was rather careful with his words as he never mentioned exactly what state I'd actually be in! In those days the operation was a huge one. The knee joint was opened and the full cartilage was removed. Nowadays, keyhole surgery does the job in quick time and you are back playing within weeks. Then, it took anything from four to six months to recover.

At the same time, I had a bed-mate, who was also having his cartilage removed – none other than my best friend, Josh Mahoney. So here we both were post-op, laid up. To make it worse Josh was one of my groomsmen. Neither of us could walk and Sue was now getting very concerned. Her mother was saluting every magpie she saw and throwing tonnes of salt over her shoulder. It may have helped my younger brother Paul, who was my best man. Luckily he didn't suffer from bad knees and so was able to give me plenty of support and encouragement as I began the long road to recovery.

Josh and I had our stitches removed the day before the wedding. Tom Sargent insisted on seeing us using our crutches before he released us the night before the big day so we hobbled around the ward putting on our bravest faces, even though we both still felt pretty terrible. It was close, but he allowed us out. Phew, we'd just about squeaked home, but you can imagine the scene at the Church of our Lady in Chains in Hartshill on that Saturday in May 1972. We had tried to keep the day a secret, but crowds turned up to see us and show their affection. That was lovely, but what they witnessed probably wasn't the picture perfect wedding that they were expecting.

Josh and I hobbled into the church, both leaning heavily on our crutches, to great amusement all round. I'm sure it wasn't what Sue had imagined for her wedding day either. It certainly wasn't how I had envisaged mine!

The wedding ceremony itself went well and the hours flew by until it was time for the happy couple (one in constant pain) to depart for the honeymoon destination in Tenerife. That's when the nightmare got even worse. I had received a bang on my bad leg during the festivities (if you're reading this Tom, I wasn't dancing, honest…). It really was giving me grief. However, I felt that, once we were jet-bound, things would settle down. Sue took on the task of driving from Stoke all the way to Gatwick airport where we were to stay before flying out on holiday the following morning. She had only just passed her driving test two weeks previously so was somewhat nervous and, don't forget, had just got married so really shouldn't have had to drive at the end of such a massive day in her life. We had a red MGB GT, a fantastic two-seater, but the wrong car if you need plenty of room for luggage and a leg which cannot bend, as I had.

We set off at 6pm to the cheers of all our family and friends. However, disaster struck. Nearing Coventry, the car started to overheat and it stopped in the middle of nowhere. I was helpless as I couldn't move, never mind walk, so Sue had to go and get help. She walked about half a mile to find a farmhouse from which she rang the AA, who were on the scene pretty quickly and got us underway again. It had been a long day and we were now really behind schedule. On nearing the hotel, beside Gatwick, Sue was going through traffic lights just as they changed to red. Fatigue had set in and she was out on her feet. This was about 3am and, typically, lurking in a layby was a police car, which proceeded to pull us in. Trying to explain everything that had happened would have taken hours. I must say the officer was most sympathetic and let Sue off the very minor offence, but commented that our tax disc had expired on 30 April. As it was well after midnight it was 14 May and in those days motorists were given 14 days to renew their tax. We were just within that fortnight's grace. Phew. A lucky escape? Just about.

I was in so much pain that sleep was out of the question. Next morning, Sue debated whether we should even fly to Tenerife, which was the destination for our honeymoon. I felt that my knee would settle down and the warmer weather would be beneficial, so we pressed on. I was given preferential treatment on embarking and disembarking, but my knee was still hurting, so on arrival in Tenerife I enquired about seeing a doctor. The language barrier proved a problem and I had difficulty explaining to the doctor that I was a professional footballer and so this was my livelihood we were talking about. Fluid on my knee was the cause of the pain. I wanted an injection to ease things. I didn't think it would hurt or cause me harm, but I was wary of receiving the wrong treatment and ending my career. If that happened what would the club do, how would they feel?

There was some confusion, but before I knew it I was dropping my trousers and bending over. I fainted when the jab went deep into my buttocks. Luckily there were some friends we had met on the flight over, who were on hand to pick me up and take me to my room. This really was the stuff nightmares are made of.

That evening we decided to return home as the pain in my knee remained constant, despite the treatment. Sue telephoned Tony Waddington, who assured her that he would sort everything out when we arrived back in the UK. We flew back to Heathrow at around lunchtime the next day as they were the only flights we could get. We had flown from Gatwick, so our car was nowhere near where we landed. Never fear, Waddo was on hand to help. He had arranged for a chauffeur-driven car to collect us on arrival and so we were greeted by our driver holding up a placard with our names on it. Typically for Waddo it turned out not to be just any old car. We found ourselves getting into this beautiful Rolls-Royce, with bundles of leg room. I started to feel better already. What an incredible man Tony Waddington was.

We were prepared for the journey of 150 miles, but you wouldn't believe what happened next. The Roller overheated just past Watford, talk about luck of the Irish. Whoever invented that saying needs his head examining. At least on this occasion. It turned out that the car was only ever used on short journeys around London and had never actually travelled long distances. Luckily for us, it just required topping up with water, and we were on our way, eventually reaching home at 1am. I was much happier now and the following day I received another jab. This time it was one of our club doctors, Sandy Clubb, a Scotsman, who drained the fluid from my knee and finally put me on the road to recovery. Sandy was a gynaecologist and I always used to say he was more familiar with the players' wives than with the players themselves, having delivered many of our babies. I recovered well enough from the injury to come back into the team at the end of August 1972.

One final sting in this extraordinary marital tale was that, amid all the wedding preparations and with me being in hospital recovering from my operation, Sue had forgotten to get holiday insurance. So what ended up being a day out in Tenerife cost me £300, a fortune in those days; at least two weeks' wages. But you know what? It was cheap at half the price. These days I just laugh about it and take solace in the fact that many writers would be paid a mint to invent a story like that. One thing is for sure, the whole malarkey certainly made for a wedding Sue and I could never forget.

Winning the League Cup at Wembley wasn't just a history-making moment in the sense that we got to bring home the club's first piece of major silverware and lay to bed once and for all that 'you've never won anything' moniker, but it also meant Stoke City had qualified for Europe. We were to play in the UEFA Cup and were among the favourites, although the first-round draw wasn't kind to us. There was no seeding in those days as there is now and we were pitched against the strong German side Kaiserslautern, when we could easily have got US Rumelange, the Liechtenstein entrants who got hammered 21-0 by Feyenoord over two legs that season.

In the 59th minute of the home leg I scored Stoke's first goal in European competition, which was quickly followed by one from Geoff Hurst, who had signed for the club for £80,000 in the summer of 1972 and said he was fed up with playing against Gordon Banks and Denis Smith. John Ritchie scored our third, but the visitors got one back to make the final score 3-1. We felt confident of progressing as we travelled over to Germany, but the return leg proved to be a sorry tale of two substitutes as far as we were concerned. One, Lothar Huber, came on early on for the Germans due to injury and scored the opening goal in the 23rd minute. John Ritchie came on for us with ten minutes left and was sent off within ten seconds of entering the pitch. We were already 3-0 down by then and on our way out so frustration was kicking in. John's temper was already at boiling point and got the better of him when Yugoslav midfielder Idriz Hosic shoved him as they lined up waiting for a free kick to be delivered. Big John retaliated by whacking Hosic one and saw red. We eventually lost 4-0 and our brief flirtation with Europe was over.

The arrival of England's hat-trick hero from the 1966 World Cup Final meant that we now had Gordon Banks and Geoff Hurst in our team. For once Stoke-on-Trent was being viewed as a glamorous place to be. But having two World Cup-winning icons sadly wasn't to last too long. In October 1972 we played a controversial game at Liverpool, which we lost 2-1. Referee Roger Kirkpatrick had enraged Banksy, who lost his rag for one of the few times in his career. So did I. I was mostly fairly happy-go-lucky on the pitch, but this day Kirkpatrick was annoying me intensely, especially as the game wore on. The Kop had this incredible ability to sway referees as they put so much pressure on them and you always knew that Liverpool were going to be given something. It was a cast-iron certainty. Now you may not believe this when I tell you, but it is true. I was reading Charles Dickens novels at the time (honestly, I was) and had recently watched the film version of one of my favourites, *The Pickwick Papers*. In a rash moment during the game I called Kirkpatrick 'Pickwick', which he didn't take kindly to and booked me. So I suppose I can claim to have engendered one of the most literary cautions English football has ever seen.

This particular day a series of Kirkpatrick's decisions got under our skin, but the final straw was a ridiculous free kick he gave to Liverpool in the last ten minutes as they attacked the baying Kop. Banksy was booked for arguing about the decision and continued to argue all the way off the pitch as Liverpool scored the winning goal from that set piece. He was devastated at having lost the game as he'd performed miracles and was in the form of his life.

At that time Gordon lived out at Ashley on the border of Staffordshire and Shropshire and I lived nearby in a town called Loggerheads. The morning following the defeat at Liverpool, Sunday 22 October, Gordon was on his way in to the club to get some massage treatment, as he often needed to the day after games as he was one of the elder statesmen of the side. As he tried to overtake the car in front of him on the approach to a notorious bend on the road into Stoke he lost control and crashed, rolling his car into the roadside ditch.

I was on my way with Sue to see her parents in Trentham and we passed by Banksy's car – a sponsored 1970 World Cup Ford Cortina – lying nose down in the ditch, all smashed up. We didn't know the extent of the damage to him as he'd already left the scene when we passed, but when the story came on the news that afternoon the extent of his injuries became apparent. Gordon had lost the sight in one eye. You immediately knew that was the end of his career. It was devastating for us. We lost our rock, the man who saved us week in and week out. Gordon was only 32 years of age and given that goalkeepers can go on for ever he probably lost out on anywhere between six and ten further years of a career at the very top. His loss had a huge effect on us both on the pitch and off it. Gordon had been at the heart of everything. He was one of the reasons why the bond between us was so strong. As a group, eight or nine couples would go out together, with our wives and families, to see shows and the like. He was also the consummate professional who was an incredibly vocal organiser. We missed that. Things would never quite be the same again.

But life goes on and the next fixture, ironically against Gordon's first club Leicester City, came around the following Saturday. As professionals you owe your club and its fans to put tragic events like this behind you and concentrate on the 90 minutes ahead. We won the game 1-0. It wasn't a great performance, but it was a result which did Gordon proud, especially the clean sheet. The biggest problem which faced the manager was that we'd been on an upward curve, but this was clearly a setback. John Farmer, an England under-23 international and also a very good basketball player, took on the mantle of replacing the world's best goalkeeper and did well, but he was prone to occasional mistakes. This meant that Waddo was never really convinced that John was the answer, certainly when he was clearly going to be compared with the great man whose gloves he was trying to fill. Consequently Waddo was always on the lookout for a new signing. He wanted Scottish international Bobby Clark from Aberdeen, but didn't manage to prise him away from the Dons. Instead he stuck with Farmer for now and brought in Mike McDonald from Clydebank as backup, but Mike only managed nine appearances in two years. Was this a conundrum which could ever be solved? How do you replace the world's best goalkeeper, a talisman who also acted as a magnet for good players to join the club?

We finished 1972/73 in 15th position in the First Division, which wasn't progress, and began the following season still in the doldrums. This was a major challenge for Tony Waddington and he began to redress the balance by pulling off one of the most successful signings in the club's history in January 1974, splashing out a club record £240,000 on the signing of midfielder Alan Hudson from Chelsea. It really was quite a coup. Huddy was the Boy Wonder, Chelsea's Golden Child, so for Waddo to sign him was remarkable. He had been a young star ever since he'd got into their side aged 18 and was still only 22. Chelsea had won the FA Cup and European Cup Winners' Cup and were one of the sides to beat in that period. Now here we were signing one of their biggest stars because he had fallen out with manager Dave Sexton. Their loss. Definitely our gain.

This transfer and those which followed, including Geoff Salmons's £160,000 arrival from Sheffield United in the summer of 1974, showed the amazing relationship Tony had with chairman Albert Henshall. They got on so well, just like Peter Coates and Tony Pulis did as the club rose back into the Premier League limelight from 2006 onwards. Sometimes Waddo would sign a player and then tell the board. You can't get away with signing players without telling the board these days, but back then Stoke's board loved the success and lapped up the attention it got them. Paying record fees was big news for our club. It got them column inches and fed their egos. The problems would come when it began to go wrong, but that's another story.

Hudson's arrival began everything, galvanising the team and shaking us awake from the slumbers which had followed the success of 1972 and the loss of Gordon Banks.

We still looked upon our club as relatively small. We were very ambitious, but we knew we weren't Manchester United or Liverpool. So this was a huge step for Stoke, attracting some of the game's best players. Somehow Waddo managed to sell the industrial, grimy landscape of the city of Stoke-on-Trent to the likes of Hudson and the others who followed. Their pedigree was such that they could have the pick of clubs and yet here they were with us. The boost was incredible.

Ours was a friendly, happy club, so we welcomed this brash cockney into our midst. The only player who had an issue with it was Mike Pejic, who thought that the club was making a mistake, but that was the rebellious side of Pej. He thought that Waddo was putting all his eggs into one basket and that the money could have been spent on several players. He also had a problem with the change in tactical emphasis Huddy's signing brought too, as he dropped deep to pick up the ball from the defence to start attacks. At first Pej wouldn't give him the ball. He was confident in his own ability to spark the creation of an attacking move. He wanted Huddy to be 20 or 30 yards further up the pitch and kept saying he should be receiving the ball there rather than coming so deep to collect and then be faced with an entire team to get past. Pej objected to Huddy being the playmaker as he felt it would be too easy to stop if it became so obvious that we were always going that way and he felt individuals' abilities were being short-changed by subjugating their own creativity. We had always had very much a team ethic and he felt that Huddy changed that, which was true to an extent. This was no reflection on Huddy himself, as it was just another example of Pej's battle with the management. He was always questioning why we were doing a particular thing.

As for the rest of us, we were delighted to have such a great talent with us. We were a very social bunch and got on extremely well. We welcomed all the new players into our dressing room as we knew it meant we had a great chance of winning something. We were on the up and Pej soon realised that Huddy brought a new dynamic to the team. He would collect the ball and then play quick one-twos with Jackie Marsh or Jimmy G to get us up the pitch. It helped that Huddy bought in to the manager and us as a team very quickly. Huddy and Jimmy G had an uncanny relationship. It was an incredible thing to see, so natural. They never really had to work on it. It was telepathic. Huddy had this incredible ability to be looking straight at you and then play the ball at 90 degrees to Jimmy, who would control it on either left or right foot equally sublimely and then return it to Huddy who had made a run forward. They could find each other wherever they were on the pitch. The really odd thing was that socially they were a million miles apart. After a game Jimmy would go to Alan and find out where he was going for his night out. If Alan said, 'I'm going to Hanley,' then Jimmy would be as far away from Hanley as he could possibly get. Generally in a completely different county if he could be. We used to laugh about that! They did not go together socially at all, but on the pitch their bond was incredible.

Huddy made an immediate impact on his debut at home against Liverpool and then also sparked a famous comeback as we turned a 2-0 first-half deficit into a 3-2 victory over eventual champions Leeds United in February 1974. I didn't play in that game, although I've since met countless fans who insist that I did. I do remember playing football that day, but it was actually at Aston Villa in the reserves, making a comeback from yet another cartilage operation. So I didn't even witness Stoke ending Leeds' attempt to break the record for longest unbeaten run from the start of the season in their 29th game.

Huddy was a level above everybody else at times. There was a banner I remember which appeared on the Boothen End which read 'Alan Hudson walks on water'. It was meant to be figurative, but he literally did seem to float across the boggy mud of the Victoria Ground at times. Some of the stuff the team played was just fantastic to watch. I was out injured for much of the first half of the following 1974/75 season and I loved watching us, especially with Geoff Salmons coming in off the wing and getting balls into the box. Waddo was purring about how we were playing. We went on a great run, winning nine games out of 18 with Hudson in the side, and finished fifth in 1973/74, which set us up beautifully for a great season in 1974/75. Our success was based on the fact that the manager trusted us to go out and play. We played off-the-cuff, cavalier football. Team talks, if we had them at all, were cursory. Waddo wasn't a great rabble-rousing speechmaker. He preferred to plan out any tactics on the Thursday before Saturday's game. These sessions would normally be more focused on how we were going to play than how the opposition would, or how we were going to stop them.

Occasionally this irked Mike Pejic, who wanted to focus more on how to deal with opponents' strengths. He always felt there was a lack of detail put into that side of planning. The rest of us were just revelling in the freedom we were given to get on and play the game. One thing that did cause confusion was Waddo's legendary ability to forget the name of just about every high profile footballer we faced. We'd always be being told to watch out for 'Mi'laddo'. That was his word. Of course some of the time we could work out who he was talking about; it might be Billy Bremner or Paddy Crerand. But often we hadn't a clue. Still, that didn't encumber us at all. Waddo trusted us to deliver. It's that simple. He put the team together and let us get on with it. It was then up to you to play well enough for him to select you the following week. There was no 20-page dossier on your opponent telling you what he'd had for breakfast or anything like that, which the likes of Leeds were being given by Don Revie to read in bed the night before a game. I didn't even know what the word dossier meant, let alone how to try to pronounce it.

Just occasionally Waddo would want a man-marking job done and that would be Josh Mahoney or Eric Skeels's job, while the rest of us could get on and play. This could have resulted in us being lazy, but in fact we knew how to play winning football. We attacked as a team and then when we lost the ball we got back and defended as a team. But generally Waddo didn't like to place restrictions on us, which we knew coaches such as Malcolm Allison at Manchester City and Dave Sexton at Chelsea were doing with their teams, insisting on a more formulaic approach, which of course has become the norm in the modern game. For example, Waddo would never tell us to keep it tight for the first 20 minutes. He'd just let us get on with it, keeping it simple with the defence winning the ball and playing it into one of the midfielders who would set the attack going and things would develop from there. The shackles were off in our day, whereas the modern-day players have to stick to the team plan. It's as much about preventing the opposition from playing as it is playing yourself today. We didn't have any such restrictions and this was the basis of our success.

I was now 26 and playing as well as any winger in the top flight. I was very much a marked man, which meant the club received some approaches from other clubs wanting to buy me. I know Bill Shankly and then Bob Paisley both wanted to take me to

Liverpool, but life was so different then. I had no desire to leave Stoke. I'd settled so well in the area, was married to a local lass and had a young family. Plus the decision wasn't down to me. We had nowhere near the freedom of contract or bargaining power the modern player has. I couldn't knock on Waddo's door and demand a move. It would have been embarrassing and also would have felt like selling my mates out. I could never have done that. Even if I had, Waddo had such a way about him that if I'd gone in to see him full of fire and brimstone demanding a move I probably would have come out apologising! Generally Waddo rejected the overtures at source and I never knew about them until much later.

I had no desire to leave Stoke, only to win more trophies with the club. Because I was deemed a threat to opponents, this also meant heavy tackles flying in and I got badly injured again in the 1973/74 season, so played only a handful of games. The operation to remove my third cartilage was undertaken by a surgeon called Mr Glass in St Joseph's Hospital in Manchester. He'd been recommended by Matt Busby, who was a big pal of Tony Waddington, and had just operated on Denis Law's knees. Matt and Tony would often holiday together in the summer down in the south of France and avail themselves of United chairman Louis Edwards's yacht which was moored there. That relationship was why Waddo, in the early days, had been able to secure the likes of Dennis Viollet, Maurice Setters and David Herd from United when Matt had finished with them. They were still very good players when they came to Stoke, albeit in the twilight of their careers. Waddo had played for Manchester United as a lad, although his career was ended by a combination of the war and knee injuries, so he was always keen to get the best treatment for his players. For some reason, though, after the operation my knee still felt very painful. A lad called John Fitzpatrick, who played for United, also had his cartilage operated on the same day as me and he came bounding into my room the next morning saying, 'Come on, there's nothing wrong with you, get up.' He was clearly fit and well. I, on the other hand, was really struggling. Even after my stitches were taken out I felt my knee lock up again. It almost felt as if the cartilage hadn't been removed. I then learned that Denis Law was having even worse knee problems following his op and it transpired that John Fitzpatrick's career ended after his operation as he never fully recovered.

I eventually got fit again, but I was never quite the same. Fast forward ten years or so to when I was training with Crewe Alexandra and my knee locked up. It was stuck at 90 degrees. I went to see a specialist who said to me, 'If I didn't know any better, Terry, I'd say you have a cartilage problem.' But we knew this couldn't be the case as I'd had all four removed by then. It turned out, though, that Mr Glass hadn't done the job properly and when my knee was opened up there was a piece of floating cartilage which had been left in there. The specialist gave me this cartilage, saying, 'There you go, Terry. There's your problem.' I've still got it at home. It looks like a bit of orange peel. I call it my fifth cartilage, so I can say in all honesty that I have had all five of my cartilages removed. There's a record which even superman Denis Smith can't beat!

Undoubtedly the injuries and that knee problem in particular did slow me down. I'd been playing at 70 or 80 per cent fitness. We didn't have big squads in those days, so Waddo would be keen for me to play if I possibly could. If only that operation had been done correctly in 1974 I could have had an even better last few years of my career, but that's life, I suppose.

We started the 1974/75 season well, only losing one of the first seven games. This took us into our next foray into European competition in fine fettle. We had been drawn against Dutch giants Ajax in the first round of the UEFA Cup. George Eastham was being groomed by Waddo as his successor, so he was sent over to Amsterdam to watch our opponents play the weekend before we were due to host them the following Wednesday, but due to fog at the airport he didn't travel and we had no report on how the Dutchmen played at all. Pej was livid about this. He felt it was utterly unprofessional and that we should have had them watched several times as soon as the draw was made. Ajax played the offside trap in the first leg at the Vic and it took us the whole first half to get to grips with it, getting constantly caught offside. By this time we were 1-0 down to a superb goal by Ruud Krol, who smashed one in from 30 yards and at half-time Pej went off on one, saying how unprofessional this all was. Poor preparation was costing us. How could you try and beat one of the top sides in Europe and not know how they played? Waddo contended we were good enough to beat them and we probably should have done. With a few changes made we played much better in the second half. Denis Smith equalised in the second half to make the score in the first leg 1-1 and then we missed chance after chance over in Amsterdam and ended up going out on away goals after a 0-0 draw. If we'd been able to start that first game as we then played the next three halves maybe we would have won. In fact both Jimmy G and Jimmy Robertson missed glorious chances in the last ten minutes in the away leg, so we probably should have gone through anyway. It was a missed opportunity, so maybe Pej was right. We should have progressed.

It hasn't been often that Stoke City have truly set the football world alight, but we did it for a second time that year when Waddo sensationally signed Peter Shilton for £325,000 in November 1974. This was another club record, a world record fee for a goalkeeper and the second largest fee for any British player, only eclipsed by Bob Latchford's £350,000 signing for Everton that February. The club had spent nearly three-quarters of a million pounds in one calendar year. It was a huge investment and statement. This was big-time stuff.

What's interesting is that our defence had conceded just two goals in the final nine games of the 1973/74 season, which does make you wonder now quite why Waddo brought Shilton in for such a vast fee. Especially when you consider that John Ritchie had suffered his career-ending leg break only two months beforehand and so maybe a striker would have been a better addition. I know he tried to sign Peter Osgood, who chose to join Southampton instead, so when the Shilton deal presented itself Waddo must have thought that he was doing the right thing. There was no better goalkeeper around. But was that what we needed at the time? I genuinely think that we wouldn't have been worse off having John Farmer in goal.

For whatever reason it didn't gel for Shilts. He proved eventually that he was up there with the best – 125 caps for England and two European Cups – but sadly his time at Stoke wasn't anywhere near a halcyon period. The back four had relied on Banksy to organise them and he had proved a hard act to follow. Shilton was very different to Banks, who could read the game and organised his back four with incessant shouting. Shilton was a keeper who looked after his own game and made great saves. He was phenomenal at that. His training routine was incredible, but he didn't coalesce with our defence, failing to give the lads that feeling of security they'd received from banks, and it showed. There is no questioning Shilton's ability as a keeper at all, but he didn't pull the strings for the back four like Banks had. That was the difference. It left an unease around the defence which never quite got sorted out.

If I'm honest, although he is a lovely feller, Peter proved easy to take the mickey out of, so we had some fun with him. He could be easily led astray and very easily fooled. One example of this came as a result of that phenomenal training regime. Shilts would always be last off the training pitch, caked in mud after doing extra sessions, particularly shot-stopping and catching crosses. He had this particular style for catching high balls which saw him take the ball as it came down and then fall to the ground with it, curled up to protect it. So he always got covered in mud and was last into the showers. It took him ages to get it all off and so was last out by several minutes, giving us plenty of time to come up with a scheme or two. This particular one was the most successful.

Back in those days we had to wash our training gear ourselves. The matchday kits were looked after by the kitman, but the training gear was yours to keep clean. Shilts's wife Sue must have had the devil's own job getting his gear clean as it was always absolutely caked in clods of muck. It weighed a ton too, which is what gave me the idea for a spot of mischief. In the dressing room was a bed for players to get massaged on and also some weights and heavy boots which were used by players to do light weights or stretches. I nabbed a couple of 2lb weights and popped them in among Shilts's muddy kit while he was showering off. Nobody could believe I would get away with it, but they egged me on to do it the first time and then when Shilts came out, dried off, had a natter with us all and then picked the bag up to go home there was a slight intake of breath as everyone expected him to notice the difference. He didn't. He trotted off home and came in the next day and didn't say anything about these weights being found among his kit.

So the lads egged me on again, this time I added another 2lb so now he had 6lb of weight. It was a bit heavier but Shilts didn't notice again and then the next time I added another 2lb so he now had 8lb extra in his kitbag and he still didn't notice or say anything. It became a running joke to see how much I could put in without him ever noticing. It also shows how strong he was to just pick up an extra 8lb in his bag without being aware of it. Everyone would wait around to see if he spotted it, but each time he headed off home with his bag and we'd collapse in laughter after he'd left the dressing room. Huddy would be crucifying him for not noticing. It went on for about a couple of months before we actually gave up because we got bored with the fact that he never noticed these weights.

Another example comes from when we travelled on long journeys and to pass the time there would always be a card school. At the heart of the den of iniquity would be Alan Hudson and Alan Bloor. We'd play brag, pontoon or poker. I remember one occasion we were on our way to Newcastle and in the time it took us to get from the Potteries to the hotel in Newcastle on the Friday afternoon Shilts lost about £1,000, which would have been around a month's wages at that time. He really did have a problem, not least because Huddy would go out of his way to egg him on and Shilts used to bite. Huddy would say, 'Go on, go blind,' or push him to increase a single bet up to £100 when the limit was supposed to be £10. Shilts couldn't help himself. He'd always bite and would be constantly chasing his losses. He was easy to read and, simply, a terrible gambler.

This gave Waddo a problem once he learned of it. It frightened him a bit. What state of mind would Shilts be in that night in order to prepare for the game? He would probably be worrying about how he could explain his losses to his wife. That might mean he couldn't sleep and therefore wouldn't be in the right frame of mind to play. Waddo was forced to put a stop to the whole gambling thing before it got completely out of hand.

We were the best team in the country in 1974/75. We could beat anyone, anywhere. We should have won the First Division title. That we didn't is something which still rankles. We were playing some wonderful, one-touch, attacking football and had a staunch defence. We could take on anyone, anywhere at any time, as our close call with Ajax had shown. The season had started well for us as we thrashed Leeds United on the opening day. The final score was only 3-0, but it could have been ten. This was particularly significant as it was Brian Clough's first competitive game in charge of the champions since their long-time manager Don Revie had been given the England job. We murdered them and I always like to think that it played a significant part in Clough's departure after just 44 days in the job at Elland Road, which has now been immortalised in that great book *The Damned Utd* by David Peace, which also became a feature film starring Michael Sheen as Cloughie.

We were in the chasing pack behind leaders Liverpool from the off, along with Ipswich, Everton and Manchester City. A purple patch in the autumn of that season saw us lose just once in 12 games. Following Shilton's arrival we kept three clean sheets and everything was going swimmingly. In fact in the calendar year 1974 our league record reads 20 wins, 16 draws and nine defeats. Not bad. We were so good that Frank Worthington, that maverick Huddersfield, Leicester and Bolton striker of the day, told me he used to come and watch us play if he didn't have a game himself, because he just loved to watch us. On 7 December 1974 we thrashed Birmingham at St Andrew's 3-0 to sit atop the league table, leading Everton and Manchester City by a point.

So, why didn't we lift the First Division title that season? There are three key reasons, I believe. The first was the occasional confusion between the new goalkeeper and our defence which destabilised things at times. It is odd that Shilts's signing didn't work out well, but there it is. It didn't.

The second was the most unbelievable run of injuries. We had four broken legs we suffered that season; John Ritchie (at Ipswich in September), Jimmy Robertson (at Coventry in December), Mike Pejic (versus Wolves in February) and Denis Smith (in the return against Ipswich in March). Plus Eric Skeels had broken his at the end of the previous season so he didn't make a comeback until late November. I guarantee if we had not lost those players we would have won those last three vital games and lifted the title that season. Plus Alan Bloor had ruptured his knee ligaments and played just twice.

I was out injured for much of that 1974/75 season and made just 16 league appearances, most of which were as a centre-forward during the exciting run in to the end of the season. I loved playing up front as I was able to utilise my strengths more, get involved in the build-up and also run on to balls played over the top. I played there because John Ritchie had suffered a terrible leg break in a challenge by Ipswich's Kevin Beattie. It finished Big John's career and I was pressed into service up front as by this time Geoff Hurst, at 33, was nearing the end of his career and the only alternative was a young, raw talent called Ian Moores, who was still being blooded sparingly.

I enjoyed playing up front as I felt much more involved in the play and hit the ground running when I came back into the side. I scored nine goals in five games in late March and early April as we forced our way back to the top of the table. This purple patch included a hat-trick as we thrashed Carlisle United 5-2 at the Vic (the second hat-trick of my career, the other having been against Halifax Town in a League Cup tie earlier in that same season). I then bagged a brace of goals – the first from the penalty spot and the second breaking clear to beat Ray Clemence at the second attempt – when we beat title rivals Liverpool at home on Easter Monday in front of nearly 46,000 buoyant fans. We also played on Good Friday and Easter Saturday that weekend, by the way, so don't talk to me about modern footballers' schedules. We regularly played three games over Easter and that year we fielded the same starting eleven in those three games save for Bluto, who missed the game on the Monday. I was in fantastic form and loving my role in a team which was challenging for the league title.

Maybe, though, the reason for our success in this halcyon period, when the team was really buzzing from 1970 to 1976, would ultimately turn out to be our downfall; the third reason for our failure to lift the league title. Our belief in our devil-may-care methods may well be why we didn't have tangible silverware to show for all that hard work. What I mean by this is that when we defeated Chelsea 3-0 the following Saturday to maintain our position at the top of the table in one of the closest title chases in history, with five clubs still involved with just three games remaining, we should have come together to sit down and discuss exactly how we were going to get maximum points from those three matches. The fixtures were kind; we had Sheffield United away, Newcastle United at home and Burnley away in that order. They were all mid-table sides with little to play for. But that meeting or get-together never happened. Waddo's theory was that because we'd had success playing off the cuff we should stick to our guns. Pej wanted us to be more professional and clinical, with less being left to chance, but then he'd been banging on about it for years. What do you do as a manager, though? Put doubt into players' minds by suddenly changing your approach? Waddo clearly didn't believe that was the way to go. Looking back now – and hindsight is a wonderful thing, I know – we were the best team in the league, but we didn't go on and win the league because we didn't talk through how we were going to get three wins from those last three games. I just think that if we'd approached them in more detail, with more forensic detail and been given a bit more guidance, maybe we'd have emerged victorious.

As it was we lost 2-0 in Sheffield and drew the final two matches 0-0. We'd run out of puff. Whether it was the injuries taking their toll or the lack of cohesion at that vital moment, who knows. We finished fifth and then lost out on another European adventure because some bureaucrat at UEFA chose that season to lift the rule which allowed only one club from each city to compete in the UEFA Cup. This allowed both Liverpool and Everton, who had finished second and fourth respectively behind champions Derby County, to qualify, when we had been led to believe that one of them would be excluded because of this 'one city one club' rule. We were only four points adrift and with a good enough goal average to know that four more points from those last three games would have seen us win the First Division for the first time in the club's history. We fell short and when it comes down to it that has to be viewed as a huge opportunity missed. We were so close. The sad thing is that with the way money has taken over the game now it's quite likely no Stoke City team will ever be in contention for the Premier League title again.

The 1975/76 season was another injury-blighted campaign for me. I only played 18 times, scoring four goals as my knees played up again and I had the fourth of my cartilages out. It wasn't a great time for me. As a team we started that season quite well, and just before Christmas stood eighth in the table, but only three points off QPR, Derby, Manchester United and eventual champions Liverpool, who were level on 28 points at the head of a very tight table. We felt like we had a chance of challenging once again as we had the previous season. In fact we now had many of our injury victims coming back into the team, even though I was rarely available, so surely we had an even better chance.

One of the games I did appear in was at Highbury in late August. It was to become an infamous example of the drinking culture which had begun to surround the club during this period. We travelled down by train on the Friday afternoon before the game to stay in the Russell Hotel. We had free time after we arrived and Waddo left it to us as individuals to decide how to prepare best for the following day's game. I got a taxi to Leicester Square with some of the lads – John Farmer, Jackie Marsh, Pej, John Mahoney and Denis Smith – and we watched a film together before having dinner around 8pm and then hitting the sack for an early night. Unbeknownst to us, as soon as Huddy got to the hotel he threw his case on the bed and took his sidekick and usual drinking buddy Geoff Salmons and Eric Skeels, who was the 13th man, travelling as an unused substitute, down to his former haunts on the King's Road.

The next morning we all had breakfast in bed and the first time we came together was for lunch at midday. Neither Huddy nor Sammy came down for the pre-match meal, but we didn't think too much of it. As we boarded the coach to go to Highbury at 1.15pm Huddy and Sammy finally made an appearance, clambering on to the coach full of the previous night's shenanigans. Huddy slapped me on the shoulder as he tottered past me and said in a gravelly voice, 'Hello TC, how are you? Guess what we got up to last night.' I could have had a good go as he reeked of alcoholic fumes, but he quickly continued on, 'We went down the King's Road last night with Chris Garland, Ossie [Peter Osgood], Ian Hutchinson and Tommy Baldwin [who was nicknamed 'The Sponge' due to the amount of alcohol he could drink] and had a few pots. We went to a restaurant [which was the only real surprise in this as Huddy wasn't a great eater]. We had to put Eric in a taxi at half ten as he couldn't stand the pace.' Huddy then went on to detail a series of lascivious tales about the amount he and his former Chelsea teammates, who were due to play Southampton at home the following day, had put away.

Huddy continued, 'We stayed out and didn't get in until 3am this morning. Me and Sammy then had hot chocolate and brandies to help us to get to sleep. I couldn't sleep, though, so I had a couple of Mogadons. I woke up at 8am and took another pill. I've had a lovely kip and can't wait to take on the Arsenal.'

With that he sat down and fell straight to sleep as the coach headed off to Highbury. It was almost impossible to wake him and Geoff Salmons was just the same. The combination of alcohol and sleeping pills had put paid to them. I turned to Josh and said, 'We're playing with nine men today. We'll get battered.'

In the dressing room before the game Sammy had to have his bootlaces tied for him as he couldn't focus at all. Denis Smith took exception to all this and pinned Huddy, as the ringleader, against the wall, accusing him of taking liberties with our livelihoods. At this the manager came in and calmed things down. Waddo asked me what was wrong with them and I just piped up with, 'It's the heat, boss. It's getting to them.' It was after all a beautiful summer's afternoon. Somehow Waddo seemed to buy this, although I do think he indulged Huddy like he was his own favourite son. Waddo had been warned off signing Huddy by other managers who thought he was a loose cannon, but he loved proving people wrong and Alan's form in those couple of years allowed Waddo to show people that he could create an atmosphere in which this incredible talent could deliver both individually and then as part of a great team. He loved the pure skill and was dazzled by Huddy's ability to a large extent and he wanted to see that on the park, so he let him have his head off it. He also knew how fit Huddy was.

Alan actually worked harder on his fitness than any of us. Not a lot of people know that. He was an incredible trainer and took it very seriously. He would often wear a couple of black bin bags, cutting arm and leg holes in them, to make himself sweat more to help him shed the extra pounds and the alcohol he'd taken on board after the game on a Saturday afternoon. Often he didn't sleep at all on a Saturday night and would keep on going for another five- or six-hour session on a Sunday afternoon. Huddy was very focused in the sense that he knew he had to pay for having that good time and he was prepared to do it. Combining the lifestyle with the way he played was, frankly, nothing short of miraculous!

Because he came from the King's Road and was glamorous Huddy had a lot of hangers-on. You'd never go into a pub or restaurant and see him on his own. At the time he was married to a model, Maureen. He was trendy and she was gorgeous. They'd be in the magazines, with photographers visiting their home to snap them as if they were the Potteries version of Posh and Becks. But never once did Huddy have a big head. He'd talk to anyone and drink with anyone. He was very popular in the dressing room because he was never nasty or bossy despite his incredible talent, he just liked to have a good time. He loved combining the two – and often did.

Of course in true 1970s footballer style this tale has a remarkable and happy ending. Typically, after ten minutes at Highbury, Huddy, still suffering from the combined effects of drink and sleeping pills, showed enough awareness to pounce on a wayward backpass and smash a shot past Pat Jennings. If you watch the game on YouTube you'll see the goal go in and then this flash of red hair arrive to give Huddy the biggest hug you've ever seen. I simply couldn't believe what had just happened. By the look on Alan's face neither could he! The defence took over then and we shut out the Gunners easily enough to cling on for the 1-0 win. The next day the *Sunday People* gave Huddy a ten out of ten star rating. If only they'd known!

Another story involving drink also occurred that season, although it doesn't involve the players having a drink, rather the directors. This happened the following April when we visited Liverpool. We never did well at Anfield – in fact in over a decade I was at Stoke we lost all but one of our games there, drawing that 0-0. I scored twice in those defeats; that special goal in August 1968 and then the opener in this particular game. Our directors tended to have a lovely day out whenever we visited Merseyside.

We'd have our usual pre-match lunch at the Adelphi hotel, while the directors quaffed champagne and wine on another table, the volume increasing loudly. Once at the ground they no doubt imbibed significant amounts more and would have been ecstatic to find that we actually took the lead for once when I found the net. No doubt another bottle of champers was popped at that moment. About ten minutes later as we defended a corner, I got whacked in the head by Jimmy Case's boot. It cut my eye and I had to go off to get it sorted out. The club doctor at this point was Sandy Clubb, who came down to the dressing room to stitch me up, although by now he was well sozzled. Before I knew it he was drunkenly sewing my eyelid to my eyebrow. Luckily enough the Liverpool club doctor was there and diplomatically said to him, 'Look Sandy, when I come to your ground you look after our players, so why don't I return the compliment. You go back upstairs to the directors' box and I'll sort Terry out.' With that, Sandy disappeared, his handiwork was quickly cut away and I got properly stitched up by the opposing team's doctor – a very unusual set of circumstances. People talk about the drink culture at Stoke in the 1970s, but it was in the boardroom as much as it was prevalent among the players.

We lost 5-3 at Anfield and Liverpool went on to win the title. We ended up mid-table that season, tailing off after Huddy got badly injured on a dreadful pitch at the Baseball Ground in March. Little did we know that something which had happened in January 1976 was about to change all of our lives… and for the worse.

9

Irish Eyes
Not Smiling

BEFORE I relate to you the sorry tale which unfolded at Stoke City in 1976/77, I'd like to divert to matters international. My career with the Republic of Ireland saw me win 27 caps and score two goals, and it lasted from my debut in October 1969 against Czechoslovakia to my final game in April 1977 against Poland. I loved playing for my country. It made me extremely proud, but the same cannot be said of the utter shambles that was the Football Association of Ireland (FAI) in that period.

I was selected by the Republic's first manager, Mick Meagan. He had only recently taken full control following something of a player revolt led by John Giles and Frank O'Neill, a famous Shamrock Rovers winger. Up until earlier that year the squad and team had been selected by committee, something most other nations had phased out in the 1940s or 50s. I'd actually been selected about a year beforehand, after my first full season at Stoke, but my first cartilage operation had meant I couldn't take part, so I was delighted when I got the news that I had been called up again to represent my country. This was truly great news. I was to be in the side to play in a World Cup qualifier against Czechoslovakia in Prague in place of O'Neill, who had been dropped, I was later to learn, in penance for his insubordination in challenging the committee's power. The Czechs were a decent side, boasting the likes of Jozef Adamec and Karol Dobias, so it was going to be a test.

To give you an idea of what international football was like in those days compared to today when there is an international calendar and the players get two weeks off, with no domestic fixtures scheduled in that period, in which to come together, train, play and then return home, let me relate to you the tale of my debut for the Republic. It was early October 1969 and I was a relatively junior member of the Stoke City team. We'd just played at Leeds on the Saturday and then for some reason had a game scheduled at West Ham on the Monday, with a home match against Arsenal to follow on the Saturday. So it was quite a hectic schedule. We drew 3-3 at Upton Park that Monday night. I went straight back to the Russell Hotel after the game and hit the sack as I was heading off from Heathrow to Prague early in the morning to make my debut for Ireland. I had a 5am call to catch the taxi to the airport and as I was leaving the foyer some of the lads were returning from their post-match night out. 'Where are you off to, TC?' they asked.

'Prague, to play for Ireland.'

'Well, good luck.'

I was going to need it.

I arrived in Prague, which is two hours ahead of the UK, at about 11am in readiness for a 6pm kick-off. The rest of the squad had travelled on ahead, but because we had the game at West Ham I'd had to follow on afterwards, which is probably why the farce that then unfolded ensued. Bear in mind this was then a country behind the Iron Curtain. There were Czech soldiers with plenty of guns at the airport, but no smiles. In fact there was a very frosty and unfriendly undercurrent. As I walked up to him, the chap at passport control demanded, 'Passport.' For some reason he could tell I wasn't Czech. I gave him my passport, which he ran his eyes over for far too long for me to be comfortable. I had never been anywhere like this before and I wasn't enjoying my first taste of cold war Europe. Then he gave me the passport back and demanded my visa. This was where it all started to go pear-shaped. I hadn't got a visa. No one had told me I needed one and the powers that be at the FAI hadn't organised one for me. I tried to explain, but as soon as I started saying that my visa should have been organised for me he lost complete interest and frostily said, 'No entry', turning his attention to the next person in the queue. So here I was stuck in no man's land due to a lack of paperwork. I could see my dreams of playing for my country evaporating before my eyes. More to the point, how was I going to get home? The FAI had my return ticket.

I tried to explain that I was here to play for Ireland that evening and eventually managed to get through to some official or other who rang up the Irish embassy. They sent a diplomat out to meet me and he managed to persuade the border guards to let me through. By what means I have no idea. It took three hours in total, but eventually I was let in to the country.

I reached the team hotel about 3pm to discover it was very sparse and to be told that my team-mate was in the room awaiting my arrival. I was expecting to see someone that I at least recognised, or maybe even knew, as if they'd been doing their homework you'd have thought that the FAI officials would put the new boy in with either an experienced international player or someone who he'd known before to help him settle in with the group. So typically I bustled into the room, full of how I'd been stuck for hours at the airport, to find someone I had never met before and didn't recognise at all. Not only that, but he didn't even look like a footballer.

That's because he wasn't. This feller got up off his bed and introduced himself as the Aer Lingus pilot who had flown the team in from Dublin the day before. I was rooming with the pilot. What a way to welcome a new cap. I got my head down for an hour or so, then went downstairs for a light pre-match meal and met my team-mates. We were very much a scratch side as many of the experienced pros who played in England were either 'injured' or 'unavailable' if you catch my drift. Back in those days players could just pull out of an international if they didn't fancy going somewhere hostile and unappealing, as Prague was back then. My boyish enthusiasm, though, got me through. I had a decent game and felt quite lively on the wing, despite the day I'd had – this was, after all, my second game in 24 hours and I'd had all that travel and been held hostage in an airport. We didn't play that badly, but were easily outclassed. Adamec netted a hat-trick and we were never really in the game after he opened the scoring in the eighth minute.

I'm sad to say that debut wasn't a one-off experience as far as the ineptitude of the organisation of the FAI went. A lot of the clubs in England viewed them as bumbling idiots. A good example is the fact that I would always receive my call-up letter in the post the day after I returned from a game. Regular as clockwork. It became a standing joke. I'd arrive home and then the next morning the postie would deliver a letter with an FAI franking mark on it congratulating me on my call-up for the game I had just played. In fact invariably I wouldn't actually receive my selection letter anyway, as I'd get the one meant for a lad called Jimmy Conway, who played for Fulham, while he would receive mine. Conroy and Conway, easy mistake to make, eh?! This farce became symbolic of the utterly ludicrous nature of the organisation which ran Irish football. In fact the players talked between themselves to ensure things got organised and the manager had to call you to let you know you'd been selected as you couldn't trust the FAI administration to do any job for you.

The mandarins at the FAI were very much your classic blazer-wearing part-timers. They loved their blazers, proudly showing off the badge to anyone who'd listen and they loved the association with us players their position gave them. But, remarkably, they could never bring themselves to actually organise well enough to make our lives easier so we could produce good results for them. Perhaps all they cared about was the hospitality they experienced and the places they got to visit with the team – either overseas or, when the selection committee was in operation, to see players in action in England to receive hospitality from clubs like Manchester United, Arsenal and Liverpool. It certainly seemed that way at times. It was a great life for them, but they were miles behind the eight-ball. Inept isn't the word. They were clowns. Well-meaning clowns, but clowns all the same. To them it was all about the four-day trip abroad. The result was secondary.

To illustrate this point I remember going to play in Hungary at the famous Nep Stadium. Because Hungary play in green and red we had to change into our all-white second strip. The game did not go well. We lost 4-0 and had John Dempsey sent off for throwing the ball at the referee in frustration. We were murdered. We came in at the final whistle worried about the seeing to we were going to be given by the manager only to find that this FAI official had turned up in the dressing room, blazer on, with badge proudly on his chest. It wouldn't be allowed these days, but, bolstered by some stiff drink, he'd come down to see us. We could tell he was well sozzled and expected to get a drunken rollicking from him. However nothing could have been further from the truth. He tottered around telling us how well we had played, 'I've never seen such a good performance from an Irish team in all my life,' he slurred. He'd only got confused into thinking we were Hungary because they had worn green and he thought they were us. He couldn't even recognise his own players, especially with the state he was in.

These clowns were led by the secretary, whose name was Peader O'Driscoll. He was a dead ringer for Oliver Hardy, except larger. His main talent was to avoid paying out money. This manifested itself firstly in us staying in two-star, not three-star, hotels wherever possible and the avoidance, if at all possible, of paying expenses. After each game we'd get an expense sheet to fill out and you just knew that O'Driscoll and his cronies would argue the toss about something and you'd end up around £5 light. Now that was a lot of money in those days, especially when you had genuinely spent it on some part of your journey to get to the game, so we all ended up inflating our expense claims in order to just get what we would be due. Getting paid the money was an excruciating experience too. It got to the stage that you had to phone up incessantly to chase up the payment, but even then this was fraught with difficulty. You'd ring up of a weekday morning before training and ask for Mr O'Driscoll only to be told he'd be in after 10am, so to ring back then. But you'd be training until around noon, so you rang back as soon as you could. 'Could I speak to Mr O'Driscoll please?' you'd ask. 'He's gone to lunch,' came the reply. 'When do you expect him back?' you'd ask. 'Two o'clock,' came the reply. Then you'd ring again at 2pm, but he'd either not be back from lunch or be in a meeting and then by 4pm you'd ring up to be told the inevitable answer, 'Mr O'Driscoll has gone home for the day, please call back tomorrow.' He was a genius at avoiding you. It was easier to get hold of Lord Lucan.

It wasn't cheap to ring Ireland in those days, so you were also paying through the nose for these peak-time phone calls you were having to make to chase your own money. The whole thing was a joke. The Irish press knew all of this nonsense was going on and often publicly ridiculed the FAI, but it had little effect. Tony Waddington soon cottoned on to how ridiculous it was and moved heaven and earth to stop me playing for them if he possibly could. He was scared I would get badly injured playing for Ireland, and in the end he was proved right. I did survive one scare in 1970 when I was flattened by a really naughty tackle from behind by German legend Franz Beckenbauer in a friendly as the Germans warmed up for the World Cup finals with a hard-fought 2-1 victory. That challenge hurt a lot, but didn't do any lasting damage thankfully. Waddo would constantly tell me in the week leading up to a game that he was going to inform the FAI that I was injured and that he would double my international match fee of £50 if I didn't go. But for me it wasn't about the money. It was about the pride. Waddo tried every trick in the book; for example, trying to play on my conscience by constantly telling me I'd be tired when I came back and wouldn't be able to play for Stoke the following weekend. But I wanted to pull on the green shirt and play, so I did whenever I could, although it was despite the FAI, not because of them, that I did so.

All this malarkey often meant we didn't have a full-strength team as various people got fed up with the situation and pulled out of games left, right and centre. Even my Stoke team-mates asked me why I bothered to go and play when all we got was third-class hotels, a load of grief and penny-pinching by the officials. Even in the summer the FAI would arrange tours at inconvenient times, not coordinated with when the clubs were going on tour themselves, so consequently most of the better players would not be available. That certainly happened to both myself and John Giles. It was almost impossible to improve the team in those circumstances and it was all a great pity really.

The team lost five out of six and gained just one point in their qualifying group for the 1970 World Cup, and fared no better in the Euro 72 qualifiers, so Meagan, disgracefully, got the boot and was replaced by Liam Tuohy, the Shamrock Rovers manager and former Newcastle winger. Liam knew what the problems were, having been a veteran player, and oversaw major improvements to the national team's training facilities and worked hard to persuade many English club sides to end their policies of not releasing Irish players for international games during the domestic season to give himself the best chance of having a full complement of players to select from, which had never happened before due to the way English clubs viewed the FAI as a bunch of jokers.

Despite this we never qualified for the European Championships or the World Cup. This was because we were almost always the lowest seeds, so we'd be in a group with several major nations, the likes of Italy, Austria and Poland. We had both the Soviet Union and France in the qualifying competition for the 1974 World Cup in Germany for example. That particular group gave me two great personal moments, though. On 18 October 1972 I scored my first international goal late in a World Cup qualifying game against the Soviet Union at Lansdowne Road, the consolation goal as we lost 2-1, slotting home a Mick Leech pass. I then scored in the next game, another World Cup qualifier, this time against France at Dalymount Park as we won a cracking game 2-1, our first home victory in six long years. John Giles headed a ball across the penalty area. I took it down, controlled it and lashed it into the net via the bar.

We were beginning to become a force on the pitch under Liam Tuohy, with the likes of Paddy Mulligan and John Dempsey (both Chelsea), Ray Treacy (Charlton), Joe Kinnear (Spurs), Don Givens and Terry Mancini (both QPR), Steve Heighway (Liverpool) and Mick Martin (Manchester United) coming into the side. Latterly Liam Brady, Mark Lawrenson and Gerry Daly bolstered the team, although I was on my way out then following my series of knee injuries.

Tuohy resigned in 1973, following a dispute over his wages, and John Giles became the side's first player-manager at the age of 32. John always says he only took the job to stop the FAI jokers giving it to someone utterly unqualified. He'd have preferred Liam Tuohy to remain in post, but in the absence of that he might as well take the job himself. The brave new world did not start well for me. In Giles's first game in charge against Poland in Dublin in October 1973 (a famous 1-0 victory over a team who just four nights earlier had knocked England out of the World Cup) I did my cartilage after just ten minutes. That led to my third cartilage operation and my real struggles with my knees. I wouldn't make another first team start for Stoke until 28 December 1974, well over a year later.

When I got back into the Republic side after I was fully fit we made a great fist of qualifying for the 1976 European Championships. We beat the Soviet Union in Dublin 3-0 thanks to a Don Givens hat-trick and hammered Turkey 4-0. This time Don went one better and scored all four. John Giles had got us playing a really good style which suited us and we ended up finishing just one point behind the Soviets, who took the only qualifying place on offer. We had a better goal difference too, so had we nicked a draw instead of slipping to a narrow 2-1 defeat in Kiev we would have gone through. John had brought a very professional approach to the game which reflected his upbringing under mentor Don Revie at Leeds. It just showed what we were capable of when we were well-prepared. It made all those ridiculous things which had gone on before all the more frustrating.

Defeat in May 1975 to a late goal in Switzerland cost us in that campaign and I have to hold my hands up and admit to my part in the only goal of a tight game. As a cross came over I got tangled up with Eoin Hand and the ball fell to Elsener, who slotted home. There were tears shed in the dressing room that night as we knew we would just miss out.

My last international appearance came in April 1977, a goalless draw in a World Cup qualifier against Poland. The previous month had seen us defeat France 1-0 at Lansdowne Road, but dropping a point against the Poles would eventually see us miss out once again and it would be another decade before an Irish team qualified for the final stages of a tournament in Euro 88 in Germany. That completed a torrid time for me as Stoke were plummeting like a stone towards relegation at the time. I was by now approaching 31 and I knew my time was up. The injuries had taken their toll and I couldn't keep on playing at that level.

I just couldn't keep away from the Irish national team, though. When Eoin Hand was appointed as the next manager in late 1981, I became his assistant. I had just retired from playing that summer and was looking for something to keep me in the game, so I took the role. My job was to keep in touch with the increasing number of players who were based in the UK. When the squad was brought together, Eoin did the coaching and I acted as his eyes and ears among the players, being their friend and supporting them; the good guy to Eoin's more austere leader. We made a good double act and put together one heck of a team.

Of course we were helped by having fabulous talent available and one of the key parts of Eoin's policy which I helped implement was to ensure that they were indeed available and weren't put off by the ludicrous administrative issues which had blighted our international careers. When I had first played for the national team we still had a large number of part-timers in the squad, mostly due to the policy of allowing a selection committee to pick the squad for the manager to then pick the team. Now, however, we had the likes of Mark Lawrenson, Frank Stapleton, Michael Robinson, Liam Brady, Kevin Sheedy, David O'Leary, Chris Hughton, Jim McDonagh, Tony Grealish, John Devine and Gerry Daly in the side. Some of these great players were about as Irish as Vladimir Putin, but we didn't care as we set about implementing the new FIFA rule which allowed grandparents to count as qualifying a player to play for a country. For example Lawrenson was about as Lancashire as they come, while Hughton was born in east London and Robinson in Leicester. We weren't quite as merciless in tracking down people of questionable Irish descent as Jack Charlton would later become, but we did unearth the likes of Londoners Tony Cascarino and Tony Galvin and future Irish football manager Mick McCarthy, a man as Yorkshire as whippets and flat caps.

Eoin's stated aim was to qualify for a tournament. However, remarkably, Eoin wasn't a full-time international manager as we are used to today as the FAI was too stingy to make him a full-time appointment. He split his time between the national team and his day job managing Limerick in the League of Ireland, where he had won the league in 1980, qualifying for the European Cup in which they played Real Madrid, and the FAI Cup in 1982. Then, later, he moved on to St Patrick's Athletic; both of these while he tried to run the Irish team as a professional a manner as he could. It wasn't a full-time role for me by any means. In fact it kept me going for just a few weeks a year. My frequent returns to Ireland did allow me to catch up with my family a lot more than I had been able to over the previous 15 years or so, and also I played a few League of Ireland games with Waterford and once for Limerick as Eoin was their manager at that point.

Qualification for the 1982 World Cup had begun with a 3-2 win in Cyprus thanks to two goals by Preston striker Paul McGee. That was John Giles's last match as Irish national manger, while the next qualifier was Eoin Hand's first game in charge and resulted in a fabulous 2-1 victory over the Netherlands in Dublin. The team fought back from 1-0 down to score twice in the last 12 minutes through Gerry Daly and the youthful Mark Lawrenson, who would earn his big move from Brighton to Liverpool at the end of that 1980/81 season. A 1-1 draw at home to Belgium, Tony Grealish levelling an early Albert Cluytens goal, was another good result as the Belgians, under manager Guy Thys, had only recently ended the European Championships as runners-up to West Germany, having seen off England along the way in the group stage. So they were a very good side with the likes of Jan Ceulemans, Paul van Himst, goalkeeper Jean-Marie Pfaff and Eric Gerets in their midst.

A third great team in our group was France, who would go on to reach the World Cup semi-finals, going out in majorly controversial fashion to West Germany. So we had three fantastic sides to try and pip to one of the two qualification places for the World Cup finals in Spain. The Republic had never qualified for anything so we were determined to give this a very good go. A 2-0 reverse in Paris saw Michel Platini, who would dominate midfields for much of the 1980s, run the game, scoring the opening goal early on. But the following month we hammered group minnows Cyprus 6-0. Things were going well, but then the controversy started.

It looked like we were going to nick a point in a goalless draw in Belgium, but then Frank Stapleton scored what we thought was a perfectly good goal, although the referee ruled it out for some unseen offence. We were holding out but then with two minutes to go the referee intervened again when Eric Gerets threw himself to the ground and was awarded a free kick. Vandereycken hit the bar and as the ball flew up into the air Jan Ceulemans fouled Jim McDonagh before nodding into the net. No free kick was given and the goal was awarded. All hell broke loose then and at the final whistle a minute or so later Eoin Hand strode on to the pitch and confronted the referee, calling him a cheat. He knew there was something wrong. I didn't want to believe it, but when further evidence emerged about Belgian clubs bribing referees in European competition I began to understand that we had actually been cheated out of that game and an appearance at the 1982 World Cup. Match fixing, it appears, was rife in Europe in those years and it was due to referees being nobbled.

So who was the referee who perpetrated such heinous crimes against us? I'll never forget his name, even though you could excuse me for doing so given its length; he was called Raúl Joaquim Fernandes Nazare. He was later shown to have been a cheat on more than one occasion in an exposé, while Eric Gerets was also later suspended for his part in a bribery scandal. That served him right as far as I was concerned as Steve Heighway had told me when the teams came off the pitch on that night in Brussels that Gerets had been laughing when he won that free kick and continued to laugh after the goal had been awarded.

That defeat was a devastating blow as we knew qualification would now be out of our hands, but with only five teams in the group and with four of us being so closely matched we knew points would be taken off each other. So it proved in the next round of games when Belgium beat France in Brussels to gain revenge for having lost their earlier meeting in Paris and we drew 2-2 with Holland in Rotterdam. That game saw us twice come from behind, once through Michael Robinson and once through Frank Stapleton, who could always be relied upon to nick a goal. That left us with eight points with one game remaining, while Holland had seven points with two games left, France were on six points with three games to go and Belgium were on the brink of qualification having already picked up 11 points, but they had just one match to play. Our final game was at home to France. Simultaneously Holland were beating Belgium 3-0 to throw the group wide open.

We started the game brilliantly when Mahut scored an own goal after three minutes, turning a cross past his own keeper. Bellone equalised just five minutes later, but a storming first half performance saw our two strikers Robinson and Stapleton both net to make the half-time score 3-1. Platini did manage to pull one back with seven minutes left, but we held on for a famous victory, with McDonagh making a wonderful save from Didier Six minutes from the end. We now had ten points, Belgium were ahead on 11 and both of us had finished our programmes. Holland were a point behind us on nine and France had just six points, although still had two games left, one against Holland and one against Cyprus. The showdown between Holland and France in Paris had to end as a draw for things to go our way. If it did, France would only be able to get nine points and Holland would draw level on points with us but would have a worse goal difference. We would be through.

Platini became our tormentor again, scoring one goal and making one for Six as France won 2-0 and they then comfortably defeated Cyprus to pip us on goal difference. It was devastating. If we'd earned that deserved point or even a win in Belgium it would have been Ireland not France in Spain and football history could have been so different. Imagine no need for the Jack Charlton revolution and no fame for Michel Platini. Wouldn't life have been different over the last 30 years?!

Despite coming so close to success, Eoin still found himself fighting constant battles with the FAI over his drive to be much more professional. One of the big problems as far as I could see was that the presidency of the FAI goes in four-year cycles. So there was little pressure in between those election times. The press used to hammer the FAI for their various continuing failures. I remember one particular press conference when the incumbent at the time wanted to scotch rumours over certain allegations which had been made against him. He called this press conference and stormed in to face the press saying, 'I am fed up with all these allegations against me and I won't rest until I find out who these alligators are.'

Now, the last time I looked in the dictionary the name for people who make allegations wasn't alligators. The press may be sharks at times, but it was the president who was an old crock. Or should that be croc?

The draw for Euro 1984 qualification saw us paired with the Netherlands once again, but this time also with Spain, who would go on to become runners-up after losing the final to hosts France. Holland were just putting together their wonderful team of the late 1980s and early 90s and we lost the opening game of the group in Rotterdam when Ruud Gullit scored the winning goal. We then beat Iceland at home 2-0 and drew 3-3 with that fabulous Spanish team, coming from 3-1 down to level thanks to two late goals from Stapleton. The crucial game would prove to be the return against the Dutch. It was at Dalymount Park in Dublin, just a stone's throw from my home in Cabra. Over 28,000 fans saw us take a two-goal lead at half-time thanks to goals by Gary Waddock and Liam Brady, who by now was playing for Juventus in Italy. Surely this would be our year. This would see us reach the first finals in Irish history.

It was especially important since the Northern Irish had reached the World Cup finals in Spain in 1982 and done so well, qualifying for the second round, knocking the hosts out along the way. Sadly Ruud Gullit came back to haunt us, scoring twice and making one for a certain Marco van Basten as Holland came back to win improbably 3-2. An 8-0 win over Malta in our final game wasn't enough, despite it being Ireland's largest ever victory in an international game. We missed out. Had we beaten the Dutch it may all have been so different.

Amid all these qualification games we played a number of very prestigious friendlies. I remember beating Czechoslovakia 3-1 in 1981 and also narrowly losing to England at Wembley in a game in which a certain Gary Lineker scored his first international goal, but the most memorable game for me was a friendly against world champions Italy the previous month, February 1985. It took place at Dalymount Park. The Italian FA had promised £30,000 for the TV rights and the perimeter advertising to place adverts for their watching millions of viewers back at home. I think they'd chosen to play us as they thought they were in for an easy game. The

Irish people were fascinated at the prospect of seeing the World Cup holders in Dublin and over 40,000 turned up to see the likes of Giuseppe Bergomi, Bruno Conti, Alessandro Altobelli and, of course, World Cup-winning goalscorer Paolo Rossi. There was a very late influx of supporters into the ground, many of which were from the large Italian immigrant community in Ireland. There was a lot of pressure at the turnstiles and several were opened to let people in, avoiding overcrowding or crushing outside the ground. But because so many of them came in late and the teams were just taking to the field they ended up sitting on the perimeter of the pitch. There were people right up to the touchlines and even against the net behind the goal. There were even people sitting on the chairs by the dugout which myself and the subs were supposed to sit in.

When we got there after the national anthems had been sung there were lads sitting in them and I asked them to move. 'Piss off, we were here first,' came the reply. Then when Rossi took the first corner of the game it was like Moses parting the Red Sea as he pushed his way through the fans to take some sort of run up to the ball. It really was mayhem. There were so many people round the pitch that the Italians ended up refusing to pay the £30,000 as no one back at home could see the carefully positioned perimeter advertising on TV due to the hordes thronging the pitchside. In fact at half-time, after several encroachments on to the pitch and having watched the linesmen being unable to run up and down the touchlines, Liam Brady came into the dressing room and said, 'This is so embarrassing. I have never been so humiliated in all my life. I'll never be able to hold my head up when I go back to Turin.'

It didn't get any better in the second half and I particularly remember two incidents which involved a cohort of people in wheelchairs who were positioned on the far touchline from where I was sitting (once I'd reclaimed my seat from those youths). The first came when Rossi realised that some of the wheelchairs were actually so close to the pitch that they were on the touchline itself. This meant that he could play a one-two with a wheelchair in order to beat left-back Jim Beglin. I couldn't believe what I was seeing. Really it was funny, but it was also ridiculous. Then came the coup de grace. With fewer than ten minutes remaining in the game the people who were looking after the wheelchair users decided they would head for the exit, rightly thinking that there would be such a crush if they stayed to the final whistle. The only problem was that from where they were positioned the only way out was blocked. They simply could not get around the pitch to reach the exit. There was only one option left open to them and they took it. They wheeled around half a dozen wheelchairs across the pitch right in the middle of an international football match. Incredible.

The whole shambles summed up the governing body's approach to international football to me; constantly chasing money in the most inept fashion. On this occasion they failed utterly dismally. There was such a ballyhoo in the papers when they found out about losing the money and the ructions rumbled on for months. For the record Italy won 2-1. Rossi scored after just five minutes, with Altobelli notching in the 18th minute. At 2-0 so early on it looked as if we'd get a bit of a tonking, but we held on and scored early in the second half through Gary Waddock. It was a memorable night in more ways than one.

When the next qualifiers came around for the 1986 World Cup in Mexico, we were drawn in Group Six along with Denmark, the Soviet Union, Switzerland and Norway. We started the group brilliantly, defeating the Russians 1-0 in front of 45,000 at Lansdowne Road in Dublin. Striker Mickey Walsh, who by now was playing for Porto in Portugal having started out at Blackpool and Everton, netted the only goal and we thought we were set fair for another great campaign. However, defeats in both Norway and Denmark saw us fail to score and when another blank sheet followed in the home game against the Norwegians, which at least earned a point in a goalless draw, it was clear we wouldn't be heading to Acapulco. Our only other decent result was a 3-0 hammering of Switzerland, but our final match saw that great Danish team who would go on to light up the finals the following year thrash us 4-1 in Dublin. Preben Elkjaer and Michael Laudrup ran riot that night and we just weren't at the races.

Once we'd failed to qualify for the World Cup, Eoin's contract was not renewed so I was also done away with just before Christmas 1985. That's fairly typical, to clear out the whole management team and the new direction the Republic took would prove to be such a magnificently successful one that I cannot be too churlish about that particular decision. The FAI brought in Jack Charlton and qualified for the next two tournaments, and indeed three of the next four. It was unprecedented and brilliant. I do believe, though, that the process of professionalisation, which had begun with Liam Tuohy, was accelerated by John Giles and then driven on by Eoin Hand, stood Big Jack in great stead for all the wonderful achievements he and his team produced.

The one thing I would say about the FAI is that it gave Jack Charlton everything he wanted in terms of him having the job full-time, having top-notch facilities, decent hotels and time to prepare, whereas when Eoin had asked for the same things he had been refused. To see them respect Big Jack more than one of their own really stuck in my craw. It was a kind of racism but in reverse. We could have achieved something really special had we not had one hand tied behind our back. But I suppose it took our transitional period to help make them see sense and give Jack what he needed in order to finally make the breakthrough.

My devotion to my country would see me go back for a third time to serve, this time as the grandiosely-titled Welfare Officer to Republic of Ireland Players, Past and Present. This was a brand new, full-time post, which I applied for and was given by John Delaney, the CEO of the FAI. In 2008, after I finished working full-time at Stoke City's Commercial Department, I got a three-year contract for a wide remit which involved looking after anyone who was Irish or who had played for Ireland that was based in the UK, but also on my travels I was responsible for sourcing second-generation players who might have Irish parents or grandparents that we could target to persuade to throw their lot in with the FAI in an international sense. This involved asking a lot of questions about parentage and grandparentage in the manner laid down by Big Jack himself.

My focus inevitably fell on Irish youth players who were coming over to England with an Academy contract at the age of 16. With a blank canvas to work with in order to fulfil this remit I made appointments at the majority of clubs in the Premier League as most had Irish players on their books; the likes of Chelsea, Manchester United, and Arsenal. In fact 80 per cent of the young

Irish players in England were at Premier League clubs. The idea was that I'd get to know the lads and offer my services as someone to talk things over with, or, as it turned out, a shoulder to cry on. I thoroughly enjoyed going to these clubs and meeting players from my era that I had played against who were now coaches and ambassadors at these clubs. For example Gordon McQueen was at Middlesbrough, Mike Summerbee at Manchester City, and Liam Brady was the academy director at Arsenal. Occasionally I'd go up to Scotland – once to Celtic and once to Aberdeen – so I was covering most of the UK. Outside the top division clubs such as Leeds and Middlesbrough in particular should be complimented on their youth set-ups. If the lads that come through there are good enough they are given a chance in the first team at those clubs, which says a lot about their belief in youth development.

It became a fascinating role, which gave me a wonderful insight into the modern youth who were coming over and finding it difficult to settle. What I felt was good for them was that advice I was giving these lads came from personal experience. I'd had my moments of homesickness, even though I loved my time at the Copes on Lime Street and on reflection it was definitely to my advantage that I wasn't one of those lads who was picked up for an apprenticeship at 15 years old, although at the time I was insanely jealous. It wasn't that I expected them to know who I was or anything about my history, but they knew enough to know that I had been there and they couldn't say that I didn't know what I was talking about. I wanted them to see me as a kind of father figure, I suppose. Someone they could turn to at any time to talk something through. Their problems were generally the same. They simply felt homesick and I could offer advice and support to those who needed help more than others.

If I got a call from someone at a club saying, 'Terry this lad needs an Irish voice to sit down with him for half an hour and chat,' then I would get on the phone, or if I felt it would be better, jump in the car and go and see them. That's all it would be, making these lads feel at home by hearing me speak (an Irish accent can be so comforting) and having me listen to their problems, gripes and issues, then helping sort them out. They might have a whinge about their digs (often dormitories rather than being in with a family like I had been as a young pro), the food, their peer group, the coaches or their girlfriends. Anything can upset a young lad between the ages of 16 and 18 it seems these days. Some were lonely. Many were quite sensitive. Others were being almost starved. One told me how after dinner was served at 6pm the fridge was locked, so he couldn't get any snack to eat after that time and he was often starving. These are growing lads, after all, with big appetites, who are training most of the day and need feeding up.

Thankfully I do have a sensitive side, although back in my day all these issues would have been dealt with by someone saying, 'Oh come on now, you big old woman you, get a grip.' It isn't like that now. The issues could become quite serious. For example, once in a while a lad would go AWOL and I would have to track them down and ensure they came back. I remember one who had disappeared that we finally traced back to his home town in southern Ireland. He hadn't actually gone home as he couldn't face what he thought would be an utter humiliation of showing up there when he should be living this glamorous life as a young Premier League footballer. He was eventually found holed up in a local hostel. The irony is that there was very little for this lad to come home to. The Irish economy is not great at the moment and there is little work for a young man who has dedicated his life to football up to that point and not got academic qualifications.

Then there was one particular instance of bullying, which blew up quite badly. I can't reveal the names or even the club involved, but it was quite a bad case. It involved other lads of the same age who were picking on him. I am the first to admit that football dressing rooms are very macho, mickey-taking environments and a lot of what went on when I was a pro would be regarded very differently if it were to happen now, for example the 'tests' Maurice Setters set for me when I first arrived at Stoke. Times have very definitely changed. But even taking that into consideration this was most definitely a sustained, targeted campaign of bullying. I'd never been involved in anything like that at all before and so didn't have any direct experience of how to deal with this scenario myself, so I called in some assistance. I had a colleague in Dublin who worked for the FAI as chief welfare officer called Mick Lynam. His background was looking for talented youngsters among inner city kids by running FAI training courses. His work had led him to have to deal with lads taking drugs or even committing robberies, so he'd really seen just about everything life could throw at you. He helped me immensely and we became a great team in dealing with this particular bullying problem. We had to get both associations involved – the FAI and the Football Association – and I'm glad to say that the club involved put immediate procedures in place to prevent this incident happening again once we'd resolved the issue.

Sometimes the lads had a gripe about the actual football itself. They might feel that their coach wasn't playing them because they didn't like them or their face didn't fit. But that just simply never happens in reality. Coaches of these age groups are retained to develop the talent and so will work towards that, honing in on the ones that produce the goods. They will be proud of those lads that make it to full professional contracts, aged 18. So if a young player wasn't being picked you could be pretty sure that it was because they weren't playing well. Explaining that scenario to a young lad who thinks the world is against him is tricky, and I relished the opportunity to help these young men see their way through the mire, revelling in the contact this opportunity gave me with the modern game.

We had some tremendous successes. Jeff Hendrick burst on to the Championship scene in Derby's midfield in 2011, scoring the winning goal in the East Midlands derby against Nottingham Forest to make himself an instant hero with Rams fans. He's now made over 170 appearances, is under contract to Derby to 2018 and has been heavily involved in propelling them into the race for the Premier League in the last two seasons. He's also won several full caps to go with his welter of international honours at every level from under-15 upwards. I would say he was one of the main successes that the scheme has helped come through. Then there's Mark O'Brien, who played in Derby's first team as a defender at the age of 16, but has been hugely unlucky since with injuries, including damaging his cruciate ligament and also having a heart scare, which meant he had to have a valve replaced at a very young age. Mark spent most of the 2014/15 season on loan at Motherwell in the SPL. It would be great to see him come through all the trauma he has suffered and settle down to have a long and successful career as he is still only 23.

I only came across about half a dozen 'new' Irishmen who the FAI were not aware were qualified to play international football for the Republic. For example, Stoke City had a lad called Ryan O'Connor. And through talking to him I found out one of his grandparents was Irish and he was more than happy to become involved, so I alerted the FAI in Dublin and they began to keep tabs on him through my reports and with Ryan being watched by Irish scouts who would come over.

The job was so important to me and I loved what I was doing. Seeing young talent develop and blossom, keeping an eye out for their names in reserve team match reports and then in first team games for those that made the breakthrough was tremendous, but so was the fact that even those who didn't make it had positive experiences, which I had played some part in, and they could go on to careers outside the game and keep playing as amateurs, or get a pro contract or a semi-pro contract further down the pyramid. Some people believe that if you get released by a Premier League club at the age of 18 then you are a failure. Far from it. Just ask the likes of Robbie Savage, who made a great career for himself after having been let go by Sir Alex Ferguson at Manchester United. There is plenty of life lower down the leagues and you can get noticed and earn a move back up to the big time if you are good enough.

The drop-out rate, though, is huge. One or maybe two players in each year group will get offered contracts by their club, that's all. The wastage rate is immense and the game needs to think more deeply about how it deals with the lads that they let go at this kind of age. In Europe they often take on the youngsters at 17, not 16 and that year, in my opinion makes a huge difference, especially in terms of maturity, both in a footballing sense and in terms of their personality and ability to cope with the big wide world. I would like to see clubs consider taking lads on one year later. I think it would help massively in terms of coping with the change that occurs when you leave home, through to dealing with issues such as homesickness and loss of self-belief. I do think these are all the greater problems for Irish lads as the devotion to their mother is so strong in Irish culture that the shock of leaving home and everything it involves is far more traumatic to cope with.

Rightly or wrongly, that certainly is the case. In fact I would say that the biggest problem that I had to deal with was those lads who came to England with a huge fanfare at 16, with vast expectation heaped upon their shoulders, then didn't get taken on as a pro at the end of their two years. Often they couldn't face the humiliation this slight would mean for them if they went home, or wouldn't face up to the reality of having to go and get a job if they couldn't win a contract with a smaller club or didn't want to bother even trying. Some of the best work I did was building these lads, who had had their dreams ripped away from them, back up, so they could look themselves in the mirror again and face family and friends. It was challenging and rewarding on a daily basis.

I very much believe that one spin-off from this role that I had created was that Premier League clubs began to take the FAI all the more seriously, because they saw the effort that was going into youth welfare and development. This brought the FAI and the clubs closer together and built a new-found respect.

But then the FAI intervened once again. In 2011, just after I'd been stricken by my aneurysm, my contract came to an end. I thought that because I'd done so well, had set up the systems, had become recognised in the role and was full of energy and desire to fulfil what I had started, that my job would continue for another period. But the FAI had other ideas. I was approaching my 65th birthday by this time and it became clear the FAI wanted a younger man in the job. I was 'retired' after being told that the official retirement policy of the FAI, written into the constitution, states that 65 is the retirement age. Now this was ironic given that the manager of the national side at that time was none other than Giovanni Trapattoni, a man who had just celebrated his 72nd birthday. I didn't bother asking the obvious question about whether Trap was also going to be 'retired', as it was clear the way this was going to go. Trapattoni didn't finish until two years later, so quite how they squared that one with their retirement policy I'm not sure. It was blatant ageism, but there were also financial considerations given the huge debt which had been accrued in the construction of the Aviva Stadium. I knew, though, that the Irish Government had also been contributing to funding my role through the Department of Foreign Affairs, so that argument never rang true to me.

The whole fiasco has ended up being something which I have become slightly bitter about – it really is the only thing in life that has left that impression upon me. The role was then vacant for about 12 months and consequently all the good work I had done and the links I had made fell by the wayside. It has since been revived but only by using part-timers, which apparently had something to do with a lack of funds to pay a full-time post's wages. This could have been believable had it not been for the five million euros which the FAI received from FIFA around the time of my departure in order to avert any potential legal action over the outrageous handball perpetrated by France striker Thierry Henry in the World Cup play-off of November 2009 which prevented the team qualifying for the 2010 World Cup in South Africa. Aside from the outrage all Irish football fans that the proffered cash was even accepted in the first place as it feels like 'hush money', it just goes to show that generations of FAI officials have had no idea how to run football for the good of the game and supporters in our country. Can that discredited organisation ever get anything right? That noise you just heard? That's me not holding my breath.

10

The Day the Roof Blew Off

W E should have won the league title in 1974/75 and if we had then Stoke City would have become a permanent fixture in the First Division, I'm sure of it. We'd have been able to attract even better players to join our already stellar squad and Tony Waddington's status and job would have been secure. He'd have been the Alex Ferguson of Stoke City. Us players would have taken huge confidence from the achievement and we'd have gone on to compete in the European Cup, which saw champions Derby lose 6-5 to Real Madrid over two legs in the second round the following season. That could have been us. Can you imagine that? Stoke City in the European Cup? Taking on Real Madrid and the like? It would have been phenomenal.

Instead, within two seasons Waddo had been sacked and we'd been ignominiously relegated. How on earth could that have happened?

It all began with a massive storm on the evening of Thursday 2 January 1976. It was officially a gale force nine, with winds gusting over 100mph, the strongest meteorological event in quarter of a century in the UK. There was damage all over the country. Railways were severely affected as overhead power supplies collapsed in the Midlands, a beech tree was blown on to the elephant house of Longleat Safari Park, causing inhabitants

Twiggy and Chiki to escape, one of the pinnacles of the main tower of Worcester Cathedral crashed through the roof and there were prolonged power outages in Norfolk, Sussex and Surrey. The storm then raged across Europe, causing 82 fatalities overall.

The following morning we assembled at the ground for a gentle training session ahead of travelling down to London to play at Spurs in the FA Cup the following day to be greeted by this mass of twisted metal and broken wood. The storm had smashed the roof of the Butler Street stand, the covered terrace on the side of the pitch opposite the main Boothen Stand. It was in a right state, having collapsed in on itself and looked even worse from the window of the train as we went past on our way to the capital.

Because of the damage, we had to play our next home game at Vale Park. We defeated Middlesbrough 1-0 and it felt like a bit of an adventure, although the facilities weren't what we were used to. The Victoria Ground reopened by the end of the month and we didn't think much more of it. We'd been inconvenienced, but it was now all cleared up and a new roof was being planned to cover the Butler Street side of the ground.

We didn't have a clue about the seriousness of the situation in terms of how it might affect the club. We had no inkling at all about the financial problems in the background which revolved around the fact that the proper insurance apparently wasn't in place for the ground. It would take a good six months for this to play out and meanwhile we finished 12th, slap bang in mid-table. The first sign that there was a major problem came when the stunning news was announced that Jimmy Greenhoff was to be sold to Manchester United for £120,000 in November 1976. This was astonishing both for us, and also for Jimmy, who clearly didn't want to go. He cried his eyes out as he stood looking at the Victoria Ground pitch for the last time. It was a dreadful moment, but even then we felt as if we had enough talent among the squad to cope with his loss. It wasn't good news, but we could cope, couldn't we?

The problem was Jimmy was but the first. One by one our most talented, and valuable, assets were sold off. First Pej went, then Huddy, Josh Mahoney and Geoff Salmons. All gone. Half the team ripped out. Key players who had made such a massive impact. When you look back it's frightening. Players were falling like a deck of cards and we went from title contenders to relegation over the course of one season. It truly was the end of an era. No more cup runs or tilts at the league title. Instead we were dragged into a terrible relegation fight as morale, not surprisingly, dipped. As each sale was announced it felt as if a little piece of us was being cut away. Our friends were leaving and the remaining squad members were left reeling, wondering where was it all going to end.

The 1976/77 season didn't start too badly, but as the players departed our form dipped horrendously. In November, after a 1-0 home victory over Birmingham we stood ninth. Even on 5 March after back-to-back wins over Ipswich and QPR we were 14th (there were 22 teams in the First Division back then), comfortably in mid-table. But of the last 15 games that season we won just one, slipping inexorably down the league until we slumped into the bottom three with just one game remaining, away at Aston Villa. We were level on points with West Ham, who had a goal difference just one better than us. We had to get at least the same result as them and improve that goal difference by the one goal. They had a tough game at home to Manchester United, who unfortunately for us had reached the FA Cup Final and so weren't really up for the fight. West Ham won 4-2, while we lost 1-0 to a penalty at Aston Villa. The unthinkable had happened. We were down.

By the time relegation came Tony Waddington had been sacked and George Eastham had taken over, first as caretaker and then permanently over the summer. All the grooming which Tony Waddington had put into George had prepared him for taking over in a time of success, not for a battle against the drop. Equally, as players and as a team we weren't prepared for life at the foot of the division. We had battlers, yes, but it's a different type of scrap when you're in a relegation dogfight. The players who were left at the club were not able to deal with the situation. I scored six goals in that relegation season to finish as top scorer, but we netted just 28 goals over the 42 games, just seven of those away from home.

To be honest we were probably too complacent. We'd always been a First Division club; well-established and long-serving. There was no one at the club who had played outside the top flight and we simply couldn't imagine relegation happening. We certainly never really spoke about it. For my part I never once thought we were a relegation team. I never conceived of it. The realisation came very late, as our results got worse and the teams below us pulled off some great wins to put on an end-of-season surge. The division was so tight that season. If you look at the 1976/77 First Division table you'll see we finished on 34 points (bear in mind it was two points for a win then and clubs often go down with fewer point these days), but Birmingham in 13th place only got four more than us. It was incredibly compressed. One more win or two draws would have seen us safe. Instead we went down in the illustrious company of Spurs and Sunderland.

The end for Waddo came when the board asked him to resign in March 1977. His relationship with the board broke down as they sought to lay blame for the unfolding nightmare scenario on the manager. I'm not sure of the exact circumstances, but they would have sacked him if he hadn't resigned, so it was a *fait accompli* as far as I am concerned. There had been a few changes at board level. For example Albert Henshall had retired and so that special relationship between manager and chairman had gone. Waddo was now being questioned more than he had ever been before as the board sought to professionalise things and he didn't like it. He'd spent a lot of money assembling the best squad the club had ever had, but now his lads were being sold from underneath him one by one. How was he supposed to replace them? They were demigods as far as the people of Stoke-on-Trent were concerned. The simple truth was that he couldn't. There were no more rabbits to be pulled out of hats. The likes of John Ruggiero, Alan Suddick and Denis Thorley were not in the same class. But then no one really was. The magic spell had been broken and reality hit home hard.

We came off the pitch at Villa Park knowing we'd somehow managed to clutch relegation from what, just a few months earlier, had appeared to be a wonderful situation. The team was unrecognisable that day. Brian Bithell was now left-back, Paul Johnson, Alan Suddick, John Tudor, Danny Bowers, Dave Goodwin and John Ruggiero were all involved. In the dressing room afterwards there was disbelief; particularly from me. For months there had been this air about the club that there were problems, not just on the pitch but throughout the entire club. There was this air of despondency which decimated team spirit.

It was endemic from the top level down. The incredible thing was how this rudderless ship had crashed on to the rocks so quickly.

As a senior player I would have been looked up to by many of the other lads. The problem was I had this innate feeling that it was all over, the spark had gone and the club would have to start from scratch again. What we'd had was gone. Over. I was 29 and I knew that I wouldn't have that many more years left in me, particularly with my cartilage issues. I still had a contract for another two years, so I had security, but when George Eastham inevitably left the club early in 1978 as we struggled to cope with life in the Second Division, I knew that any new manager who came in would be looking to sweep the broom through and clear out players who had both been part of the last regime and of the sudden decline. That was understandable, not least because we were still shell-shocked, quite frankly.

The opening day of the 1977/78 season saw the nightmare continue. We lost at promoted Mansfield. I got a cut eye which made my day even worse and before we knew it the club had sold Peter Shilton to Nottingham Forest, the last of the high-profile departures of players who could command decent fees. Shilts fetched £250,000. Within three years he had won the European Cup twice. Meanwhile George's inevitable sacking was quickly followed by one of the most horrendous days in the club's history when we lost to non-league Blyth Spartans in the FA Cup fourth round. At home. Worse, we somehow contrived to let a 2-1 lead slip to these Northern League part-timers by conceding two late goals to go down 3-2 at the Vic. I remember trudging off the pitch at the end of that game numbed into thinking that it was just another defeat; the most recent in a whole series of them. When I thought about it, that worried me. It didn't hurt as much as it should have done. I knew there was something seriously wrong with me then. I should have been utterly embarrassed like Jackie Marsh was. He always says he couldn't leave the house for two weeks after that. The fans were devastated, but I came off the field without it having too much of an impact on me. It just shows how much the fall from grace had affected me. It was as if I was expecting these bad things to happen to us. And to continue to happen. It was almost as if that dreadful result had to happen to shake things up. Surely we couldn't go any lower than this?

It was very difficult for George Eastham to follow Tony Waddington as manager. It was the 1970s equivalent of David Moyes succeeding Sir Alex Ferguson at Manchester United. Equally Moyes inherited many problems, which Eastham also faced. Some of those were to do with the rapidly disappearing talent, but even before that you got the feeling that George was going to struggle as he would be undermined at times while he was being groomed. For example, we were drawn against Second Division Sunderland in the FA Cup in February 1976. Before the home game we spent the Friday night at Seighford Hall near Stafford as a little getaway to prepare us. Waddo was there, but he put George in charge as part of his preparation. The problems began when it became clear that the rules changed a bit when George was in charge. He immediately barred us from drinking alcohol at mealtimes, whereas Tony would let us have a glass of wine with the meal if we wanted to.

This outright ban caused a ripple. It didn't bother most of us, but it did unsettle some. Geoff Salmons approached George on the quiet and told him that he had always drunk two pints the night before a game to settle his nerves and allow him to get off to sleep (he should have said at least two if he was being completely honest, but he wasn't looking for a session this particular night). George refused. His new rule was no alcohol and that was that. Sammy complained that he wouldn't sleep and he'd be next to useless the next day if he didn't have the beer. George didn't care. 'I'm sorry, Sammy, I have to bring some form of discipline to this club and I don't believe in it. You're not having them.' Geoff was devastated. Now, as Waddo was there Sammy went up to him and told him what had happened. Waddo hated conflict of any kind and always moved to appease people. Josh and I were rooming next door to Sammy and Huddy and so I heard a knock on the door and a softly spoken 'room service' as we were bedding down for the night. We poked our heads out to see there were two pints of Guinness on a tray outside Geoff's door that had been brought up for him. I turned to Josh and said, 'George has a battle on his hands here.'

He was on a downer from day one, as he would never be able to break that link to the manager who was moving upstairs. There is always that shadow there. Players find it difficult to adjust to a new gaffer at the best of times, let alone when the old one is still around. So, the handover was fraught with difficulty as Waddo's way of dealing with things was so different to how George saw things.

In any case, it turned out that George wasn't really cut out for management. Waddo did have, when it came to it, a ruthless streak. He knew that if he had to move you on then you had to go. He didn't have a problem with that. George, on the other hand, found that side of management very difficult. He couldn't face the fact that one day he'd be eating with a player and the next he'd be having to sell them to another club and cause a whole load of upheaval for him and his family. He couldn't find it within himself to sell players who needed to go because he couldn't face telling them that there was no place left for them at Stoke. I was the same. I would never have been able to do that. So I suppose you could say in some ways that Waddo's judgement was off in identifying George as his successor.

Of course, it didn't help that all of a sudden George was having to deal in Poundland rather than shopping in Harrods as Waddo had been able to do in bringing in the likes of Greenhoff, Hudson and Shilton. The funds had completely gone, swallowed up by the rebuilding of the uninsured stand. All in all it was a right mess… as they say in Fegg Hayes.

After the disaster that was the Blyth Spartans horror show, the board moved quickly to appoint a new manager. Coach Alan A'Court had been acting as caretaker, but the new man was a complete new broom. His name was Alan Durban and he had previously been the manager of Shrewsbury Town. Durban's playing career had seen him be an integral part of the Derby County side which won the Second Division and then First Division titles in the late 1960s and early 1970s. He'd also won 27 caps for Wales, so was very experienced and would prove to be just as tough as a manager as he had been uncompromising as a midfielder. He'd led the Shrews to promotion from the Fourth Division in 1977 and left them in mid-table in the Third Division when he joined Stoke in early March 1978.

We were 18th in the Second Division table when he arrived. The mighty had well and truly fallen. We won our first two games with Durban in charge and rallied to finish the season in seventh place, having picked up 19 points from a possible 32 in the run in. Suddenly there was hope around. You could sense it in the air as preparations were being made for the new season. There was talk of a promotion challenge as Durban's brand of no-nonsense, pragmatic football ensured plenty of clean sheets and lots of victories. He brought great organisation to the club and shook us out of our mordant introspection, moving quickly to shape the club in the way which he knew could get us near the top of the Second Division.

However none of this was good news for me. I had just one more year left on my contract, as did Alan Bloor and Jackie Marsh. I was not really suited to Durban's style, so I knew I wasn't going to be involved much in this renaissance, and was too heavily associated with the previous regime. I also didn't fit his plans. Durban wanted me to play as a midfield player rather than a winger, asking me to come inside and keep possession, rather than risking losing the ball by taking on the full-back in an attempt to cross from the byline. It was not how I'd played the game throughout the career and I was too long in the tooth to adjust. Durban brought players in to fit his vision, such as Paul Randall from Bristol Rovers. That was fair enough. As he proved by winning promotion that season, Durban knew exactly what he was doing.

My time was rapidly coming up. I knew it. There was no hiding from my age, the state of my knees and the impending end of my contract. Durban was very fair with me and told me early on that I would not be offered another contract so that I could make alternative arrangements in plenty of time. From March 1979, I therefore spent most of my time trying to find a new club, rather than cheering on my team-mates to achieve promotion back into the First Division, which they did thanks to a late winning goal at Notts County on the final day of the season.

I'd played 333 games and scored 67 goals for Stoke City, which puts me 15th on the all-time goalscoring list, level with a chap called Jimmy Broad, who by all accounts was a bit of a maverick back in the 1920s. But there is no room for sentiment in football. While the players and supporters celebrated promotion, I was packing my bags on my way out.

11

Hong Kong Fooey

AS soon as I'd learned that I was not going to be required at Stoke City after May 1979 I had cast around for where I might be able to go next. I spoke with John King, the Tranmere Rovers manager, and received an offer from non-league Worcester City. However, I still believed I could do a job above the level of the Fourth Division or non-league pyramid. Maybe my knees stopped any clubs higher up the divisions getting in touch, even after my details were circulated on the free transfer list via the PFA to all the clubs in the country. That list was also circulated around the world and it came to the attention of a gentleman in Hong Kong who worked for a club sponsored by his boss's company, Bulova, the watchmakers. He contacted me and I arranged to meet him in London. I was intrigued. Hong Kong sounded so glamorous and I fancied it. It felt like it would be such a complete change. I wanted to see how the other half lived and also the job on offer was a player-coach role, so it would stand me in good stead for the future career as a coach which I was planning on. The money was the same as I had been on at Stoke and the two-year adventure appealed to me. There was also the temptation of being a big name in a small pond as my arrival would make news headlines in Hong Kong.

It was explained to me that the Bulova club owner was one of the wealthiest people in Hong Kong, but so was his brother, who owned the other major club, sponsored by his watchmaking company, Seiko. So there was a major family rivalry between the two. The main club were Seiko, who had been champions with a side containing a number of Scottish lads, but Bulova were the new pretenders. This appealed to me and I was impressed at this incredible family, who had spawned two major watch brands. My ultimate boss would be a man who the Chinese players and coach of the club looked up to with great reverence, which was ironic as he was only five feet three inches tall. But boy was he a powerful man in Hong Kong. You didn't mess with him, as I was to find out. His name was Mr Chim. He was an accountant by trade and wouldn't know whether a ball was pumped or stuffed.

I flew over on my own and then Sue joined me about a month later along with Tara, our first daughter who had been born in 1974. Even before they arrived I had realised quite quickly that I had made a major boo-boo. It simply wasn't at all what it was cracked up to be. The food was poor and the accommodation was poor, so I had to ask to be moved. Eventually we lived in a tenth-storey flat in Happy Valley. There was an expat community, but it wasn't anything like as close as the players and wives at Stoke. In fact Sue hated Hong Kong, every minute of it. She could not wait to go home. We had still kept the house in Clayton, but I expected that I would have to see my contract through. So I thought I'd better get on with things. I tried, but the five months we were there seemed like five years.

Despite the issues surrounding our daily lives, the biggest problem was the standard of the football. I had taken two young lads with me as fellow British professionals. They had just been released by Bolton and a third one came from Manchester City. They flew out with me, but we couldn't raise the standard from a pretty appalling level, which was roughly equivalent to lower non-league in England. The young lads struggled to make any impact at all.

On top of that the crowds in Hong Kong were quiet. The people just wanted to watch good football, but did not have any tie to a particular club. That was quite the opposite to the partisan nature of English supporters, so there was no chanting and no raucous home support, just polite applause for whichever side played a good bit of football every now and again. Not only that, because Hong Kong was such a tiny island the games were mostly played in the one stadium, the national stadium. So there was a nominated 'home' team, but it wasn't really home at all. Maybe the showpiece game between my team Bulova and Seiko, the great watch rivals – the 'Time Derby' if you like – would see about 10,000 fans attend, but other than that there would only be around 2,000 supporters in a stadium built for over 30,000. Combine the lack of supporters with their natural reserve and sometimes you could hear a pin drop. It was almost as quiet as the Emirates Stadium!

Training was a joke. We had no proper training facilities. We had to train in the park by running and playing around people doing their own personal jogging or an outdoor tai-chi class. You couldn't train during the main part of the day, either, due to the heat and humidity. We mostly trained at 7am for a couple of hours and then again in the early evening. The training was almost exclusively woeful and this simply wasn't what I was used to or had signed up for.

But the major problem was that the players didn't want to improve. Worse, the Chinese culture was such that you couldn't even hand out a rollicking as they took offence. Now, it was my role as coach to do this, to try and ensure some sort of standard in our play, but as soon as anyone made a mistake and you raised it they took huge offence and it got very heated very quickly. This was ridiculous as all I was trying to do was help them. It was my job, after all. Very quickly this became an issue. Their average ability meant that not only could I not coach these players, but I couldn't shine myself as on the pitch I was trying to do the job of about half a dozen men. I had arrived to quite big headlines as I had transferred from a team that had been one of the best in the English First Division, but now here I was being part of a distinct failure. There was such expectation on me to lead them into being a better team, but they didn't want to be led and I ended up having to bite my tongue.

The discrimination we received was astonishing given that we were supposed to be there to help. When it came to hard work on the pitch during a game this turned out to be completely foreign to the Chinese nature, so us professional Europeans were expected to do all the donkey work. The part-time Chinese players were treated by the coach as if they were on a pedestal. He would tell me that they didn't really need to train because they were naturally fit, which was laughable. Us Europeans, however, would be made to train like dogs. The coach's idea of a training session was for us to do 20 laps of the park. I remember the first day he made us do this when we hadn't even got used to the change of time zone yet, let alone the heat and humidity. The young lads who'd come over with me looked to me for some sort of lead and I protested that we needed to build up to this, but the coach wasn't having any of it. This mindset was atrocious. We could only go slowly due to the exhaustion which set in quickly as we weren't acclimatised yet. Also what he was demanding was completely alien to how I had been used to training in one of the best leagues in the world, but when I tried to point this out he wasn't interested at all.

In fact the coach didn't really seem to want my input. He had limited English so we couldn't really communicate. One day the coach was giving a team talk on how he wanted us to play, illustrating his points by drawing arrows on the board. I remember clearly laughing to myself as what he drew reminded me of Custer's Last Stand. There were arrows all over the board which seemed to go round and round the pitch, like circling the wagons. I remember thinking to myself, 'How did I get involved in this,' as I took to the pitch after that particular piece of tactical inspiration. We lost.

On top of all of this was the huge expectation on us to win a trophy due to the ballyhoo which had surrounded my signing and the fact that we were supposed to be able to topple Seiko off their perch. The pressure was on, we weren't very good and it was inevitably going to lead to a confrontation. I just never expected it to play out the way it did.

Just before Christmas I got injured with a bad hamstring tweak. The coach made allowances for Chinese players to get injured, but not for the English. He insisted I played in the next game, but I'd been to the acupuncturist (a treatment which I believe in and has stood me in good stead over the years, especially with my knees) and had been told to rest. So I had a medical opinion which I thought the club would understand and agree with. I was signed off for about two weeks, but because the owner wasn't happy with our results he put pressure on the coach, who told me he didn't accept that I was injured. Of course Mr Chim was the paymaster and on top of that as he was the owner I was supposed to show him deference and respect, especially as a foreign national. I had always tried to put my views forward as that was why they had employed me, but I should have paid more heed to the culture in which I was now living and working. That was a mistake. It ended up with Mr Chim coming into the dressing room and saying something to me in front of my fellow players which questioned my desire to play due to my injury. He thought I was swinging the lead. It really got my goat. Everything which had been building up during my five months in Hong Kong boiled to the surface and broke out into the one major act of my life which I feel ashamed of. I pushed the chairman. He staggered back, but didn't fall. The look on his face said everything, though. The looks on everyone else's faces told a similar story. They were flabbergasted that Mr Chim had been pushed by the Englishman (OK, I'm Irish, but they didn't discern).

Now I'd created a situation which is one of the most dangerous when in the Far East. I'd made a very powerful man lose face. He'd been lowered to my level in both his eyes and those around him. This was not good. He could not accept this. He stormed out, but the next day he summoned me to a meeting. Sue was worried because she knew I was still angry about being accused of faking the extent of my injury and warned me not to do anything stupid, as we might never get off the island. I realised then that never a truer word was spoken as Mr Chim was the kind of man who could make us simply disappear. I hadn't come across anything to do with the Triad while I was in Hong Kong until now, but I knew of their reputation and wasn't about to put my family in that kind of danger, so I calmed down and went to meet him.

I arrived on my own to face the music to find that Mr Chim was sitting in his office in a massive chair behind a huge desk, surrounded by his henchmen. The whole scenario made him look like a Bond villain. I half expected Oddjob to walk through the door and fling his bowler hat at me. I did manage to resist the temptation to say, 'The name's Conroy, Terry Conroy' as I wasn't in anything approaching a humorous mood. I was still too hopping mad at the whole situation, but I'd decided to keep schtum and let him do the talking.

'Mr Conroy,' he said. 'You made me lose face. I cannot accept this. I have to do something about this. I have many friends who could make life difficult for you...' he left a gap here for this to sink in, but he didn't have to as I knew what he meant. 'You can no longer live a safe life in Hong Kong,' he continued.

I had a two-year contract, so I wasn't going that easily, but I was going... I had one chance to take a parting shot and I took it.

'Mr Chim,' I said, showing at least some politeness. 'You know you come to London regularly on business?' Mr Chim nodded. 'Well, I have many friends there...'.

I left the inference for him to consider. He didn't rise to it and we quickly moved on to sorting out the contract. He paid me up including our flights home. We would be getting out. Pronto.

Chim's parting shot as I left was, 'Be careful, Mr Conroy.'

The next day, 20 December 1979, we booked the flight and then we flew back to the UK on the 23rd, arriving home at Heathrow on Christmas Eve. Sue hadn't wanted to spend Christmas in Hong Kong anyway as she was really pining for home. It was sunny and warm in the Far East, but she wanted cold and snow. On top of that it would have been her first Christmas away from her home and family, so Sue was delighted to reach the UK once again. While I was waiting for the luggage to come round on the carousel she raced to the nearest payphone and rang her parents to give them the good news that she would be back in Stoke that night and to reserve three places at the family Christmas table for the next day. Before I knew it she was racing back to me with news.

'Terry, Tony Waddington has been on the phone to my mother.'

'Really?' I said. 'What does Waddo want?'

'He's just joined Crewe Alexandra as manager and he wants to know what time you'll be back in Stoke and if you'll ring him to discuss terms.'

This was great news – my old manager coming to save the day. We never did find out how Waddo even knew I was leaving the Far East and flying home. Perhaps he too had friends in Hong Kong!

I signed for Crewe just after Christmas and made my debut in January 1980, scoring in my second game at York in a 2-2 draw.

Some things are just meant to be. When I arrived at the club they were flat bottom of the Football League – 92nd out of all 92 league clubs. In those days there was no automatic relegation to the non-league divisions. Instead the bottom four clubs in the Football League had to seek re-election from a vote of the other 88 members. This generally resulted in the existing clubs being re-elected rather than the one non-league club which was up for election replacing one of them. Crewe were perennial re-election specialists, regularly finishing in the bottom four, and the directors had called on Waddo to try and get them out of the mire as by the law of averages eventually they would have to get unlucky and would lose their status as a league club.

I spent 16 happy months with Waddo at Crewe. I was delighted to be back, both in the UK and with my manager. He had so many connections he managed to bring together a team of experienced pros like myself, Jimmy Greenhoff, Danny Bowers and Kevin Lewis from Stoke. I also played alongside an attacking midfielder by the name of Mark Palios, who would go on to find fame and notoriety as the chief executive of the FA from 2003 to 2004 after being a part-time player who ran his accountancy career alongside playing football. Mark is now the owner of Tranmere Rovers where his financial skills are going to be fully put to the test to make the club the success once again it had been in the 1990s.

There was also a goalkeeper called Bruce Grobbelaar who joined us after failing to get a work permit after a trial at West Brom. It was obvious Bruce was going to be something special. He was funny and eccentric. He would hang on the crossbar while the ball was up at the other end during games, or do acrobatic flip-flops in his area. He even had the nerve to step up and score a penalty in our final game of the 1979/80 season. The fans loved him clowning around as he later went on to do at Liverpool. The most famous was his wobbly leg routine in the penalty shoot-out of the 1984 European Cup Final against Roma in Rome. Bob Paisley pounced to sign Bruce after seeing him play for us. It wasn't a surprise when Bruce went on to become one of the best goalkeepers and biggest personalities in the game.

Having won just three games before Christmas and being massively adrift of the other 23 clubs at that point, we improved quickly and had a decent run, ending that 1979/80 season in 22nd place, narrowly missing out on avoiding having to apply for re-election. The following season was even better. We were in the top half of the table, which was almost unheard of at Crewe! I was playing in midfield, rather than on the wing, which suited my legs at this late stage of my career. I knew this was my last shot and I revelled in it, playing 37 games and scoring five goals in my 18 months at Gresty Road. We had good crowds for Crewe and the team spirit and camaraderie were akin to that we'd enjoyed at Stoke. Of course with so many players who had been with me at the Potters this was no surprise. We did really well and in fact at one point we were doing so well we hit the heady heights of fifth in the Fourth Division table. At this point one of the directors had to take Waddo to one side and say, 'This isn't on, we can't go up. We can't afford to win promotion.' Can you imagine that?! So Waddo blooded some youngsters in the final games of that 1980/81 season and we ended up 18th, although only eight points off seventh position.

It took a while for Crewe to transform into the club we know today. That was all the work of Dario Gradi, who arrived at the club just a couple of years later, but I like to think Waddo had a small part to play in that by playing those kids at the end of that season. By now I was assisting Eoin Hand and so decided that my time was up and I finished at Crewe in the summer of 1981.

You know when it's time to finish. Your body tells you. You also know that time will come, especially as you pass the age of 30, but you hope and pray that the life you have been leading will never end. I think particularly for me I staved off thinking about the end of my football career for as long as I could. Even after formally retiring in 1981 I kept my hand in playing over in Ireland, as I mentioned earlier. There's nothing that beats playing, and I knew I wasn't cut out to be a manager, so I saw a future for myself in coaching. That was the natural progression for me.

I'd done a preliminary coaching badge as I was coming to the end of my time at Stoke and I just thought someone would take me on. I didn't realise I'd have to really work to get an opportunity. I did write to several clubs, but no one ever got back to me. I expected clubs to jump at the chance of having Terry Conroy as a coach, but it never happened, mostly because I didn't push myself enough. I thought my name and reputation would get me a job. I needed practical experience, but didn't go out and get any. Just being Terry Conroy wasn't good enough and I wasn't persistent enough. I was very naïve, really. The phone didn't ring because I didn't make it ring by chasing down every contact I had and pestering them into giving me a job. It is a salutary lesson to anyone to make your own luck. I'd never have accepted that lack of application on the football field. I'd have got stuck in and made something happen. It just shows how footballers are not ready for the big wide world as much mentally as anything.

I had to build a new life outside the game. This was incredibly difficult as nothing can substitute for playing football. You talk to any pro and they will tell you that. The buzz is very difficult to describe, but it's a tangible, gripping thing. You could be forgiven for getting slightly bitter that the game hasn't continued to give you a living, but I kept my hand in by appearing on the after-dinner speaking circuit on and off, meeting many of my colleagues from my era as I went. I could not make a proper living out of that. It was pin money and not regular enough. You need to be a major world star and be able to relate your experiences to a corporate audience to be able to pull that off. I'm more down to earth. I love speaking with your average supporter who loves the game and specifically Stoke City and who will have been at most of the games and know the players about whom I am speaking. I am not so into speaking to faceless, monied men who aren't really that interested.

A year later and I was still sending off the occasional application letter for coaching positions, but not working my contacts at all. I couldn't see myself doing anything other than football, but now, with nothing happening for me on that front, I had to admit that reality was starting to bite. It's the one thing I would really change. Instead of painting myself into a corner by failing to make a move into coaching I would have made sure I made the transition out of football into a proper career. Of course I had qualified in printing due to my father's insistence in me getting a trade back when I was a teenager, but that industry was changing and I didn't see myself getting back into that as I'd have to effectively start from scratch. I'd worked on old-fashioned machines and the technology had come on leaps and bounds in 14 years since I'd last touched a press. Perhaps I should have gone back in to it as at least I knew something about the print trade. I avoided it, though, as I thought that there was something better out there.

The problem is your mind and body are not trained for life outside of the game at all. It's a stark realisation and one which some former players just can't cope with. Having a life training two hours a day, with plenty of rest and then a game on Saturday is, simply, the perfect existence. By this time I had three daughters; Niamh was born in 1982 and Sinead in 1986 to add to our brood, so there was quite an imperative for me to be bringing some cash in – the mortgage had to be paid and mouths had to be fed.

There's obviously a world of difference these days in terms of the money players who have played consistently at the top level for over a decade would have saved up. I hadn't earned a huge salary during my football career, although I will never complain as it was perfectly decent. But we were now surviving on my paltry savings. My back was against the wall. I couldn't face working in a factory. Even the thought of the nine-to-five grind of an office put the fear of God into me. So I did one of the two things open to me. While Huddy and Geoff Hurst, when they retired, got involved in pubs and bars, which wasn't really my thing, I went to work on a market.

I suppose there comes a point in every life story that the protagonist is down on their luck. It gives the hero time to reflect on the fortune he has enjoyed in life to that point and reassess his future before emerging from the dark times into the light. Usually, though, it's rare this period lasts quite as long as mine did. Once I'd finished working with Eoin Hand and Ireland in 1985, my luck wouldn't turn for another 12 years. During this period everything I did was a means to an end. It was just to pay the bills. I thought there was something out there waiting for me, but, try as I might, I couldn't find it.

I do always look on the bright side. A bit like Del Boy in *Only Fools and Horses* I'd be saying 'This time next year…' There was no luck of the Irish for me to fall back on, however. Just cold winter mornings as I got by selling pottery on the markets. This was only ever intended to be a short-term measure to bring in some money, but it lasted for three years.

It wasn't just me who had to go out and work. Times were tough, so Sue got a job as well. Sue is a down-to-earth, typical Potteries lass and so she just got on with things without any complaint. She worked in the Stonehouse Hotel in Stoke and often did two shifts a day – arriving at work at 6am in order to wait tables at breakfast, coming home and doing the school run, then going back to the hotel in the evening to do dinner from 6pm to 11pm. It was hard, but Sue was never anything other than realistic about having to do what we needed to in order to get by.

I really felt as if I was in the wilderness and only just surviving. I didn't get any satisfaction out of selling pottery on the markets and the biggest thing for me was I didn't have any attachment to the work I was doing in any way other than it was money to feed and clothe my family and pay the bills. I needed to feel as if I was deriving something from the job on top of the plain cash I was able to take home. It was a very difficult time.

I still thought something would turn up which suited me and eventually something came my way which was better than running a market stall. A friend of a friend of mine asked me what I was up to. When I told him he asked me to come in and have a word with his manager who was based in Newcastle-under-Lyme. This ended up with me spending five years selling insurance policies, life assurance and pensions. I had to do qualifications to get that job, but at least it was a step up from the markets. I wasn't doing nine to five, either. I was self-employed and did a lot of evening consultations to discuss people's requirements. The job gave me freedom and allowed me to manage my own time. That at least was a step up, but this all came to an end when I realised that more and more advisors were getting into the insurance market and it was becoming extremely competitive. I was approached to work with a different company in Stoke, selling mortgage insurance, so I became an expert and did quite well. That all ended in 1991, though, in something of a fall-out which I won't go into. Simply put, I was at a loose end again, looking for a fifth career.

A friend of mine heard that I was out of work and approached me to help him out. He worked for Hassell Homes, a company which developed new homes, and he asked me to organise a full clean of each new house before the occupants took possession.

There were quite a few houses to clean so I ran the business and coordinated the four to six ladies who did the cleaning for me. I would often help out, as I'm not too proud to get my hands dirty. The business was my way of life for six years and I inventively called it TC Cleaning! We did a lot of seasonal contracts. For example, each Christmas season we tidied up every morning following the festivities at the Tatton Park Christmas Parties. There would be a month's worth of bashes celebrating the festive season, with 900 or so guests in a tented area. We cleaned up each morning and then set up in readiness for that night's event. We also cleaned refurbished Marston's pubs all over the country and one year we did the Cosford Air Show.

I did think about making TC Cleaning grow, but somehow I didn't have the drive and aspiration to go big in that business. I knew it was possible, but I kept it within an easy scope of what was doable, rather than push things to the limit. By this stage I have to admit that there was an element of a lack of confidence after over a decade of doing work which I felt was purely a means to an end. There was pride in some elements of it, but the grind over that period really did get to me and I was becoming increasingly listless.

I stopped going to watch Stoke too, as I felt I had to beg and I feared the rejection of someone at the club telling me I couldn't have tickets for this week. The thing is you become a nobody if you are not being seen around. Consequently, I distanced myself even more. My fondness for the club had left me and I really wasn't bothered. As a former player if you go through a significant period of time without being involved in the game you lose the hunger. Matchdays don't mean anything to you and you become indifferent to what's going on. In the years that I was out of the game entirely I rarely went down to the Vic to watch games and I lost track of the goings-on at the club. I was engrossed in trying to work out a life which not only could sustain myself and my family, but also one that I could enjoy. For the most part I just about managed that. The problem was, though, that I could never quite leave aside the fact that football had been my life. It had to play a part still. I could not shift that something in the back of my mind which told me that I'd get that call, the one I'd been waiting for all these years.

The problem was I didn't know how to make that happen.

12

Conroy's Coming Home

IT was May 1997. Three big things happened. Labour won a landslide victory at the General Election and Stoke City were leaving their home of over 100 years, the Victoria Ground, for pastures new; namely the shining edifice of the Britannia Stadium up on the hill at a new development which had been named Trentham Lakes. It might not have been in Trentham or have any lakes anywhere near it, but it was to be the new home of Stoke City FC.

Now the observant among you might have noticed that I've only mentioned two things. Well that's because I'm saving up the third one for a minute.

First I have to take a moment to say a fond farewell to the Victoria Ground. It had been my home for 13 happy years. I'd had many successes there and I'd grown up from a young lad of 20 to become a First Division footballer, husband and father with the Vic as a central part of my life.

From my first digs over the road to the social club to the dressing rooms, my past was everywhere I looked as I said a fond farewell to the ground as the 1996/97 season drew to a close. I'm not overly keen on sentiment as I prefer to look forward, but this period did give me pause for thought about what part the old ground had played in my life.

Of course this was the same for many other former players and thousands of supporters, who enjoyed a wonderful final game at the Vic, defeating West Brom 2-1 in the last league match of the season to finish slap bang in the middle of the First Division table. At that point Stoke seemed in decent shape, but over the summer manager Lou Macari left and star striker Mike Sheron, who had scored 39 goals in under 100 games having joined City from Norwich in one of the deals of the century as Lou Macari swapped misfit Keith Scott for him, was sold for £2.75m. In addition young full-back Andy Griffin would be sold to Newcastle United for £1.5m the following January in order to raise funds to pay for the construction of the new stadium. Meanwhile the Vic was fast disappearing amid a flurry of demolition work and auctions, which saw fans buy everything from turf to the turnstile through which they had once entered the ground.

While it was true that the option to redevelop the Victoria Ground site was not viable, it was a very sad moment to say goodbye. The future, though, seemed an exciting prospect as the 1997/98 campaign moved into view with a new stadium to call home.

So what was that third great happening of the summer of 1997? It came in a phone call made by the marketing manager of Stoke City FC, Tony Tams, to me just after the club had moved into the Britannia Stadium. Tony asked, 'Terry, we are looking for a compere to look after guests in our new hospitality suite at home games, are you interested?'

'Of course,' I replied. 'I could do that with my eyes closed.'

I'd never compered so much as a tiddlywinks championship at this point in my life, so I was taking a complete flier on whether I'd be able to pull this off, but I was delighted to have been asked and loved the thought of being involved again. I could feel the fire rekindling in my belly as I put the phone down at the end of that conversation. I was coming 'home', despite the fact that I'd flirted with my other home in Ireland at the very end of my playing career.

The new stadium, dubbed the Britannia originally as part of a long-term sponsorship deal with the Britannia Building Society, opened with a low-key League Cup second leg against Rochdale on Wednesday 27 August 1997. It seemed that first game set the tone for what was to follow. Stoke could not even beat the Third Division team, who had been easily swept aside 3-1 in the first leg at Spotland. Despite Graham Kavanagh scoring with ten minutes to go, Rochdale equalised late on.

Never mind, things would really get going the following Saturday with the official 'first' game at the Britannia Stadium. It was against Swindon Town in front of a 23,000 crowd. But the portents got even worse that day. It was our first real experience of the windy conditions which would eventually cause the Brit to become the bane of so many visiting team's lives. We weren't ready for it then. The three open corners of the exposed stadium meant that the wind swirled into the ground, turning it into a maelstrom with its own weather system. That day the idea was that, before the actual match kicked off, by way of a ceremonial 'christening', Sir Stanley Matthews would 'score' the very first goal at the ground in front of the new Boothen End, the home section behind the goal at the north end of the ground. However, the wind was so strong and swirled so violently that the ball the now 82-year-old Stan side-footed from the penalty spot was blown off course and never made it into the net. That would prove to be typical of the team in that first season in the new stadium. Despite opening the scoring that day through a scrappy goal by Richard Forsyth, Stoke lost 2-1 and ended up getting through three managers as they plummeted towards ignominious relegation. What a way to christen a brand new stadium!

Chic Bates had been first team coach under Lou Macari and Stoke had taken the cheap option of promoting Chic to replace Lou that summer as a way of saving enough money to pay for the stadium's construction. It didn't work and Chic was sacked just after Christmas with Stoke in 16th position, having earned just 29 points. This was the culmination of a dreadful week in which the team had been thrashed 7-0 at home by Birmingham and then lost at West Brom in the FA Cup. There had been a piece in the local paper leading up to the Birmingham game about the bonuses the players had been promised which were not paid. The players were demotivated and it set the scene for a dreadful day. Jez Moxey, the chief executive, who is now at Wolves, was the purveyor of this bad news to the players and was painted very black in the aftermath of the incident. The fans were already angry at the asset stripping of the squad which the building of the new ground had meant, but as the 7-0 humiliation unfolded the mood turned very black indeed.

I was in the Waddington Suite, hosting the 150 or so people in there, but as I sat watching the slaughter unfold I was growing increasingly worried by the chants of sections of the crowd. Sure enough after the final whistle a mob of about half a dozen people, desperate to get their hands on members of the board, stormed in from the West Stand area near the dugouts, climbed up the stairs and forced their way into the Waddington Suite, which was barely guarded by security at all. They assumed it was the boardroom as the stadium was very new back then and people didn't know where things were. These fans thought they would be able to confront the board or even chief executive, but instead found themselves in the main corporate hospitality suite.

That didn't stop them. They set about doing as much damage as they could, pulling things off the walls, even the lights from the sockets in the ceiling. They threw wine on the floor and smashed glasses on the tables as frightened customers dived under them to avoid getting hurt. There were children in the room, but the rampage continued. It may have only lasted five minutes or so, but it was a frightening experience. These were our own supporters, not the opposition. That was the hardest thing to take. It didn't matter who I was. I couldn't pacify them. Eventually security came in and dispersed them, but that incident took quite a bit of recovering from. I always say that since that day the club have made it a rule never to sell 7 Up in the bars…

It was around this time that Peter Coates stepped down as chairman, with Keith Humphreys taking up the reins. Mr Coates remained as a majority shareholder, though. Little did anyone know he was busy building up a business empire in the shape of Bet365, the online betting company, which would stand Stoke City FC in very good stead for many years to come. That was all a very long way in the future and lot of choppy water was still to flow under Stoke City's bridge. It's fair to say that Peter was very unpopular with fans at this point. His stock in the Potteries was very low; a situation which did not improve as the season wore on and Stoke lurched from one disaster to another. In fact over the course of the season City would lose 11 home games. Often painfully. Chris Kamara came and went as manager in the blink of an eye. My former boss Alan Durban, now aged 55, was given the role of caretaker manager and asked to try to engineer some sort of bid for survival. To an extent he did well to get what was by now a rag-tag set of loanees and young pros into a position whereby winning the last game, at home to Manchester City, would see Stoke safe.

But the 5-2 thrashing in that match consigned Stoke to another spell in the third tier of English football. This was not what had been envisaged by the board or supporters when the move to the new stadium was made. In fact it seemed as if the Brit was a millstone around the club's neck at that point, far from the tremendous asset and intimidating fortress it was to become a decade later.

Amid all this mayhem I was trying to sell the club to people as I also joined the commercial department full-time, having proved my worth to them as matchday host. This was not easy. It was one of the most difficult periods of the club's history and the level of disillusionment was unprecedented. I think the hope dealt out by having the new ground made the speedy fall from grace all the more painful. It was my role to try and sell sponsorship packages, which included picking the man of the match. The sponsor would also get a signed programme and signed ball as well as a meal and their business name all over the programme and scoreboard. There were few takers and in those years down in the third tier which ensued it was often the same local businessmen who I could turn to as regulars to keep things ticking over for us.

To boost things I decided to get a former player in to sit with the sponsors on their table. It was often a Stoke legend like Josh Mahoney or Harry Burrows from my era. As matchday guest he would also chat with supporters, sign autographs and we'd do a little interview in the Waddington Suite to entertain the guests while they ate. They would also end up being introduced on the pitch at half-time, often to a hero's welcome from the stands. Stoke fans' memories are very long and so they love players of old, especially those who come back after some time. This all proved very popular and we began to build a client base who liked feeling just that little bit closer to the club that this experience allowed. I loved this job and had the freedom to make it what I wanted it to be as long as it worked. Generally it did, and well. The guest players were my contacts who I invited and they'd do it for me as they were only getting a free lunch and their expenses paid, not actually getting an appearance fee. They'd really be coming to have the interaction with the fans again. Much like me, most players who have felt that connection yearn to have it again.

I was reawakened and reinvigorated by the whole experience. This job was what I had been waiting for all these years. It had taken me almost two decades to become an overnight sensation. Outside of matchdays it was now also my job to find sponsors for everything from the match ball to the programme, sell advertisements for the hoardings round the pitch or the programme, mascot packages for kids and matchday suite packages. Now this all sounds quite easy to do with a sexy product like professional football, but then you have to take into consideration the fact that we are talking about Stoke City FC who at that time were at one of the lowest ebbs of their history having just been relegated to the Third Division (as I still think of it), which is called League 1 today.

Selling Stoke in those circumstances was hard. You were going cap in hand to people. Some heavy discounts were applied in order to get people through the door. You had to. People were turning their nose up at paying £400 for a package to sponsor the match ball and have six people in the suite, for the tour and a meal. On top of that the Potteries was struggling. Factories were closing, unemployment was rising and the area had an air of depression about it. It wasn't a great time at all, especially if you were trying to generate revenue like I was.

The product on the pitch wasn't great. Having Kyle Lightbourne or Wayne Thomas as man of the match isn't the same as Bojan Krkic, Ryan Shawcross and Peter Crouch, let's face it. Peter Thorne, Kevin Keen and Graham Kavanagh were saleable assets, then later we had Clive Clarke and James O'Connor as stars of the team. We may only have attracted 100 or so people to the Waddington Suite for smaller opponents, and the room holds

350. These days it's always packed out, so it just shows how being successful on the pitch relates directly to generating income.

I loved it all. It was natural to me. But I especially loved the matchdays, meeting supporters of every type, age and experience. I might have been talking with people who had been supporters for donkey's years or those who were only just finding their love for the club. Often it was both, as dads brought wide-eyed youngsters along to teach them all about Stoke City. I was delighted to play a part in capturing the kids' hearts for the lads in the red and white stripes. This process would begin on the tour of the stadium which the sponsors and their guests have to kick off their day when they first arrive. The tour was completely made up by myself. We greet guests with a Buck's Fizz, then show them a DVD about the history of the club. It starts with a welcome message from the manager. When Tony Pulis was in charge he recorded a piece in which he said, 'Welcome to Stoke City Football Club. I really hope you have a good day… despite the fact you are being shown around by Terry Conroy.' It also included welcome messages from some of the players. It's very personal as only people who go on the tour ever see it.

We then go into the directors' box and sit in their plush, padded seats, then visit the press box and TV gantries, showing fans where the Hawkeye cameras which judge the goal-line decisions are sited. The guests then move on to have a photograph in the dressing room next to the shirt of their favourite player and see their boots up close. Then we'll head into the media suite and do a mock post-match press conference. I love interviewing kids. 'So, Crouchy,' I'll say. 'Another hat-trick today. Tell us about the goals.' And the kids will go on about these amazing goals they have scored. They are often hilarious.

We then go down on to the track surrounding the pitch, with more photographs in the home dugout, before ending up in the Stanley Matthews Lounge to talk about the great man's career, my favourite subject. I'm very conscious of the need to send people away thinking how much they have enjoyed the tour, and how much they have learned. It's very important to make people feel they have had a special day. It's a fantastic opportunity to win friends and influence people, even those who are fans of other clubs enjoy the opportunity to learn about the club and its history, especially Stan.

Nowadays, I am now officially known as the 'matchday ambassador'. I do the man of the match's post-match interview and present the sponsor's awards. My additional duties also see me visiting the various hospitality suites and corporate boxes to say hello to people accompanied by the guest of honour for the day to brighten their day. There's never a dull moment when you've got someone like Mickey Thomas, a well-known raconteur, in tow. Sometimes he can be in one box for half an hour, let alone getting round all of them! I too can talk all day about football and my experiences. I get asked every week about the team I played in, the goal at Wembley and winning the League Cup. And of course, almost inevitably, someone will approach me, hand extended in warm greeting and utter the immortal line, 'You don't remember me, do you?'

It's always a great day, whatever the result and I feel that for me it's just as good as the involvement I had as a player, just in a very different way. I really feel the benefit of getting instant feedback from happy customers throughout the day, and also sorting out any issues which crop up. I've done the role for almost 18 years now, so it's actually longer than my entire playing career.

The major issue through the first decade I had the job was that the club was still all over the place. If I summarise in one sentence that in the first ten years at the Brit, Stoke went through nine managers, suffered one relegation, two play-off semi-final defeats, survived a last day must-win relegation scrap, won the Autoglass Trophy at Wembley and a play-off final at the Millennium Stadium, buried the greatest player in its history Sir Stanley Matthews in moving fashion, and the club changed hands twice, you'll see that in comparison to *EastEnders* Stoke was a real soap opera.

One of the main episodes was the seven years which saw an Icelandic consortium buy the club. When they purchased Stoke on 15 November 1999 they were effectively saving a club which had been sliding towards oblivion. Their impact was instant, a 4-1 victory at Wycombe providing some hope for a revival, but then came those successive play-off defeats and the policy of bringing

Scandinavian players into the team did not pay off. Some like Brynjar Gunnarsson and Bjarni Gudjonsson were successes, but others simply weren't. I remember Rikki Dadason being built up as this international goalscorer when the club announced he would be joining from Viking Stavanger, where he'd scored a hatful of goals, at the end of the Norwegian season in November 2000, but then I became completely deflated when I saw him on the pitch. He had, after all, only been finding the net in Norway. There were many more like him, the most infamous of which were nicknamed Triggy and Ziggy by then manager Tony Pulis, who simply refused to play sub-standard signings.

I didn't have much contact with the new owners. Chairman Gunnar Thor Gislason would only bother to come over to England on a Friday and just pop into the commercial department and say hello. I'm fairly sure he didn't know who I was or even the fact that I had played for Stoke during a very successful era. They knew Stoke were a very big fish in the third tier of English football, but clearly had no real idea about the history of the club or its traditions – for example they brought in a new club badge in 2001, which caused a lot of angst among traditional supporters.

I also had very little contact with Gudjon Thordarson, the new Icelandic manager, but I was delighted for him after successive play-off failures against Walsall and Gillingham when he again steered Stoke to the play-off semi-finals, this time against Cardiff City, who had become huge rivals as the board had seen fit to sell both star striker Peter Thorne and midfield playmaker Graham Kavanagh to them. I remember the first leg of those play-offs very well. Cardiff went two goals up through Robert Earnshaw and Leo Fortune-West and everyone thought that was it for another year. But then on-loan striker Deon Burton snatched a late goal after a sustained spell of pressure and the roof nearly came off the Brit. You just felt the pendulum swing Stoke's way. I remember in the Waddington Suite after the game telling everyone that, even though they might feel a little down in losing the game, Deon's goal could be really important.

On the face of it Stoke had no chance of winning at Ninian Park, but that's exactly what happened. James O'Connor scored in the 89th minute to send the game into extra time. I was watching the match along with about 4,000 or so delirious Stoke supporters on a big screen at the Brit. It was a fabulous evening. We'd sold the place out and it went crazy when Jimmy netted that goal and then even more ballistic when his free kick deflected in off substitute striker Souleymane Oulare's backside to send the Potters through to a comfortable victory over Brentford in the final to achieve a promotion which at times had felt as if it would never come.

The Icelandic owners must have thought that because, bizarrely, four days later they sacked the Icelandic manager who they themselves had installed in 1999. There had been problems between Gunnar and Gudjon for some time. As people working within the club we knew the relationship was fiery, but you assumed that this was just the way it was with colleagues who were in it together. The truth was, by the end of that season, Gudjon hated Gunnar. He felt the chairman was always completely anti what he wanted to do with the team. He had been becoming more vocal about dismissing Gunnar's talents in the press and by the time the end came it wasn't that much of a surprise. The timing, however, was.

For their next manager the Icelanders turned to a young up-and-coming English coach. Steve Cotterill had propelled Cheltenham Town up from the non-league wilderness into the Football League. He had earned a shot at a higher level, but when I met him I realised immediately that he was, to put it mildly (and politely), extremely confident. In fact for someone who had achieved nothing in the game really, I felt he was an arrogant individual who came to a big club like Stoke thinking it was just a stepping stone to bigger things. He told anyone who would listen that he was going to manage England. I had very little contact with him, but was probably among the few people who were not surprised when, after just a handful of games, in early October Cotterill announced his resignation. He was off to join Premier League Sunderland – not as manager, mind you, but as number two to Howard Wilkinson. Sunderland would go on to set a new record low points total for the Premier League of 19 and both Wilkinson and Cotterill would be out of a job after just 27 games in charge in which they recorded just two victories, losing every game after 5 February that season.

For this desertion Stoke fans dubbed him 'Quitterill'. An apt name. That move to Sunderland shows you just what a good judge of a situation our friend Mr Quitterill is. He's found his level with Bristol City now as he has finally achieved something tangible by winning promotion to the Championship in 2014/15, although it's taken him long enough to do something with a club.

To be fair to Cotterill he experienced what each of the managers who worked under the Icelanders did, that the club was being run from afar with no one linking things together in the UK on behalf of the board. Everyone within the club felt the decisions were being made elsewhere with no reference to them, not just on the footballing side, we felt that too in commercial. Apathy followed and it was a sad time.

It now felt like the club was a long-forgotten dinosaur, especially after the ensuing episode of respected manager George Burley being offered the manager's job, even going so far as to attend a game, but then turning it down. Perhaps George was canny enough to spot the trouble coming. The board then had to scrabble around to find a fourth- or fifth-choice appointment in the form of former Gillingham and Portsmouth boss Tony Pulis. I wasn't over the moon with any of this. Tony's record at Gillingham had been good, but subsequent to that he'd had a very chequered history, including legal battles with a couple of clubs which had only just ended. My feeling was that we should have been appointing a much bigger name, to make a statement, to say we're Stoke City and we're a big club. Instead we had what felt like a low rent option. It was quite soul-destroying in many ways. Not that Tony was a bad manager, but he wasn't the name that former Ipswich boss George Burley was. The brutal truth was that Stoke City could not attract that kind of manager anymore.

So, it's fair to say that I was quite underwhelmed by the appointment of Tony Pulis.

Once I met Tony I immediately bought into him and felt we had a chance of survival against all the odds. Tony was a different character to the previous aloof managers. He was always chivvying staff along, with his optimistic approach permeating around the club. He'd visit departments and be bubbly with all of the staff. He infected them with his enthusiasm and you could feel the tide begin to turn. People warmed to him and were supportive of him. We all wanted him to succeed, whereas previously there had been a feeling that a lot of staff were indifferent to the club being successful as they weren't invested in the club and what was happening on the pitch. Tony changed all that for the better. Everyone at the club felt he was their friend, which made a huge difference as the club was battling relegation in this first season after winning promotion.

Tony took over on 31 October 2002, with the club having won just three games and standing in 21st position in the table, one spot above the relegation zone. We would eventually stay up on the final day of the season thanks to a 1-0 victory over Reading, through a goal by on-loan striker Ade Akinbiyi. That season was great for us in commercial to sell as The Great Escape and the fans were galvanised once again. After managing to pull off an unlikely survival bid, Tony was also talking about taking the club into the Premier League within five years. It felt like paper-talk then, but in fact he would prove to be spot on.

The immediate aftermath of that survival season saw Tony slowly build the squad through loans and free transfer signings. The likes of Mark Crossley, Peter Hoekstra, Peter Handyside, Darel Russell, Ed de Goey, Gerry Taggart, John Halls and Michael Duberry contributed to making Stoke a mid-table side. But that's all we were and the Icelanders were clearly getting frustrated with things, especially their relationship with the manager, who simply refused to play their Scandinavian signings. In the 2004/05 season – forever known to Stoke fans as the 'Binary Season' – their relationship broke down completely. Tony's decision to play increasingly defensive football, which resulted in long sequences of games which ended either goalless or in 1-0 victories for either side, didn't particularly bother me as what was refreshing was that there was at least a coherent plan. You could see that Tony was biding his time to develop the club and find the players that could get us up the table. The likes of Gifton Noel-Williams and John Eustace were early signs of this; both were quality players, but both had major injury issues. It was a means to an end on a very restricted budget. It wasn't great for sales, though.

It also turned into football to make a point. No fun, no foreign players, but actually this was a major achievement when you look at the overall context. I suppose supporters weren't aware of the huge tensions behind the scenes. Gunnar wanted players from Iceland to come over and TP simply point-blank refused. He wanted no part of it, preferring instead to control who he had in his squad as he rightly argued that if he was going to be judged on results he wanted to field players he himself had signed. Tony will never be the foreign-style coach who makes the best of players who are imposed upon him. He just doesn't work like that. If his head is on the chopping block he wants to stand and fall by the players he brings in. He suffered constant harassment to bring in Icelanders but resisted.

It all ended inevitably with his departure from the club at the end of that 2004/05 season. I always thought the bizarre thing was that when Gunnar Gislason announced Tony's departure the reason he gave was for 'failing to exploit the foreign market'. Do you know who the last signing Tony Pulis made in that first spell at Stoke was? Mamady Sidibe, a Mali international striker, who'd grown up in Paris. Now I know geography isn't my strong point, but neither Paris nor the Malian capital Bamako (yes, I looked it up) are that close to Trentham, are they? For me, Gunnar was trying to make it sound faintly racist and I think nothing could be further from the truth. The Icelanders that were being foisted upon Tony simply weren't good enough. Had they been then TP would have been delighted to utilise them.

So, Stoke City were managerless once again. This time, though, the upset was all the greater as the Icelanders overtly stated that they would have one last season in which to try to win promotion, but were now actively looking to sell the club. They wanted to see some fun in the football, though, and so appointed a little-known Dutch manager who had been in charge at clubs such as Anderlecht, Ghent, Dinamo Tbilisi and even coached the Georgian national team, as well as out in the Middle East at Al Wasl in Dubai. His name was Johan Boskamp and with him around there was never a dull moment.

Initially I felt his appointment was a real kick in the goolies for the fans as Boskamp was an unknown quantity. No one had ever heard of him and this weighed heavily on his shoulders. Funnily enough I had a lot more to do with him than most other managers. He would come in to the commercial department with a big smile on his face and seek me out. It seemed that he thought I could relate to him because of my age and past. I enjoyed the fact that he had bothered to find out my background. In fact he knew I'd played against Ajax back in 1974 as he had been playing at Feyenoord back then. I found him a jovial, entertaining and enjoyable character. He was, though, very quirky. For example, his idea of a typical working day ended at lunchtime with a hearty meal, and a bottle of Coke followed by an afternoon watching DVDs; not necessarily of either Stoke City or our forthcoming opponents.

Boskamp gave the Icelanders their new direction and the open football they craved. He was happy to win 5-4 and we had a lot of high-scoring games. The only problem was he never quite got to grips with how to deliver consistent results at the Brit. In fact, we won ten at home and nine away that season. Our home form was relegation, but our away form was promotion. Again, it didn't make for the best sales.

During our chats Boskamp would ask me what I thought of the previous weekend's game and I'd offer my opinions. Often I was telling him we were too attack-minded. For me to say that was quite something! I love pushing forward and playing off the cuff, but I also know that you have to earn the right to play that way in the English game, especially in the Championship, which is a battle every week. Johan loved his defenders having the freedom to roam forward and would talk about midfielders breaking to support the strikers and even forwards being able to defend. He was looking for a brand of Total Football, which he had played in his spell in the Dutch national side alongside Cruyff, Neeskens and Rep at the 1978 World Cup. It's the Dutch way to be gregarious and adaptable and this shows in their style of play. This was quite the opposite to Tony Pulis, who was all about organisation and defensive solidity.

Boskamp kept the press endlessly busy with a ream of stories, none more famous than that Coventry incident. He had been brought to the club by director of football John Rudge, who had also identified Dutchman Jan de Koning as first team coach. The trio had a massive fall-out during a match at Coventry in November 2005. Rudge had been sitting in the stands but spotted a weakness in the Coventry defence which he felt Stoke could exploit so came down to the touchline to communicate it. As Boskamp was out in the technical area Rudge discussed it with de Koning who then implemented the change. He hadn't run it past the manager who felt undermined and threw an absolute paddy. The working atmosphere was terrible after that, all the more so I believe because the change actually resulted in the team turning a 1-0 deficit round into a 2-1 victory. Boskamp really didn't appreciate that. The outcome was that Johan had this feeling that everyone was ganging up on him, the world was weighing heavily on his shoulders. He could never get past it and it blighted the remaining time he had at the club. He consistently banged on about how unhappy he was. It was yet another Stoke City own goal.

In keeping with the board's vision, Boskamp had brought in players such as Carl Hoefkens, the silky Belgian right-back, Belgian midfielder Junior, Czech winger Martin Kolar and Australian midfielder Josip Skoko. Domestic-developed talents such as Luke Chadwick, Peter Sweeney and Kevin Harper complemented those foreign signings. This surely had made the Icelandic owners happy?

Actually it turned out they wanted more than that. They wanted promotion or nothing. Boskamp's brand of helter-skelter football certainly may have been more entertaining, but it was no more successful than his predecessor. Stoke finished 13th in 2005/06 as opposed to 12th the previous season. More entertainment, but the same result. Boskamp signed off with a typically swashbuckling 5-1 away win at Brighton, with teenage striker Adam Rooney grabbing a hat-trick, then waltzed off into the sunset, chuntering away to himself as he had done pretty much all year about how the whole world was against him. I wasn't surprised he went when he did, as I knew all about the discord behind the scenes. It had been a hoot, though.

Late in the 2004/05 season as it became apparent that the Icelanders were looking to prepare the club for a sale it had been decided there had to be cutbacks and it was announced some staff would be made redundant. I knew I would be a casualty as people looked upon me as an ex-footballer, rather than having any intrinsic value to the club. I felt many very senior people would look at me and ask themselves, 'What does he really do?' I felt this was unfair as I believed, and still do believe, my value to the club is tangible in many different ways as I know countless people in the Potteries and am accessible as someone people can relate to, which is why they bought sponsorship from me. Sure, I had my sales figures to point to and those at least saw me offered a choice of either full redundancy or to reduce my hours to two days a week. I wasn't happy at all about this as I felt I deserved better, but chose the two-day week option, plus keeping up the matchdays, and began to cast around for something else to do, although it would be a while until the Irish FA job came up and I left the commercial department entirely.

It hurt a lot that my role was being so restricted by this change to two days a week, but it seemed to sum up where the club had got to under the Icelanders. They were treading water at best, desperately looking for a way out. It was now the summer of 2006 and Stoke were a million miles away from being the club we know today. The owners wanted to sell and there was no manager. What a truly sorry mess my club was in. Again.

What we needed was a local benefactor, who had pots of money and the club's best interests at heart. Fortunately for Stoke, the fans, players and entire city (Port Vale fans excepted, of course) just such a man strode on to the scene and changed everything.

13

Back in the Big Time

ENTER Peter Coates. It's fair to say that the news the former chairman was to buy back the controlling interest in Stoke City FC from the Icelandic consortium to whom he'd sold it several years earlier was met by a mixed reception in the Potteries. There were some fans who were just glad to get rid of the Icelanders. There were others who thought Coates was the only option as no one else would take on the club and its huge debt, lack of ownership of its own ground and not even having a proper training ground to call its own. Then there was a sizeable proportion of the fanbase who simply didn't trust Coates following the events of his chairmanship in the 1980s and 90s. A very vocal debate followed, which only intensified when the 'new' owner announced that the 'new' manager of Stoke City was to be someone the fans knew all too well, former boss Tony Pulis, who had divided opinions greatly towards the end of his previous spell in charge. I would say about 80 per cent of the supporters were not in favour of the new regime, with about half of those being vehemently against this turn of events.

They were worried that it would be a return to the same old same old.

How wrong can you be! Before we knew it Stoke would be challenging for promotion in just their first season back at the club, while the Coates/Pulis dream team secured a sensational return to the Promised Land of top-flight English football the following campaign.

It was a remarkable, incredible turnaround, the like of which has rarely been seen in the game of football. Yes, I rate what Peter and Tony achieved together that highly.

Back in the summer of 2006 you would have been hard pushed to find a Stoke City fan of any long standing who could visualise what would occur over the following decade or so. If you'd said to any of them that they would get promoted to the Premier League, would win 5-0 at Wembley on the way to a first FA Cup Final appearance, would play in Europe and would sign a player known as 'the new Lionel Messi' you'd have been carted off by the men in white coats. Nurse, someone's escaped!

The preceding 20 or so years of mediocrity, minor success and huge disappointments had conditioned fans into a mentality whereby winning at the likes of Wigan was perceived as a major success, especially after a dreadful 6-1 hammering there in November 2001. That was one of many humblings these supporters have had to endure since the wind took the roof off the Butler Street Stand. It had been a very bumpy ride since then and there didn't seem to be anything different in prospect when Coates and Pulis took the reins again.

But, things were in fact very different. No one really knew what a phenomenal success the Coates family, with Peter at its helm, had made of Bet365, the online betting company, based in Stoke. His wealth had been transformed and the family had also bought into his vision for the football club when he told them he wanted to buy it back from the Icelanders. It was a huge gamble on their part and Stokies everywhere should be truly thankful that they took the risk. Looking back now it's apparent that the period of Icelandic ownership was a low period that had to happen to allow Peter Coates to come back to the club and propel it into the stratosphere, for that is what happened.

If I'd been underwhelmed the first time Tony Pulis had been appointed as manager then to see him return just felt like a retrograde step; more of the same sterile football. He had a plan, but it was difficult to see how that plan could achieve anything more than mid-table mediocrity in the second tier. There is also a rule of thumb which says 'never go back'. But how wrong could I be. Tony had spent his year away as manager of Plymouth identifying players of the calibre of Ricardo Fuller, Rory Delap, Liam Lawrence and Danny Higginbotham, and now with Coates's backing he brought them to Stoke. His template stood the team in such great stead. The fulcrum in attack was the role played by Mama Sidibe, the player who TP had signed but then not been able to work with back in 2005. City went on a great run and finished eighth in 2006/07, then won promotion on the back of a fabulous 2007/08 season, finishing second to West Brom. Hard work, organisation and sheer grit were the basis of success. That base allowed the flair of Lawrence and Fuller, whose superb hat-trick defeated West Brom 3-1 at the Brit just before Christmas, to shine through.

From my point of view the way the club was being galvanised threw me back in time to the arrival of Alan Hudson in 1974. The city was stirring in just the same way and the backing the supporters gave the team was incredible, like we had experienced back then.

You could just feel the good times coming rolling back, especially as the run-in to the 2007/08 season saw tense, titanic victories at home against promotion rivals Bristol City and away at Coventry. A final-day draw against Leicester ensured Stoke were promoted into the Premier League to end 23 years of pain and anguish for Stokies everywhere, me among them.

Of course, selling the club as this all unfolded was a breeze. Life in the commercial department had now completely turned around. Previously I'd been trying to scrape together a few sponsors here and there, now business came to us. We actually couldn't fit enough of the LED advertising boards around the pitch. Local businesses loved bringing clients to games against Liverpool, Manchester United and Chelsea and to experience the unique Britannia Stadium atmosphere.

Where matchdays had been a chore for so many people over the preceding 20 years or so, now there was the delicious temptation of the Premier League to attract people, including many women and families to the Brit. Everything was changing and for the better. Season tickets flew out of the box office over the summer of 2008 and the buzz was immense. Despite doom-mongering 'expert' predictions of the team finishing bottom by miles, you just knew that we would give most teams a good game at the Brit, especially with a packed house backing the team.

Of course we had a secret weapon with which to take on the Premier League; the incredible long throw of Rory Delap. In the last minute of the very first home game of that remarkable first Premier League season Delap launched the ball into the Aston Villa penalty area and Sidibe nodded it home to secure a famous 3-2 victory. Mayhem ensued and it set the tone for some remarkable home wins that campaign, including over Spurs, Manchester City and Arsenal. This was little Stoke, socking it to all these big boys. I revelled in every moment.

I got to know Tony Pulis reasonably well during his two spells at the club and discussed his approach to the game with him on many occasions. He is renowned for playing a direct game, but this is because he plays to the strengths of the players he has at his disposal, organises them brilliantly and utilises every possible method to get something out of the game. He discovered and then deployed Rory Delap's throw as a central part of Stoke's strategy for surviving that first Premier League season, something which Rory's previous managers had ignored. It led to countless goals and I loved the whole theatricality of each set piece. The expectation when we got a corner or a throw-in saw the place came alive. The noise the Brit made when Rory had the ball in his hands saw it at its rumbustious, raucous best. That tactic alone became synonymous with Stoke City across the globe as it made great TV. Opposing teams were scared of it and would try to find people who could throw like Rory so they could practise defending against it. I remember Carlo Ancelotti once telling a press conference that his Chelsea team had spent all week practising defending against the long throw. The only thing was Rory was injured that week and didn't play!

Many of the scribes who came to the Brit that first season had never experienced anything so visceral and just plain loud as the Brit. It took them aback as they'd become comfortable in their Premier League cocoon. They took to writing about the whole experience as intimidating and I always think that helped us massively as it built the windy old place up in visiting teams' minds. I used to play on it as much as possible in my build-up to the day's game when speaking to the sold-out Waddington Suite crowds, which often featured a smattering of fans from the visiting club. Having discovered how much opponents in my era hated playing at the Vic far too late for it to be of use, I was determined to leverage every possible advantage out of this particular scenario. So, I banged on and on about Rory's long throw, the gaps in the three corners of the Brit and how the visiting nancy boys wouldn't fancy it today. It made a real change from pretending to auction off the company timeshare apartment in Beirut to keep people amused as I often had to during the slim years.

The hostility created by the Brit surprised many visiting players. I'll never forget the spectacle of Spurs goalkeeper Heurelho Gomes crying as his side succumbed 2-1 early in the season, with Gareth Bale being sent off and Ricardo Fuller missing a penalty to boot.

Croatian defender Vedran Corluka ended up in hospital after that game, having become so disorientated he challenged his own goalkeeper for a cross and got his lights punched out. I'm fairly sure Mr Wenger blamed Stoke's rugby playing tactics for that particular hospitalisation, as he often does, even though it wasn't a game in which he was involved. But then that's Arsene for you. In fact it was a combination of the swirling conditions, intense pressure and good old fashioned 'up-and-at-'em' tactics which caused Corluka to end up at the North Staffs. Oh, and the right fist of his own keeper.

Teams weren't just being beaten at the Brit, they were having the life sucked out of them and conversely the crowd and the stadium itself seemed to energise our players all the more. There was a particularly brilliant example during the immense 1-0 victory over Manchester City in January 2009. Waves of intense vocal support seemed to tangibly lift the players and helped Stoke's ten men (Rory Delap had been sent off in the first half) to victory.

When I played I used to love hearing what they used to sing on the Boothen End. The fans took to celebrating our success then in typically tongue-in-cheek fashion by rewriting 'Land of Hope and Glory' to 'Land of Smoke and Glory':

Land of Smoke and Glory
Home of Stoke City
Higher, higher and higher
On to victory

Famously, another chant back in my day was in honour of one of Stoke's leading fans, John Bayley, aka Zigger Zagger. You could hear it tumbling down from the Boothen End, 'Zigger zagger, zigger zagger, Stoke City' it went. In the early 1970s there was a lot of interest in the media about terrace culture, so much in fact that Jimmy Hill came and made a TV programme about Zigger, while Stoke playwright Peter Terson wrote a play called *Zigger Zagger*, which was performed by the National Theatre.

Nowadays the Stoke crowd's sense of humour spills out from the stands in various different ways. There's rarely a game goes by in which I don't find myself laughing at something the Boothen End comes up with. There are standard songs such as the ironic celebration of having won the Autoglass Trophy (hardly the most glamorous prize in the world) twice:

We won it two times
We won it two times
The Autoglass Trophy
We won it two times

Mind you, for my money the Watney Cup should get more of a mention, although we did only win that the once.

The same song was used as the basis for a great chant following the triumph of that BBC TV programme Marvellous about former kitman Neil Baldwin. By this time Neil had become something of a local celebrity and there had even been one match in the 2014/15 season dedicated to him as Neil Baldwin day. After the show won two BAFTA's in early May 2015 Stoke fans immediately cannibalised the Autoglass Trophy song turning it into:

We've won it two times
We've won it two times

Stoke at the BAFTAs
We've won it two times

I remember during the Europa League campaign of 2011/12 another amusing ditty saw Stoke fans promoting British tourist venues by singing 'Turkey's a shithole, I wanna go Rhyl' to visiting Besiktas fans. Of course, there is always something amusing to chant at opposing players. Everton goalkeeper Tim Howard has been known for his shiny bald head for years, however since his heroic performances in the 2014 World Cup in Brazil for the US national team he has also sprouted a decent-sized beard. Naturally when Everton visited the Brit in early 2015 the Boothen End picked up on this and informed him, 'Timmy Howard, you're head's upside down.'

My favourite, though, is what has become known as Wenger-baiting. Each time Arsenal visit the Brit and dismally fail to perform the Stoke fans come up with something brilliant with which to mock the hapless visiting manager. In 2011 when Arsene got very worked up and flapped his arms around in his technical area the fans behind him started copying him and before you knew it everyone around the stadium was doing it while chanting 'let's all do the Wenger'! Even Gary Lineker laughed about it on that night's *Match of the Day*. It helped, of course, that we were 3-1 up and cruising at the time, much to Mr Wenger's eternal chagrin.

That first magnificent season saw Stoke finish 12th. That isn't avoiding relegation. That's finishing mid-table. Four further mid-table finishes followed. We are now an established Premier League club. The success has been phenomenal – at least in Stoke City terms. We may not have any silverware to show for it yet, but there have been great wins, a European adventure and pride has been fully restored to a magnificent club which had been in the doldrums for almost a quarter of a century.

In the seven seasons that Stoke have been in the Premier League clubs such as Newcastle United, West Ham United, Portsmouth, West Bromwich Albion and Blackburn Rovers have been relegated. The likes of Leeds United, Nottingham Forest, Sheffield Wednesday and Derby County – top-flight fixtures in my day – haven't even played in the Premier League in that time.

There have been many major casualties too. By that I mean clubs who thought they were too good to go down, or who thought they would come straight back up if they did get relegated – the likes of Bolton, Wigan and Blackburn, for example. Relegation for Stoke during those first five years probably would have been curtains. The club would not have been strong enough to recover from the disappointment and the fans would have thought that another quarter of a century in the wilderness would be about to ensue. So for me the fact that Tony Pulis kept Stoke comfortably in the Premier League has now set the foundations for a very long stay indeed. Stoke are among the top ten clubs in the country now under Mark Hughes and are officially one of the top 30 richest clubs in the world. That is incredible considering where we were when Messrs Coates and Pulis returned in 2006. Nowadays clubs who come up look enviously at Stoke as the best example of how to survive and then thrive in the Premier League. In the season during which I am writing this book, 2014/15, both Burnley and Leicester have adopted a similar approach. Neither club should have a hope of staying up – just as Stoke seemingly didn't in 2008/09 – but have given it a good go.

In 2008 I was offered the job working as liaison officer for the Football Association of Ireland, so I resigned from the commercial department at Stoke City, although I remained as matchday host. Retaining that link has given me a unique perspective on how the media works. Earlier in the book I had a rant about the appalling standard of reporting which pervades the modern game. I actually get the chance after every home game to redress the balance as the sponsors' man of the match is brought up to the Waddington Suite after each match and awards are handed over and photographs taken; the usual stuff. Then I get a couple of minutes of interview time, during which I try not to ask the obvious questions. Having been in their position I know it's the last thing they want to be doing, so I try and make it fun and interesting for both them and their adoring public.

On this one particular occasion Stoke had drawn 2-2 with West Ham in early November 2014 and the sponsors had chosen Bojan

Krkic, the little wizard brought to the club by Mark Hughes the previous summer who'd had a cracking game, as their man of the match. Now the Spaniard wasn't confident in his English, having only moved to the UK three months earlier, so requested to only have two questions put to him. Even then with my Irish accent being quite strong poor Bojan literally hadn't got a clue what I was saying. I'd put something to him, hold the microphone out to him to respond into and he'd look at me, turn to look at the 300-strong audience, and shake his head. There were howls of laughter. After the third attempt he actually said, 'Que?' Now for those of you who have never seen the comedy *Fawlty Towers*, featuring Basil Fawlty, his awful hotel, his ogre of a wife and the Spanish waiter Manuel, from Barcelona, this will mean nothing. But I'm sure most of you have. So, I turned to the audience and said, to great hilarity, 'I feel like I'm at Fawlty Towers.'

I could see Bojan was rather bemused, so I tried once more, this time some real pidgin English with a very slowed-down delivery, asking him if he was settling into Stoke-on-Trent. There was a brilliantly comic pause and Bojan once again said, 'Que?' His eyes twinkled at me and I knew he'd caught on that all he had to do was respond in that way and he'd bring the house down. He had that audience eating out of his hand. I then followed up by asking him if he was now able to understand since I'd switched to speaking in Catalan and he gave the most deadpan 'yes, of course' you've ever heard. The whole place fell about laughing. It was one of the most hilarious post-match interviews I've ever done and Bojan clearly enjoyed the experience, although just as clearly had no real idea why.

After the next home game against Burnley, Bojan was also given the man of the match award. He was receiving some treatment after the game and so didn't want to come up, but I persuaded him by telling him I'd ask him about the referee, with whom he had exchanged a few angry words at the end of Stoke's surprise 2-1 defeat to the relegation strugglers. 'Did the referee upset you?' I asked. All Bojan had to do was another one of those pauses and say simply, 'Yes' and nod his head dramatically; again the whole Waddington Suite crowd, who had also been upset by Martin Atkinson all afternoon, launched into applause. This was then doubled with my second and final cheeky question, 'Bojan tell me, when you were a kid growing up in Barcelona did you dream of playing at the Britannia Stadium?' The reply came instantly this time, 'Of course.' Well, that brought the house down. Job done. Another hero established. No need for asking inane questions about being disappointed with a result.

Being in the Premier League for a sustained spell means that Stoke City have so many foreign players now and their English isn't as bad as some of them make out. Sometimes I think they like to hide behind it in order to get out of things they don't want to do. Steven N'Zonzi is one who occasionally does this, but the first time he won the man of the match award and came up to the Waddington Suite to receive the presentation from the sponsors I put him at ease right away. Steven got up on to the stage and immediately said to the crowd, 'Ladies and gentleman, I am sorry, but I do not have good English.' Of course I immediately followed this up by saying in my heaviest Irish accent, 'It's OK, Steven. Neither do I.' We got a good conversation going after that and the crowd loved him.

Asmir Begovic and Johnny Walters are very eloquent and, of course, Peter Crouch is always up for a laugh. He is very witty and fans adore him, especially after his wife Abbey won *Strictly Come Dancing* in 2013. They have become Stoke-on-Trent's new golden couple. Captain Ryan Shawcross is very down-to-earth when he is being interviewed, while Charlie Adam is quite dry and witty. Spaniard Marc Muniesa also has a great sense of humour and has been a major reason why Bojan has settled so quickly at Stoke. Because I get to meet so many of the players I can tell that it feels as if the dressing room has the same kind of characters in as we had in our day and that helps because people want to stay, to be a part of the very special club that Stoke City has become.

There is something else I want to vent my spleen about, though. Something which has crept into the game in the modern era; diving. I hate it. I never dived, even though the opportunity would have presented itself on countless occasions. The reason I never dived is simple. It's cheating. I was brought up to play the game the right way and it would never once have entered my head to go down if I wasn't brought down by a tackle. I fought to stay upright and continue playing. I never went looking for a free kick, a penalty or to cheat my opposing professionals. I simply can't abide seeing it, and these days it does seem to happen almost every week. I like to think it's one of my key principles, but then as Groucho Marx used to say, 'If you don't like my principles I've got some more.'

In my day if you got a reputation for taking a dive you would be treated like a leper; the lowest form of professional cheat. You would be shunned by the footballing fraternity and that was enough to stop people from doing it, generally speaking. It was rare, although striker Francis Lee, who played for Manchester City and Derby, did get a bit of a reputation for it and he got slaughtered for it by the press. All the more reason then to get up and get on with the game.

I was delighted when Stoke City chairman Peter Coates came out so strongly in stating that he didn't like diving and would not tolerate it at our club in the autumn of 2014. It certainly isn't something that the Stoke crowd like either, even if it is their own player who benefits from it. The Britannia crowds may be partisan, but they are also sporting and fair. My biggest concern about diving is how youngsters are influenced by seeing professionals diving around the place like swans. I see it getting replicated when I watch junior games now. It's a worrying development.

Huddles are something else which I don't understand. As professional footballers you live in each others pockets, train together, spend all week preparing for a game, then the manager will pep you up with a few words before you walk out of the tunnel. What can possibly be achieved by a huddle taking place just before kick-off? Are they not already prepared enough? Do they really need to say to each other, come on we're in this together? Are the players asking each other how they are? What would happen if in the huddle someone said, 'Look boys, I can't do this. My wife's left me and my brother has died, leaving me with three kids and a goat to look after'? It's a very odd thing to have come into the game. It never happened in my day and I simply don't understand how it can benefit anyone. Sermon over.

The media loved to make villains of Stoke under Tony Pulis. Take Mickey Quinn on the radio for talkSPORT, for example. He'd be forever on about Stoke being a pub team. Even when we were beating Arsenal and Spurs he'd accuse TP of playing pub team tactics. To be fair to Mick, he's well acquainted with pubs, so he should know. But the point is that certain people couldn't bear the thought of little old Stoke beating these big sides. It wasn't in their script. I know for a fact that TP and the boys revelled in stuffing predictions down these people's throats, just as much as we all loved watching it happen. There wasn't a media pundit on the planet who didn't predict Stoke to finish bottom of the league, well adrift in our first season up, 2008/09. But TP engineered Fortress Britannia, where Stoke only lost four games and we ended up finishing 12th. Meanwhile the angst which greeted the relegation of media darlings Newcastle United was astonishing. It was as if the world had ended; glamorous Newcastle relegated, while nasty little Stoke stayed up!

Then we reached the FA Cup Final via a record 5-0 semi-final victory over Bolton. That didn't suit many people either. Neither did signing quality players such as Peter Crouch, Steven Ireland, and now Bojan Krkic as the team has morphed its style under Mark Hughes. Even though we play a very attractive game nowadays, much of the media loves to denigrate the mighty Potters. It simply doesn't suit a lot of people for Stoke City to be in the top flight, but that's the way we Stokies like it, isn't it? Stuffing people's words down their throats. We've been doing it for years and long may it continue. In many ways we thrive on it and it drives the whole club on.

I would love to see Stoke City win another trophy in my lifetime. We came so close in 2011, only losing the FA Cup Final 1-0 to Manchester City. It was a fantastic achievement to get that far and it must be on the board's and the manager's minds each year that some tangible success could come Stoke City's way. The chairman has gone on record as saying that he wants to get back into Europe and that taking part in the Europa League doesn't phase him at all. Certainly it was a great adventure when Stoke qualified in the 2011/12 season and visited places like Split in Croatia, Thun in Switzerland, Kiev in Ukraine, Tel Aviv in Israel, Istanbul in Turkey and Valencia in Spain. It reminded me of our heady days touring the world playing exotic opponents and spreading the word of Stoke City.

Each trip saw Stokies travel in their thousands and return with incredible stories. My personal favourite is the one that saw the fans standing on an open end in Israel while the heavens opened, relatively unusual in the Middle East, and few were ready for the biblical deluge which soaked the lot of them. Sopping wet, but buoyed by a famous 2-1 victory, the fans emerged on to the street and found a launderette just over the road from the ground. Locals were then greeted to the sight of countless supporters stripping down to their undies in order to dry their clothes off, before heading out into the night to celebrate.

So can Stoke achieve another trophy win? I see no reason why not. New manager Mark Hughes has taken the club on a step forward from where Tony Pulis left the team and with a fair wind can get up into the mix for seventh and eighth place in the league. That has to put you in the frame for cup success at some point. What a victory would do is allow people to give the team of 1972 a rest. We get resurrected year in and year out even now, well over 40 years after the event. It's because it's the only tangible success the club have ever had. It's also based on the fact that most of us live close to the Potteries and are game for media pieces or celebratory dinners. That's all nice, but wouldn't it be great to be able to say that the club have moved on and achieved success in the modern era. That's something that a decade ago, before the return of Peter Coates as chairman, could simply not have been conceived of. It's no wonder people around Stoke-on-Trent call him Saint Peter.

14

The Old Boys

WHEN I had my scare in March 2011 it was during the build-up to the biggest match Stoke City had faced in years – the FA Cup semi-final at Wembley against Bolton Wanderers. The city was ablaze with excitement. It really did remind me of the old days. I suppose you can't help but reminisce in that way when the good times come round again. Although I was devastated I had to miss it, I just wasn't ready to attend the semi-final on Sunday 17 April. There was no way I could attend so soon after such major surgery. It was as much the potential over-excitement during the game as the travelling down which posed the problem, so I had to watch Stoke's 5-0 thrashing of Owen Coyle's Wanderers on TV, not that it was any the less exciting for not being there. Every time a goal went in and it looked as if I might be thinking of getting up from my sofa and dancing a little jig round the living room Sue cast a steely glance in my direction and I behaved myself.

In the build-up to the game Tony Pulis and David Kemp had come to see me while I was convalescing at home and promised me that if we won through to the final, then I would be coming to see the game; no ifs or buts. They gave me that as a target to get well, so the semi-final victory aided my recuperation process in more ways than one. As did walking around the lake at Trentham Gardens, one of my favourite beauty spots in the area. It's about two miles in circumference and at first Sue was unsure about walking round with me on her own as she reasoned that if something happened to me she wouldn't be able to do anything to help, so Jimmy Greenhoff, who lives in Cheshire, volunteered to accompany us. We walked a couple of hundred yards the first day – which was more than enough – sat down for a rest and then returned to the café for a coffee. I have to say I couldn't have managed those first steps without the help of Jimmy G. He was there that first time with Sue, helping me slowly to take the exercise needed to aid my recovery and then each subsequent week. The whole process took me back to my childhood, learning how to take a step at a time, daring to go quicker, but with no great confidence. Anybody meeting the pair of us would have wondered what we were doing. Sue and Jim were patient and within a few weeks, we were reaching the heady speed of one mile an hour. So thanks, Jimbo, for your help and support during that period.

Before we knew it we were being joined by other former players resident in the area who fancied a stretch of their legs. From these walks has come what is now known as the Tuesday Club. It is now the 11th Commandment for all former Stoke City players from our era: thou shalt not miss Tuesday morning at Trentham. Hail, rain, snow, gales – it doesn't matter. So you'll find Denis Smith, Gordon Banks, Mike McDonald, Jimmy Greenhoff, Harry Burrows, John Ruggiero, Brendan O'Callaghan and myself, plus a few friends, pottering round the lake. It's quite an illustrious crew that can be 16–20 people strong. It's wonderful to have a chat and a laugh with the lads and it's a social occasion we look forward to every week. It shows how strong the bond between us was in our team group as the camaraderie of the dressing room is still as strong as ever, even if our bodies aren't.

We have all now got various ailments and to the untrained eye we look like a right bunch of misfits. Jimmy has had an operation on his ankle so hobbles along, and Denis Smith can barely bend any of his leg joints as most have been fused together in his bid to become the Six Million Dollar Man. I swear you can actually hear his various body parts clanking, and the same goes for Harry Burrows, whose knees are shot to pieces. Mine aren't great, but I look comparatively fit and sprightly compared to them! Ahead of us all strides Gordon Banks. For a man of 77, his fitness is incredible and we have trouble keeping up with him on our walks.

He also plays golf twice a week and is fitter than most of his World Cup-winning colleagues, some of whom are in declining health.

It's great testimony to them all that they wanted to come and support me in my recovery efforts and I'm so pleased that this has all stemmed from my scare. It was not only great exercise, but also the best form of therapy for me in my efforts to make the FA Cup Final at Wembley on 14 May and take TP and Kempy up on their promise.

Sure enough I was pronounced fit enough and the manager more than delivered on his side of the bargain. It turned out that Sue and I were to be the club's special guests on FA Cup Final day. We were treated like royalty, being chauffeur-driven from our home to Wembley and back. We were guests in one of the hospitality suites at Wembley and had fantastic seats to watch the biggest game in the club's history. I relished everything about that day and I know that Stoke fans will understand when I say that the occasion was the most memorable thing for me. The result would have been a bonus. My mind wandered through that 90 minutes, realising how fortunate I was just being there. But we all know that fairytales rarely exist in sport, so the cup went to Manchester City. However after the disappointment of the final whistle I watched with enormous pride as our supporters stayed to a man after the game and showed their unfailing sportsmanship in applauding the winners and remaining for the presentation of the cup.

It was a lesson in dignity and humility which supporters of many other so-called 'big' clubs who lose finals should take a great lesson from. All too often the end containing the losers' fans is almost empty as the trophy is being awarded. Not that day. Stokies were almost as loud and boisterous in supporting their own team and then acknowledging the victors as the Manchester City fans were. My admiration for our incredible, passionate and knowledgeable supporters only grew all the more. Long live all Stokies.

I now know that both chairman Peter Coates and chief executive Tony Scholes had a part to play in making that one of the most wonderful experiences of my life and I would like to take this opportunity to thank everyone involved from the bottom of my heart. It was a very special day and I will always remember their kindness. It's yet another thing which shows me how special a football club Stoke City is.

Of course special clubs are made by special people and I cannot finish this book without taking a moment to talk about the man that is Tony Pulis. Of course Tony and I played against each other that once in April 1978, although that game didn't go well for Stoke as he kindly mentioned; 1-1 at half-time became a 4-1 hammering at Eastville. My knees are still recovering from the tackles the young pup put in on me that day! I'm sure I still have a scar from one of them…

When he came to Stoke as manager we got on well. I lived around half a mile away from the training ground and I'd go in at least once a week to see how things were going and would also pop down when I had to get things signed by the players for the commercial department. TP loved meeting up and talking about the old days. We'd have lunch together and if I had a guest like Jimmy Greenhoff or George Eastham then Tony would sit with us and chat. He loved to hear the stories from old-timers like us and treated us with such respect. For example, he would often get visitors a signed shirt to take back for their young relatives, which was great. He always wanted to make us former players feel involved and that worked particularly well in the context of Stoke City.

People underestimate the importance of David Kemp in that relationship. He and Tony Pulis are a double act. Their relationship is very strong. Kempy is far quieter and doesn't get involved in the fans, while Tony is the figurehead. David concentrates on working with the players and is the straight man to TP's constant banter. Once they are outside work that changes and Kempy is more than a match for Tony. He's very witty. In fact his sense of humour is very dry, but he just prefers to stay in the background. His contribution to the cause at each club at which they work is priceless.

If you turn to the photographic section of the book you'll find a fabulous picture of Tony and I sitting on the bench by the pitch at Lyme Valley before one of Stoke's traditional pre-season friendlies against Newcastle Town. On our knees are various of my grandchildren and it's testament to the man that he allowed us to sit on the bench with him that day.

Tony is also renowned in the Potteries for his support of local charities such as the Donna Louise Trust. For anyone who doesn't know about the Donna Louise Trust it is a Stoke-on-Trent-based charity which cares for children with life-limiting conditions. They have a constant drive on to raise much-needed funds, so Tony took up the baton and walked up Mount Kilimanjaro, nearly killing himself along the way, and cycled from John O'Groats to Land's End, among other things. I suppose we are similar in that we will both go above and beyond for the right cause. That's such a positive thing and I think often those kind of things get a lot less exposure in the modern press than some of the more negative stories about footballers and managers which do the rounds on social media these days.

The other major cause which Tony helped with was one that is very dear to me; Stoke City Old Boys' Association (SCOBA). It was founded by former Stoke left-back Geoff Scott, who played with me at the end of my time at the club in the late 1970s. We raise money to help look after the club's former professionals, especially those who have fallen on harder times and need help. Tony was incredibly supportive of us. He helped us persuade Ricardo Fuller to be the star attraction at our first annual dinner in 2010. It was a great, sell-out night, with Ricky providing some amusing anecdotes during an interview by yours truly.

The second year the guest of honour was Tony himself. I grilled him with some really tough questions like, 'Why do you wear that baseball cap?' and he had the sell-out crowd hanging on every word as he rarely does personal appearances. Tony is a very funny man, which I'm sure people have come to realise by listening to him on the radio working as a pundit as he's been between the jobs at Crystal Palace and then West Brom since leaving Stoke.

If there's one last thing to say about Tony then it's that he even agreed to write something vaguely nice as the foreword for this book, so I must have done something to impress him over the years!

Another event which I helped set up was a celebration of the careers of one of Stoke's greatest ever players and servants; club president Gordon Banks. The event was called 'Gordon Banks: A Hero Who Could Fly' in honour of a book of the same name written about the inspiration which one young boy in Northern Ireland took from watching Banksy play for Stoke and England. The writer, Don Mullan, was already an acclaimed author for his book *Eyewitness: Bloody Sunday*. In honour of Gordon's 70th birthday, Don then wrote a very different book all about how his admiration for Banksy had helped him leave behind his difficult upbringing in Derry and become a journalist. Don had wanted to be a goalkeeper and had grown up idolising Gordon. It had always been his dream to meet him. Now as it happened Don attended the same church as my nephew and they got talking after Mass one Sunday. Don shared his dream and my nephew said he might be able to arrange it through his Uncle Terry. Before I knew it I was on the case sorting out the meet up and then helping create a statue and special event to honour Gordon's career and achievements. BBC Radio Stoke helped publicise things for us and made a feature about the meeting between Don and his hero. It was quite emotional being able to help bring them together.

We then formed a committee and set about having a statue of Gordon Banks built. We had experience of this from when the wonderful statue of Sir Stanley Matthews, which stands outside the Britannia Stadium looking over where the old Victoria Ground stood, was commissioned. Its co-sculptor Andy Edwards is a superb craftsman and was brought on board. Gordon did a bit of modelling for him and Andy produced a small statue in bronze of Gordon's famous save against Pele. But eventually we decided that it would be better to have a life-size figure of Gordon standing upright, rather than diving, so Andy did us a small version of it so we could use it to raise some funds. It was fabulous work and Andy is a fantastic talent. I was delighted when, finally in May 2015, the statue was given a home on what's become known as Gordon's Bank, outside the corner of the Britannia Stadium where the south stand and east stand meet, where the big screen stands.

The fundraising came to fruition in July 2008. Don set up a carnival day at the Brit, which the local council got involved in as it was such a wonderful event for the city. We invited personalities such as Nobby Stiles, Roger Hunt, Peter Bonetti and George Cohen from the 1966 World Cup team to make it a memorable day, which included a match between two celebrity teams.

The *piece de resistance* was getting Pele there. We did have to pay him a fee to come, but he was delighted to be involved in both the fundraising event and the dinner that evening. It did lead to one of the most magical moments of my life when I was introduced to him. This was the great man himself. Incredible.

But even that was surpassed by the fact that, because Don had been doing a lot of charity work in South Africa and had met Archbishop Desmond Tutu there, he was able to persuade him to come over to England for the unveiling of Gordon's statue, combining it with a whistle-stop tour of the country. To meet this most incredible and gracious man was astounding, all the more so because of what happened next. We were putting the Archbishop up at the Manor House Hotel at Hanford. Myself, Don and Sue were invited to meet with him at the hotel on the Sunday and this somehow ended up with us taking communion with him as he said Mass in his room. As a regular churchgoer this was an incredible privilege for me. It really was remarkable and it's fair to say I've never met anyone like him. He is the most charismatic man I've ever met.

Not many people know this, but during the event on the Saturday Archbishop Tutu paid a visit to the Donna Louise Trust, slipping quietly away to visit for an hour or so. The impact he made in that visit was inspirational. I don't know how he'd heard of the Donna Louise Trust, but it was such a wonderful act by a truly magnificent and noble man.

I can't stop working for such great causes. There is so much to do. Whether it be a statue to honour Gordon, the Donna Louise's wonderful and much-needed provision for children who need our help, raising the awareness of testing for AAA or the work we do for SCOBA raising money for former players who need assistance, I'm always on the go, promoting good causes. What's wonderful is the support which the city of Stoke-on-Trent gives to them, and that people such as Tony Pulis and his successor as manager at Stoke, Mark Hughes, Peter Coates and a whole host of celebrities constantly give us.

There are various campaigns which are going on in football at the moment. One of the key ones for me is in honour of Jeff Astle at West Brom, which sees their fans applaud in the ninth minute (Jeff wore number nine) to bring attention to the degenerative brain disease which killed him aged just 59. Albion have called the campaign 'Justice for Jeff' and it is a fitting tribute to a great player who was the top scorer in the First Division in 1969/70 and who scored the winning goal in the previous season's FA Cup Final.

There is a very personal reason why I support that campaign to provide financial support to ex-players and their families who have had to suffer as a consequence of Alzheimer's disease or dementia. That is that I saw the same degeneration affect a close friend and former playing colleague of mine; John Ritchie. After his forced retirement due to that broken leg at Ipswich in 1974, Big John set up a very successful pottery business. He was bright and breezy and always chatty during our frequent meetings. But things changed, and quickly. John began to become uncommunicative and angry. His family realised that he was not well, but before they knew it he had deteriorated so badly that he wasn't able to run the business or go out in public. It was devastating for all concerned and I am convinced that football was a contributing factor in his illness, although it may have acted to bring on earlier a condition to which John was predisposed. We'll never really know.

He died in 2007 aged just 65. It was an awful time. Back when we played we just weren't aware that playing the game we loved could cause these types of conditions. You just didn't ever feel that in the long term you would have health problems. Firstly we were footballers, fit and healthy. But secondly, everything was about the here and now. It certainly wouldn't have helped either Jeff or John that they were heading those old leather balls every day in training and then in matches.

Witnessing John's quick demise gave me pause for thought that no matter how much money the current players earn it cannot protect them from similar issues. Perhaps the progress of medical science and the lighter balls, which do not soak up as much moisture, will help reduce the incidence of these problems, as will the banning of indiscriminate cortisone injections in terms of making knee and ankle injuries worse. It was simply standard procedure in our day, but doesn't happen now.

As a proud tribute, I'd like to quote part of the inscription on Big John's statue outside the Boothen End at the Britannia

Stadium. It reads, 'He is Stoke City's top marksman of all time and lives on in our hearts as one of Staffordshire's greatest sporting heroes.'

Hear hear.

At the moment at SCOBA we are concerned with older players' knees, hips and ankles, and the fall-out from all those cortisone injections we had, but I do worry about the modern professional and what awaits him after retirement too. I believe we could be storing up some significant problems for ex-players in future and it's the other big thing which gives me cause for concern, alongside my work publicising Abdominal Aortic Aneurysms.

Of course modern pros will have plenty of money, we know that, but life isn't only about the amount of cash you have in the bank. During the writing of this book Clarke Carlisle has survived a well-publicised suicide attempt, by walking in front of a lorry on an A road in Yorkshire. This is a lad who has only been out of the game for a couple of years, who is only in his mid-30s and has so much of his life ahead of him. He is bright too, having been the chairman of the Professional Footballers' Association and, famously, appeared on both *Countdown* and *Question Time*. He is, though, clearly suffering badly from the withdrawal symptoms of not being involved anymore, despite plenty of media work and the like. When you've been adored by the paying public for 15 to 20 years as a young man, and had all the trappings of the footballing life which the modern era bestows upon you there can often be a gaping chasm left when it all ends. I had it in part during my wilderness years which saw me running my market stall and cleaning houses to make ends meet, although I was often so busy I didn't have the time to think and brood upon it that Carlisle will have. Maybe the modern pro suffers from a bigger drop-off than we ever did because the difference is so vast now. Perhaps that's one blessing in not having earned so much money. I couldn't afford to have that kind of reaction. I just had to get my hands dirty and find any way I could to earn cash to feed my family.

Unlike our era, there has to be less of a support network in terms of true friends as the profession is so transitory now and there are so many foreign players in the English game. While they greatly enrich the Premier League they also generally return home and so would never be found supporting a stricken colleague by turning out for a walk round Trentham Lake in the sleet and snow one January morning, for example.

The culture of wanting or engineering a move is such an integral part of the game now, whereas in our day firstly there was a lot more loyalty and secondly we didn't have freedom of contract, so it was up to the club whether you stayed or went. Now, though, the mindset of professionals, especially those who come from abroad, is to stay three or four years at a club and then move on. Not only does that generate signing-on fees and the like, but it also means they can experience football in different countries and under different coaches. It isn't just about the cash. It's no criticism of the modern professional, just that their circumstances are very different to ours.

At Stoke, because I am involved there, I know that there are really only three or four of the current squad under Mark Hughes who understand the history of the club or have taken the trouble to really understand the area. One of those is Asmir Begovic. The big Bosnian, who kept goal at the 2014 World Cup in his country's first appearance at the finals, is often thought of as being a prime target for Champions League clubs – having been linked with Chelsea, Manchester City and even Real Madrid. He's certainly good enough to make that kind of leap – if he wants to. You would think he would be fairly mercenary, but far from it. Asmir is a very devoted and eloquent young man. He is tremendously loyal. He is also lucky in that his position of goalkeeper often has a far longer career and so he doesn't have to rush to take the first opportunity which presents itself. Often keepers play on at the top level until their late 30s or even early 40s. Just think of Peter Shilton or Brad Friedel or, for the really old among you, Dino Zoff, who captained Italy to the 1982 World Cup at the age of 40.

Asmir actually lives in the Stoke-on-Trent area, just a couple of miles from the training ground, and has set up a charity called the Begovic Foundation, which helps children by providing great sporting facilities for them to use. For example, Redgate Clayton, a minor non-league club in Newcastle-under-Lyme, received a £10,000 donation from the Begovic Foundation to help them improve facilities at the club and reinstate their Sunday morning under-six, under-nine and under-11 teams, so they think they've won the pools. He is also building new sports facilities at a Special School in Sarajevo, the capital of Bosnia. He believes so much in supporting local causes, both at home and in Stoke. It is wonderful to see. It came as no surprise that Champions League clubs across the continent of Europe began to show an interest in Asmir, with rumours of Real Madrid and Roma being interested in his services. Throughout it all Asmir has showed just what a gentleman he is. I'm sure all Stokies join me in wishing this great club servant all the best in his new adventure when the time comes.

Of course, once Asmir moves on he will become eligible to become a member of Stoke City Old Boys' Association. One of the key functions of SCOBA is to allow ex-players to have a continuing attachment to their club. We are there to help them with whatever they need. Often it is not just physical assistance which our members need, sometimes it can be bereavement counselling. Whatever it is, our association is there when they need to call us.

I think it says a lot about the area of Stoke-on-Trent that so many former players have stayed in the area, even though we didn't hail from north Staffordshire originally. Gordon Banks, Jimmy Greenhoff, myself and even Alan Hudson, who just can't keep away, are all in the area. None of us originated here, but this has become home. This is as much due to the nature of the people, their warmth and welcome, as it is to the beauty of the countryside in which we all live. It would be fantastic to see some real investment going into the city in terms of redevelopment. The profile of the club having been in the Premier League has a huge part to play in Stoke-on-Trent's future. People around the globe are becoming tuned in to Stoke City. We are the second oldest league club and have a rich heritage, but the modern era has icons such as Peter Crouch, Bojan Krkic, Rory Delap and his famous long throw, to offer to complement Banks, Matthews, Greenhoff and Ritchie. Despite that we are consistently regarded as underdogs. Stoke City will never be glamorous, but that's one of the appeals and we play on it. If you love blood and guts, and love upsetting the applecart, you'll love the Potters.

It's important that clubs recognise the contribution these players have made and that link is crucial. When our ex-players come and watch the game, they meet fans and act as ambassadors for the club. It's great publicity and brings in extra cash for the club as well as for the charity work we do. I am so grateful to Stoke City FC for recognising the benefit that this brings to them. The Coates family should be applauded for the continuing support they give to SCOBA and its many causes. It helps our club stand apart in yet another way. There are so few Premier League clubs which are owned by British citizens and who reflect the nature of their area so closely. It's rough, tough, working class, friendly, passionate, loyal and there is an amazing bond between club, fans and players. It really is an honour to be a part of that very special relationship and long may that continue.

I would never want Stoke City to go the way of so many other clubs such as Manchester City who have literally sold their soul to the Sheiks. It's very sad to see how that has affected the fabric of the club and its move towards a fully corporate environment. I believe it severely affects the atmosphere on matchdays too. As soon as they are not winning the silence kicks in. At Stoke if the opposition score first the Boothen End kicks in, lifting the players to get back into the game. That's how it should be and certainly how it was in my day. It's special and wonderful. A bit of a throwback maybe, but thank heavens for that in this day and age of same-old, corporate Sky TV sanitised football as a product. It isn't. It's a sport.

All this manifested itself in something quite special while I was writing this book. At the start of the 2014/15 season myself and a number of other former players from my era were invited over to Norway by the chairman of the Stoke City Norwegian Supporters' Club. These are a very unique kind of Stoke City fan who worship the team from afar and make trips over once or twice a year to visit the Britannia Stadium for a game. They are crazy too. Seriously. I love them.

A party of six of us – myself, Gordon Banks, Jackie Marsh, Denis Smith, Jimmy Greenhoff and Josh Mahoney – travelled over to Oslo for four days. It turned out to be a fantastic experience. We were treated like royalty. It all began as soon as we walked through immigration. We were met by a reporter from the national TV news station, who wanted to interview the great Gordon Banks.

Banksy's piece made the second item on the Norwegian national news that night. Stoke City were item two on the news in Norway! It didn't stop there. One of the first dignitaries to greet us at the airport was the local mayor who ripped off his suit jacket and shirt to reveal to us his Stoke City top underneath!

We did various appearances and events and they were packed each and every time. Everywhere we went there seemed to be Stoke fans. The attachment these supporters have is incredible and it all dates back to our era when *Star Soccer*, the central ITV football programme, was sold to Scandinavia and broadcast each Sunday. There are 700 paid-up members of the Norwegian fan club even now and they revel in the fact that Stoke are a club built in their kind of image; earthy underdogs, blood and guts football, sticking it to the big boys.

We loved every minute of our time there and got on famously with everyone we met. We might have been heroes to them before we arrived, but we were all friends by the time we left. I was constantly being told that they were surprised at how just like them we all are, but that's because of our togetherness as a group which stems from being a Stoke City player from my era. It helps me look back so fondly because for me that feeling isn't yet a dim and distant memory. We have it still today, whether it be on trips like that, our Tuesday morning walks round Trentham Lake, when we meet up for dinners or just give each other a ring for a chat. My goodness I am a lucky man to have such wonderful people to call friends.

The last home game of the 2012/13 season saw Stoke City FC celebrate the club's 150th anniversary with a special day of celebrations prior to the match against Spurs. It saw a gathering of around 90 former Stoke stars introduced to the crowd. It did get me wondering what is the collective noun for a gathering of former Stoke players? A wallop? A hobble? A giggle? I'm sure Mick Quinn would just call us the biggest pub team ever. On the day, over 90 former players were on show, walking three abreast from the tunnel out on to the pitch to receive a commemorative scarf from chairman Peter Coates, then marching off to sit by the side of the pitch. Each trio walked out to huge applause. I was one of the last three and next to me was goalkeeper Gavin Ward, who played for the club in the early 2000s, but is now coaching at Shrewsbury. Gavin turned to me as we were waiting to stride out and said, 'I'm glad I'm walking alongside you, TC. It means I'll get a good cheer as they'll be cheering for you because they won't remember me.'

'Gavin, trust me,' I said, 'they never forget here.'

Sure enough Gavin got a tremendous reception when his name was called out. Many other players like George Berry, Adrian Heath and Ade Akinbiyi also remarked upon how they were astonished how each time they returned to the Potteries they were met by this great clamour and a welter of people thanking them for their service to the club and recalling incidents from games. I've never asked any of them if they have the same experience of people approaching them and saying, 'You don't remember me, do you?'

One question which has become a significant thing for me during the process of writing this book is what measure I place on success? Especially over the entirety of your life. I had an ambition from an early age to become a professional footballer. I achieved that by overcoming all the obstacles life put in my way. But that doesn't make what I did any better than anyone else who realises their childhood ambition, whatever that may be. My football career had come and gone by the time I was 36. I'm approaching 70 now and have had several attempts at 'second careers' since retiring from the game.

At those 150th anniversary celebrations I was voted in to the best ever Stoke City squad. It was a great honour, having fought off the likes of Harry Oscroft, Mark Chamberlain, Jermaine Pennant and Liam Lawrence to claim a place alongside the likes of modern heroes Ryan Shawcross, Asmir Begovic and Ricardo Fuller, players from my own era such as Big John, Jimmy G, Banksy, Huddy, Smithy and Pej and my boyhood heroes Neil Franklin and Sir Stanley Matthews.

As wonderful as it is to be appreciated, it embarrasses me when people tell me I'm a legend. All I've done is take what opportunities life offered me and made the most of them. I'm blessed that my talents lay in the world of football, which is a game millions of people love. I don't necessarily buy into the whole legend thing. I suppose this bashfulness relates back to my upbringing. I was never one for the glory. I simply loved football and was determined to make it my life because of that. My success has brought me medals and plaudits, but I played the game for the love of it when all's said and done. The fact that I earned a good living from it allowed me to meet my wife and bring my family into the world. If anything I hope that this book has allowed you the reader an insight into what our era was like to play in, and also simply to live through. Times were very different in the 1960s and 70s. We had so much freedom and far less inspection or intrusion by the media. There was never any major issue with people wanting contact with my family, for example, which I think players these days have to be very wary of. It was never an issue for me.

In a way I was pleased I had three girls as there would have been a lot of pressure on a son of mine. He'd have had photographers round with a ball at his feet almost from the womb. Instead Sue and I have been blessed with three wonderful girls, each of whom has been through university and is now making their own way in the world. Our eldest, Tara, went to the University of Sheffield and is a housewife with three young kids; my grandchildren, two girls and a boy. Niamh has been working in Sydney for over two years managing major accounts for a media agency, for example looking after advertising and promotions for clothing store New Look or Emirates Airlines. Sinead is also in the media as she works for various radio stations in Manchester including Heart, Capital, XFM, Smooth and Classic. The girls all love what they do and I am so proud of them and their families. They all grew up in Stoke-on-Trent and are proper Potters. Sue and I finally moved out to the country a few years ago, but we still regularly get back into the Potteries and enjoy the warmth of the people who never seem to have had enough of me!

It embarrasses me sometimes – what right do I have to write this book for example? I've just lived a life and done my best, that's all. Sometimes when I'm introduced as an after-dinner speaker or when presenting awards I think they're actually talking about someone else. The plaudits are all wonderful, but they are also slightly embarrassing. I find it difficult to come to terms with at times. But then the process of writing an autobiography has caused me to reflect on my achievements. I've played football at the highest level and had a role in winning Stoke City the first major trophy in their history, scoring a goal at Wembley to boot. I've travelled the world and had tremendous amounts of fun along the way. It's been a great ride.

I never expected life to owe me anything. I do think there are former players who believe that the game owes them a living even after they've stopped playing. You can certainly understand those who are jealous of the wages players earn these days – especially millionaire modern players who are distinctly average in comparison to some of the superstars of yesteryear – but I'm not among them. Good luck to them, I say. There are pros and cons to having played in any era and I'm glad I played when I did. It was wonderful and I wouldn't change it for the world. I've always taken whatever challenges I have faced since I left football as something that I just have to overcome. I'd never dwell on something and think that this shouldn't be happening to me. I think this attitude was instilled in me by having grown up in a big family and having to survive having nine brothers and sisters and a strong, if wonderful, mother. It was a fantastic grounding and so was my early years playing football in the street.

Someone showed me a clip on YouTube recently. It was of a Stoke versus West Ham game from August 1976, the start of the season when it would eventually all go horribly wrong. We won the game 2-1 and the highlights show me scoring one of the goals and creating the other. I watched the clip – it's about six minutes long – and d'you know what? We were really good. My goal flies in from over 25 yards out right into the corner of the net at the Boothen End, while I set the other up for some young striker called Garth Crooks (whatever happened to him?), his first for the club. We created countless chances that day and should have won by more. We were playing superb, off-the-cuff football and West Ham couldn't live with us. Those were great days and I am so honoured, privileged and proud to have been involved in them and now to have shared all the fun and laughter we had behind the scenes in those wonderful years with you in the pages of this book.

I want to finish off by talking about the future. My grandson is six as I write, but he's a chip off the old Conroy block and is currently playing at the Crewe Academy. He has some of my genes;

good dribbling skills and he dips his shoulder to take on his man, going one way first and then the other. That's what I used to do and I can see it in him, even at this early age; the same ability and natural talent as I had. He's so dedicated, too – just like me. He's fascinated by any reading material he can get hold of that mentions football. He knows UK geography and the countries of the world fantastically well because of football. I get huge enjoyment out of watching him play. He's keeping the bloodline going as it's been dormant for years because, as I had three daughters, Rafa does not bear the Conroy name. Tara married a half-Spanish, half-English gentleman called Mike, so Rafa's surname is Sanchez-Montez. Look out for him in ten years' time or so; Rafael Montez. Just remember who taught him everything he knows!